Christian Justice

There aren't two categories of people.

There aren't some that were born
        to have everything,
    leaving the rest with nothing,
and a majority that has nothing
    and cannot taste the happiness
that God has created for all.

The Christian society that God wants
    is one in which we share
        the goodness
that God has given for everyone.

Archbishop Oscar Romero

Christian Justice
Sharing God's Goodness

Julia Ahlers and Michael Wilt

Saint Mary's Press
Christian Brothers Publications
Winona, Minnesota

Nihil Obstat: Rev. William T. Magee
           Censor Deputatus
           5 May 1994
Imprimatur: †Most Rev. John G. Vlazny, DD
           Bishop of Winona
           6 May 1994

The publishing team included Barbara Allaire, development editor; Kevin LaNave, Stephan Nagel, and Robert Smith, FSC, consulting editors; Mary Duerson Kraemer, copy editor; Barbara Bartelson, production editor and typesetter; Stephan Nagel, art director; Penny Koehler, photo researcher; Genevieve Nagel, photo research assistant; Jayne L. Stokke, Romance Valley Graphics, page designer; Tim Foley, color illustrator; Tom Wright, cartoonist; Maryland Cartographics, mapmaker; and Alan M. Greenberg, Integrity Indexing, indexer.

The acknowledgments continue on page 293.

 Genuine recycled paper with 10% post-consumer waste. Printed with soy-based ink.

Printed in the United States of America

Printing: 9 8 7 6 5 4

Year: 2004 03 02 01 00 99 98

ISBN 0-88489-330-8

Contents

1 Envisioning a World of Justice

Carolyn volunteered two afternoons a week at Mercy Nursing Home. She spent part of the time helping the nurses, and she always took time to visit with some of the residents. She would join them in the recreation room, where a few men were always playing checkers, other residents would be listening to old music, and some might be dozing with a magazine open on their lap. And then there was Mr. McCormack. He was the oldest person Carolyn had ever had a conversation with—much older than her own grandparents—and she always looked forward to hearing his funny stories about his days as a conductor on the railroad. He enjoyed talking to her, too, and he insisted that she call him "Mac"— "Just like all my friends do."

One Thursday afternoon Carolyn arrived a little late, and from across the room Mac seemed agitated. When he looked up and saw her, though, he smiled and waved for her to come over. "I've been waiting all day for you. I almost called your school and told them to give you the day off. I've had such a memory, I couldn't wait to tell you."

Carolyn was intrigued. She sat beside him and asked, "What did you remember, Mac? You seem so excited."

"Oh, I am," he said. "It was a dream I had when I was twelve or thirteen years old. It was around the time I made my confirmation at church. You know how old I am now, right?"

"Of course I know. You're eighty-two years old. You're always bragging about it!" said Carolyn.

"And I'll brag even more when I'm eighty-three. But this dream. I'm kind of a religious person. Always went to church. I was friendly with the priests, and they helped me and my wife out a whole lot when our youngest boy, Jimmy, got killed in Vietnam. But I'm not one of those mystical-like people. Know what I mean? I mean I never saw an angel or anything like that. But back when I was kid, I had this one dream, and I probably never thought of it again since then, until this morning, I was lying in bed just daydreaming." He closed his eyes and took a deep breath.

"Mac, I'm all curious," Carolyn said. "What was the dream?"

"It was Jesus," he answered. "I was walking on a street near my family's apartment—in the dream, I mean. We lived in a run-down neighborhood. No one had much money. Everybody's parents had to work hard just to keep the family going. It wasn't a pretty place. But I was walking on this street, and this guy comes up next to me. At first I was scared. He kind of snuck up on me, and there were some kids in the next neighborhood who were always looking for any excuse to pick a fight. But this guy didn't pick a fight. He looks me in the eye and says, 'So Mac, how are you?' So I say, 'How do you know my name?' and he says, 'I recognized you right away, that's all.' 'Well, I don't know who you are, so maybe I oughta get going,' I said.

"Then I noticed he had these bloody scars on his forehead. At church we'd been learning about the Crucifixion of Jesus and the crown of thorns they put on his head. And the nuns told us how his own blood stung his eyes. I started staring at the blood on his forehead, and he says, 'That's right, that's who I am.' I believed him—there was no doubt in my mind. Then Jesus says to me, 'So how are things with you, Mac? How's your life going?'

"So I told him how it was going. It wasn't going great, I told him. My father worked long hours at the paper mill, so that I hardly ever saw him, and when I did he was too tired to talk or play. And that he drank, and was drunk a lot of the time, too. And how hard it was on my mother, who had to take care of all us kids practically by herself, with not enough money. A lot of times there was nothing for supper but old bread. I told him how hard school was because there were always other kids threatening to beat me up just because I was Irish. I told him how crowded our apartment was, with ten of us living in two rooms, and how filthy and ugly the neighborhood was, with garbage in the streets 'cause there was no place to put it. Jesus just nodded and listened. He put his hand on my shoulder—his hand had dried blood on it, but it felt warm and strong.

"Then Jesus says to me, 'What can I do for you, Mac? What do you need?'

"'I just want a better world,' I said. 'Just a happier place to live.'

"'I'll do what I can,' Jesus said. 'You help me out, all right?'

"That was the last thing he said. He smiled and walked off to the next street, where some kids lived that I was scared of, but I didn't warn him or anything. I figured he knew what he was doing."

Mac stopped talking. He had tears in his eyes, and Carolyn reached over and took his hand.

"You know," said Mac, "he asked me to help him out. I'm not sure if I did a good job of it or not."

"I'll try to help too," Carolyn said. "I'll help too."

Longing for Justice

In the story you have just read, it might seem that Mac was not asking for very much. "I just want a better world," he told Jesus in his dream. "Just a happier place to live." Mac's longing, though, is much like that of millions of people who want nothing more than a good, dignified life. Without directly saying it, Mac was expressing a desire for a world characterized by justice.

In a just world, the conditions needed for all people and all of creation to survive and flourish are met. Humankind, at its heart, longs for a just world, and the vision of Jesus and the church is a vision of justice. To make that vision come true requires our participation in building a world of justice. Like Mac, it is good to consider whether we have done a good job.

Here in the Real World

Visions of a just world may seem pleasant, but those who seek justice are often regarded as unrealistic dreamers. "That's the way it's always been," people might say of injustice. "Things will never change. The world is a really rough place."

The World *Is* a Rough Place

Many of us, looking at the realities of our lives, might be inclined to agree with this assessment of the world: it *is* a rough place. The stories on the evening news often confirm this view, as do the difficult experiences of these three young people:

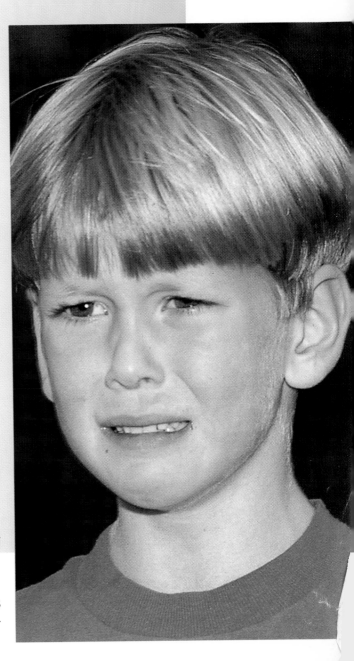

> The strain of her parents' divorce shows in Andrea's eyes. She looks like she needs a week of sleep. But she is mostly concerned about how the divorce has hurt her seven-year-old brother, Trevor.
>
> "It's like he's living in his own little world. He doesn't want to be around people because he figures no one wants him around. When I look at him, he stares angrily at me. Whenever my mom asks him to help out with the house, he yells at her and punches at her.
>
> "The night my dad finished packing up and was about to leave, Trevor held tight to his leg and screamed and cried. It was a scary thing. His face turned all red. Then he sat on the back steps for two hours straight, just staring. He was afraid he'd never see our dad again. Trevor's so afraid of being hurt again."

•

When asked to describe something she dislikes about her life, Jodi, a high school junior, responds:

"I can't stand gym class. On gym days I dread going to school. I mean, it never fails—the same girls are always team captains, and I always get picked last. Always. Every time. It's humiliating. I admit, I'm not a great athlete. But so what? It's just gym class, not a state tournament. You'd think there's a better way to divide the class into teams, something a little less embarrassing and more fair. It's enough to give some kids a real complex."

•

Stefan is a twenty-three-year-old prison inmate. At the age of eighteen, he was caught in a drug bust and is serving seven to ten years for dealing cocaine.

"Dealing drugs was an easy way to make money," he says. "With that money I could dress up, buy jewelry, impress women. Plus I could pay for my own coke habit. I thought all of that made me a real man.

"Now I'm starting to see how fake all that was. I thought what I was doing was giving me dignity, manhood, acceptance, when all that was really happening was that I was abusing myself. And others. That weighs on my mind every day now."

Parallels on a Larger Scale

Without stretching our imagination too far, we can draw parallels between the hardships faced by these young people and situations found on a larger scale.

From divorce to war: Many divorces are similar to situations in which nations are at war. In both divorce and war, innocent people get caught in the crossfire. Both situations create casualties and refugees, people uprooted from the security of their homes. But neither marital problems nor conflicts among nations have to be so destructive and harmful. As we will see in upcoming chapters, conflicts can be resolved more positively than many people assume.

From gym class to "business class": On the grand scale of justice, Jodi's feelings about being picked last for teams might seem fairly insignificant. But when we take a closer look at what is going on in her example, we see that it involves the matter of respect: all people deserve a basic level of respect no matter who they are, what talents they have, or what benefits they may offer to others. A parallel situation

1. Write a brief description of a problem from everyday life. Then make a parallel between that problem and a problem on a larger scale.

exists when a corporation, without regard for its workers, moves its factory to a foreign country where it can operate more cheaply and make larger profits. As a result, the workers face the humiliation of unemployment, poverty, and possibly even homelessness.

From self-abuse to earth-abuse: Stefan's desire for acceptance is shared by virtually every person. It is a healthy human desire. Unfortunately, we often engage in risky and self-destructive behavior in our efforts to gain acceptance. Usually these avenues of behavior turn out to be dead-end streets. We fail to fulfill our needs, and we put ourselves and others at risk. Our tendency toward self-abuse is similar to our abuse of the earth. In the interest of ease or profits, we engage in practices that save us effort or money but harm the environment.

How Did the World Get This Way? Lessons from Genesis

Reading about these examples of harmful conflict, lack of respect, and destructive practices has perhaps brought to mind examples of injustice and hardship in your own life and in the world at large. You may even agree with the conclusion that the real world is simply a rough place and that this is just the way it is.

Is injustice "just the way it is" in the real world, or can we do something to change the world? To answer that question, we need to consider first, How did the world get this way? For help in answering this question from a Christian perspective, we can look to **Genesis**, the first book of the Bible.

God's Original Intentions

In Genesis, we find the biblical stories of Creation, of Adam and Eve in the Garden of Eden, of Cain and Abel, and of Noah and the Great Flood. These stories do not give us scientific knowledge about creation, but they do offer insight into the religious meaning of creation. From these stories we can discern a lot of truths that pertain to justice.

Genesis opens with the story of **Creation**, but first, a description of emptiness: "In the beginning when God created the heavens and the earth, the earth was a formless void" (1:1–2). The account continues with an introduction of all the elements of creation: light, water, plants, animals, and so on, including humankind.

"God saw everything that he had made, and indeed, it was very good" (1:31). When all had been made, God declared that all creation is good—simply because it is the work of God, who is the very essence of goodness. The **Garden of Eden** symbolizes the whole of this good creation; it is a world of life and well-being. Creation thrives. God entrusts **Adam** and **Eve** with the upkeep of the Garden. They are to make sure it remains the place God intends it to be.

The truths about justice that can be discerned from the Creation story include these:

- God wants the whole of creation—people, plants, animals, the earth itself—to flourish.
- God wants creation to be a place of goodness and beauty, a place that is deeply satisfying.
- God wants creation to be a place where human beings, as caretakers, interact with one another and with the whole creation out of love. They are to act out of concern that all people and creation continue to survive and thrive.

Above: God declared that all creation is good. This sixteenth-century woodcut depicts God watching over "everything that he had made" (Genesis 1:31).
Right: In the story of the Great Flood, God seeks to end a vicious cycle of sin. The dove returns to Noah in this nineteenth-century painting by James J. Tissot.

Human Beings Can Choose Love or Sin

God created humankind with a genuine **capacity to love,** as well as the **freedom to choose.** Because we are created as free persons, we can choose to love or not to love in any given instance. Making a choice opposed to love, opposed to God's intention for creation, is **sin.** The Book of Genesis gives us several examples of the effects of sin on creation.

In the third chapter of Genesis, God gives the first man and woman access to the whole Garden, with one exception: "'You shall not eat of the fruit of the tree that is in the middle of the garden'" (3:3). However, they yield to temptation and commit the sin of taking an action opposed to God's desire. For this, they are banished from the Garden.

The biblical story of the first sin provides us with a vivid image or metaphor of what happens when human beings go against God's intention: they lose the "Garden of Eden." In a way, they turn their back on it. The term *original sin* refers to the human tendency to make choices that violate God's intention. The world's history of wars, persecutions, discrimination, and exploitation demonstrates how often people have made shortsighted, self-serving choices that have dire consequences for God's world.

Sin Leads to More Sin

The Book of Genesis continues with the story of the killing of **Abel** by his brother **Cain.** Here we learn another important lesson about justice: sinful, unloving actions lead to additional sinful actions. Cain becomes jealous of his brother Abel and kills him. This sin is multiplied when Cain is confronted by God: "'Where is your brother Abel?'" asks God, and Cain answers, lying, "'I do not know; am I my brother's keeper?'" (4:9). The same thing happens in everyday life. A child lies to her parents and finds herself having to tell more lies to keep them from discovering the previous ones. A manufacturing company disregards environmental protection laws and harasses and even fires an employee who speaks up about it.

The biblical story of **Noah,** the ark, and the **Great Flood** illustrates how a vicious cycle of sin can be set in motion. By the time of Noah, according to Genesis, sin had become widespread. "The LORD saw that the wickedness of humankind was great in the earth, and that every inclination of the thoughts of their hearts was only evil continually" (6:5). Under these circumstances, the conditions of justice deteriorate: creation can no longer survive and flourish. In the story, God makes the difficult decision to eliminate all of humankind except for Noah and his family, the only humans who are living for the sake of justice. It is God's great desire to restore the world to a state in which the well-being of all creation is no longer threatened but is fostered and nourished.

2. Describe in writing an experience from your life in which a harmful action led to another harmful action, and so on. What steps could have been taken to break the cycle?

In a world dominated by sin, realities like this slum in Sao Paulo, Brazil are considered to be "just the way things are."

The Dominance of Sin

When the world is heavily dominated by sin, as in the story of Noah, people can easily be drawn into sinful ways. Often, our choices seem to be dictated by the "way things are," and we can hardly see any other way than to follow along. Even seemingly minor situations can become infected by the dominance of sin. Consider Joel's story of being drawn into sinful, unloving behavior:

> I really started to love music and singing in my sophomore year. That year, we had a new choir director, Mr. Weller. We rehearsed four times a week, and I could hardly wait to get there. He chose good, challenging music that I really enjoyed learning. We had great concerts, and Mr. Weller had us sing in small groups at nursing homes and hospitals. But a lot of people assumed that he was gay. He just had that "way" about him, they said. Some of the kids who had been in choir before didn't join again because of it. And some parents heard the rumors and there was talk of starting a protest to the principal.
>
> Even though I stayed in the choir, I have to admit I went along with some of the jokes about him. I mean, if I hadn't gone along, if I'd defended Mr. Weller, the other guys would've probably said I was gay too. Finally all that kind of talk and bad feeling must have had an effect. Mr. Weller resigned at the end of my junior year. The rumors were so mean by then, I guess he just had to move on.

Almost against his own wishes, Joel found himself participating in an attitude that says it is better to look out for yourself than to stick up for someone else, that it is better to go along than to risk having different ideas. In spite of all that he was learning about music, Joel's main concern was himself and his image. Similarly, Cain, looking out for himself, killed Abel out of jealousy. And the people of Noah's time were corrupt and wicked, relating to one another in ways God had not intended. They put themselves first, even if that caused others harm.

Sin as the Norm

Many people are caught in the grip of a societal attitude that justifies looking out for one's own interests at any cost. If we think honestly about this attitude, we can probably find it somewhere in ourselves. What is so disturbing about self-serving behavior is that after a while, we begin to assume there is no other way of operating. "Looking out for number one" is the name of the game. We can either play by the rules or lose out. This self-centered attitude becomes even further entrenched because so many individuals and groups gain great benefit by acting out of self-interest.

Sin as the Root of Brokenness and Injustice

From a faith perspective, Christians believe that the refusal to be concerned about anyone or anything except one's own interests is the basis of the rough and broken character of the world. Sin—acting out of self-interest and refusing to be concerned about the needs of all of God's creation—is the root of injustice.

The world *is* a rough place. Christians acknowledge this and recognize sin as the cause. The brokenness is very real, deep, and widespread. But the Christian vision sees further—it also recognizes that hurt and brokenness do not make up the whole picture of reality. They are *not* inevitable. The world does *not* have to be that way.

3. Write a paragraph or two agreeing or disagreeing with this statement: *The refusal to be concerned about anyone or anything except one's own interests lies at the root of the rough and broken character of the world.*

For Review

- What conditions are met in a just world?
- What can we learn from the Book of Genesis about God's intention for creation?
- Briefly describe the role of human freedom in fulfilling God's intention for creation.
- Define *original sin*.
- What do Christians recognize as the cause of the world's being a rough place?

The Christian Vision: Sin Is Not the Only Way

A truly Christian view of reality sees something at work in the world that is more fundamental than sin. This fundamental element is **grace**—God's transforming love, or self-communication, that has visible effects through human actions. Grace is more powerful than sin, as we see in this encounter on a New York City street, remembered by Kathy Petersen Cecala:

> Once I was approached by a somewhat shabby, elderly woman who greeted me with a hug and a strange greeting: "Lydia, how nice to see you again!" I was about to shake her off, thinking her senile, when I noticed lurking behind her several unsavory looking characters. I quickly escorted her into a store, where she told me the men had been following her for several blocks, taunting her. When the coast was clear, I walked her to her destination, and I still remember her tearful gratitude. (Pierce, editor, *Of Human Hands*, pages 61–62)

Ms. Cecala's loving, grace-filled response proved to be more powerful than the sinful actions of those who were harassing the old woman. Love has the power to transform sinful situations into opportunities for good.

The belief that grace is more fundamental and more powerful than sin is not just based on wishful thinking. It emerges out of a deep well of sources from which Christians and all humankind draw insights about justice and morality. Let's look at the most general source—natural law—and then continue with specifically Christian and Catholic sources—the Scriptures, Jesus, and the church.

Grace is more powerful than sin.

Natural Law

The concept of **natural law** refers not to a law that is written down, but to the moral order that is built into creation by God. Following natural law means doing what nature, and thus what God, intends. This source of insights about justice and morality is available to all who seek the truth with sincerity. We learn about natural law by observing nature and reflecting on human nature. These are aspects of life that people share no matter what age, culture, or ethnic group they belong to, no matter what philosophy or religious tradition they follow, and no matter whether they are rich or poor, male or female.

Because natural law draws on universal human experience, it is a key part of Catholic teaching on justice and morality. The Catholic Tradition sees God as the author of natural law. By reflecting on natural law in the light of the Scriptures and the example of Jesus, Catholic teaching can enable us to understand what God desires for us and for all of creation.

The Faith Witness of the Hebrew Scriptures

As Christians, most of our understanding of Jesus and his Good News comes through the Gospels and other writings of the Christian Testament. Christian belief in the power of grace over sin is also rooted in the faith experiences of the people of ancient Israel. These are recorded in the portion of the Bible called the **Hebrew Scriptures.** The following examples from the Hebrew Scriptures are just a few of the events that demonstrate the power of God's love to transform and bring goodness to life.

God's Promise and the Exodus

In the Book of Genesis, God makes a **covenant,** or promised agreement, with **Abraham** and **Sarah,** which gives them and their descendants the identity of God's **Chosen People.** God tells them, "'This is my covenant with you: You shall be the ancestor of a multitude of nations. . . . And I will give to you, and to your offspring after you, the land where you are now an alien'" (17:4–8).

Before this promise is fulfilled to the Chosen People, however, the descendants of Abraham and Sarah are forced into slavery in Egypt by the wicked Egyptian pharaoh. But when these powerless slaves cry out from their misery to the God of their ancestors, God hears them and is deeply moved. Working through **Moses,** God demands that the pharaoh "'Let my people go'" (Exodus 5:1), and the Hebrew people are eventually freed from bondage in a great event called the **Exodus.** After this, God leads them to the land promised to them through Abraham and Sarah.

Coming into the Promised Land

The Hebrew Scriptures describe the **Promised Land** as "a land flowing with milk and honey" (Exodus 3:8). This phrase is a rich symbol. It tells us that the land promised to

4. God's covenant with Abraham and Sarah is an important element of the Jewish and Christian faiths. In a paragraph, write about other covenants, or agreements, that influence the way communities, such as your school, are organized.

the Chosen People will be a secure home. It will overflow with the resources needed to guarantee that their basic needs will be met both now and in the future. In the Promised Land, life will be less exposed and less vulnerable, making it possible to truly thrive. The Promised Land will be God's gift to every member of the community. As long as they work to maintain its well-being, God's people will not lack what they need for a good, satisfying life.

The stories of God's promise and the Exodus focus on the power of God's love to liberate and transform. The gift of the Promised Land shows the purpose behind God's transforming, liberating work: God is determined to secure well-being for creation, which was God's intention from the beginning. The stories also show how the transforming power of God's love turns a situation of death (slavery in Egypt) into an opportunity to grow toward new, full life (life in the Promised Land).

Jesus' death on the cross was not the end of his story. After three days, God raised him from the dead as a testimony to the power of God's love.

The Life, Death, and Resurrection of Jesus

The Christian view of reality finds its deepest source in the life, death, and Resurrection of **Jesus Christ.** We learn about him, his message, and his early followers in the writings of the **Christian Testament.**

Meeting God in Jesus

The Gospel of John opens by proclaiming, "In the beginning was the Word, and the Word was with God, and the Word was God" (1:1). A few verses later we read, "The Word became flesh and lived among us" (1:14). In other words, God became human in the person of Jesus, who is the Word of God, the fullest expression of God. All four Gospels are filled with stories of Jesus touching the lives of people in ways that helped them turn away from sin and follow in his footsteps. Jesus embodied God's grace for everyone he came in contact with. Meeting Jesus, and being touched by him, meant meeting and being touched by God.

"Follow Me"

Throughout the Gospels, we hear Jesus call many to be his disciples. Time and again, to Levi, Philip, Matthew, Peter, and many others he said, "Follow me." Then and now, following Jesus means doing as he did—embracing a life of loving service to others. Jesus lived and breathed the command to love your neighbor as yourself. He said to his followers, "'I have set you an example, that you also should do as I have done to you'" (John 13:15). As the Gospels show, what Jesus did was heal the sick, comfort the dying, feed the hungry, and challenge oppressors. His whole life, Jesus did the work of justice.

Transforming Love and the Paschal Mystery

The brand of love lived and taught by Jesus proved to be very costly. As a result of the love he taught and the way he lived, Jesus was put to death by those in power. But his death on the cross was not the end of Jesus' story. After three days, God raised Jesus from the dead as a testimony, once and for all, to the power of God's love. The forces of love overcame the forces of sin and death and brought new life. Abundant life, not death, is what God wants for the world. Ultimately, nothing can stand in God's way: Even death can be the means for bringing about new life.

The Christian term for the reality of new, abundant life emerging from death is the **paschal mystery**. The church celebrates the paschal mystery in the seasons of Lent and Easter, but the emergence of life through death is a year-round reality. We witness it in the changing seasons when trees lose their leaves, only to return to green in the spring. In a similar way, when people give up sinful activity in order to act justly, they die to their old ways and are born to a new way of living. When love overcomes sin, life overcomes death.

The **Good News** announced and embodied by Jesus carries this message: God, creator of the world, gave human beings the freedom to choose love or sin. That same God is also actively involved in helping people turn away from death-dealing, sinful ways to base their relationships with one another and creation on the ways of love. This is the reality of God's grace at work in the world.

The Witness of the Church

The belief that love is more powerful than sin has as another source the **Christian church**, the community of God's people who believe in Jesus Christ. The **Catholic church** has had a continuous Tradition for almost two thousand years. Beginning with Jesus' command to his Apostles to spread the Good News "'to the ends of the earth'" (Acts 1:8), the church has profoundly affected human history.

5. Choose any Gospel story in which Jesus' teaching or actions have a clear influence on another person. In a one-page essay, describe Jesus' influence on the person and how Jesus' teaching or actions in this story might touch your life now, two thousand years later.

6. Take a few moments to reflect on the meaning of the paschal mystery. In a paragraph, relate how the transforming power of the paschal mystery has touched your life in any way, small or large.

The Church's Mission

The Good News proclaimed by Jesus calls for a world in which all of creation flourishes. Jesus said of his followers, "'I came that they may have life, and have it abundantly'" (John 10:10). The church's mission is to proclaim God's desire for all creation's "abundant life" and to help that life come about. In the centuries since its beginning, the church has developed a number of ways to proclaim the Good News and fulfill its mission. These can be discussed in two general categories: **service** and **teaching**.

Proclaiming through service: The earliest Christian communities structured their life together so that the needs of all members were met. In the Acts of the Apostles we learn that "everything they owned was held in common. . . . There was not a needy person among them" (4:32–34).

Catholic religious communities such as the Missionaries of Charity, founded by **Mother Teresa of Calcutta,** have come into being specifically to provide for those in need—orphans, sick people, poor people, prisoners. Catholic communities also go beyond attending to basic survival needs. The **Christian Brothers**, for example, have founded schools that enable people to grow and develop to their full potential. Doing service also gives the church the opportunity to proclaim the Good News by being a visible sign of grace in the world.

Proclaiming through teaching: Whenever the church teaches as an institution, it also fulfills its mission as an instrument of love. The official documents of **Catholic social teaching** reflect on the wisdom developed and handed down by the church throughout the centuries. Documents like *Economic Justice for All,* the U.S. Catholic bishops' pastoral letter on the economy, bring the teaching of the church into public discussions of issues facing the wider society. In this way, the effect of God's transforming love is furthered in the world.

Mother Teresa of Calcutta and the Missionaries of Charity provide for the survival needs of marginalized people—those who are poor, sick, orphaned, imprisoned.

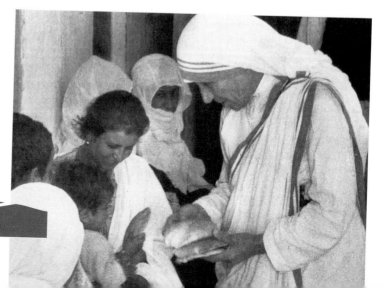

Strong Words from the U.S. Bishops

This excerpt from the U.S. Catholic bishops' pastoral letter *Economic Justice for All* (1986) describes the Christian vision of economic life:

> The basis for all that the Church believes about the moral dimensions of economic life is its vision of the transcendent worth—the sacredness—of human beings. *The dignity of the human person, realized in community with others, is the criterion against which all aspects of economic life must be measured.* All human beings, therefore, are ends to be served by the institutions that make up the economy, not means to be exploited for more narrowly defined goals. Human personhood must be respected with a reverence that is religious. When we deal with each other, we should do so with the sense of awe that arises in the presence of something holy and sacred. For that is what human beings are: we are created in the image of God. . . . Wherever our economic arrangements fail to conform to the demands of human dignity lived in community, they must be questioned and transformed. (Number 28)

The lived experience of the Christian community serves as a testimony to the truth about God's love, the truth passed on to the church by Jesus Christ. God's love can truly bring new life and well-being to a sinful, weary, and broken world. This is so because God's people are actually making it happen every time they answer the call of Jesus to "follow me."

For Review

- How can sinful situations be changed into opportunities for good?
- What is natural law?
- Describe God's covenant with Abraham and Sarah.
- Define the term *paschal mystery.*
- What is the message of the Good News proclaimed by Jesus?
- What are two ways the church proclaims its mission?

Accepting God's Invitation to Justice

Mrs. West is a veteran at helping people mend their fractured lives. She has worked in the chemical dependency unit of a public hospital for nearly twenty years. Unlike most of the other staff members, Mrs. West is not a social worker and has no professional training in the field. She is self-taught.

"I guess you could say I just have a way with people," Mrs. West explains. "Listening, letting them cry on my shoulder when they need to, that sort of thing."

Mrs. West explains how she became involved in her work: "I was just a young woman when my first husband drank himself to death. He was a good man, but he couldn't find the strength to overcome that weakness. A while after his death, I heard about this ward, and I started volunteering. Soon I was invited to join the staff."

Working with people one-to-one has definite rewards, but Mrs. West is most proud of the substance-abuse prevention program that she helped establish for her county. "We start with young kids, because this is not just an adult problem. We go to the schools and teach kids that alcohol and drug abuse are no substitute for a fulfilled life. We show them how advertisers mess with their minds and their self-esteem with the commercials they put on TV. We show them how to take responsibility for their health."

Her feelings are constantly challenged by the stories and experiences of the unit's patients, but Mrs. West seems to always find more strength. "My faith as a Christian picks me up," she says. "I'm trying to do what Jesus would have done, what God wants—help those in pain, and do what I can to stop the cause of their pain."

Working for Justice: Essential for Christians

Mrs. West's straightforward statement that her faith gives her strength for her work seems rather simple, but it also captures the essence of what living the Christian faith is all about: loving your neighbor by working for justice. As one longtime advocate for justice put it, "If I'm going to call myself a Christian, I don't have any choice but to be concerned about justice. What's love without justice? It's empty and meaningless."

Throughout the centuries, the church has taught this message that love must be linked with justice. Justice, in the words of **Pope Paul VI**, is "love's minimum requirement." An act of justice is a sign of love, but it also creates conditions that enable love to grow. In other words, justice originates in love and causes love to increase. Love is at the center of the Kingdom of God preached by Jesus, and we know this love because it is made visible through justice.

Justice and the Kingdom of God

When Jesus taught about the **Kingdom of God,** he was referring to the world as we know it—not some place apart from our earthly existence, but a world transformed by God working through human beings. In the Kingdom, or Reign, of God, life is lived to the full.

God is present in the human heart and therefore in human actions. The Kingdom of God occurs wherever and whenever God's intentions are fulfilled, and all of humankind is invited to participate in the Kingdom. Jesus told the parable of the great feast to help his listeners understand their need to respond to God's invitation.

7. Write a brief description of a situation in which the Kingdom of God is made evident by an act of justice. The situation can be fictional or based on a news event or an actual experience from your life.

Paul VI, who served as pope from 1963 to 1978, taught that justice is "love's minimum requirement."

8. Rewrite the parable of the great feast in a modern setting. Be as imaginative as you wish.

"Someone gave a great dinner and invited many. At the time for the dinner he sent his slave to say to those who had been invited, 'Come; for everything is ready now.' But they all alike began to make excuses. The first said to him, 'I have bought a piece of land, and I must go out and see it; please accept my regrets.' Another said, 'I have bought five yoke of oxen, and I am going to try them out; please accept my regrets.' Another said, 'I have just been married, and therefore I cannot come.' So the slave returned and reported this to his master. Then the owner of the house became angry and said to his slave, 'Go out at once into the streets and lanes of the town and bring in the poor, the crippled, the blind, and the lame.' And the slave said, 'Sir, what you ordered has been done, and there is still room.' Then the master said to the slave, 'Go out into the roads and lanes, and compel people to come in, so that my house may be filled. For I tell you, none of those who were invited will taste my dinner.'" (Luke 14:16–24)

Responding to the Invitation

Like all of Jesus' parables, this one has many layers of meaning. It shows us a group of people who have been invited to a dinner. But when the time for dinner arrives and all the preparations have been made, everyone refuses to attend. They tell their host, "We have better and more important things to do." Jesus is making a connection between the host's invitation to dinner and God's invitation to participate in the Kingdom. When people sin by relating to others unjustly, without regard for others' well-being, they are refusing God's invitation. It is as if they are saying to God, "We have more important things to think about—ourselves."

The Church Teaches About Surviving and Thriving

In his encyclical *On the Development of Peoples* (1967) Pope Paul VI discussed survival and thrival rights. He did not use those specific terms, but spoke in terms of "human conditions":

What are less than human conditions? The material poverty of those who lack the bare necessities of life, and the moral poverty of those who are crushed under the weight of their own self-love; oppressive political structures resulting from the abuse of ownership or the improper exercise of power, from the exploitation of the worker or unjust transactions.

What are truly human conditions? The rise from poverty to the acquisition of life's necessities; the elimination of social ills; broadening the horizons of knowledge; acquiring refinement and culture. From there one can go on to acquire a growing awareness of other people's dignity, a taste for the spirit of poverty, an active interest in the common good, and a desire for peace. Then man can acknowledge the highest values and God Himself, their author and end. Finally and above all, there is faith—God's gift to men of good will—and our loving unity in Christ, who calls all men to share God's life as sons of the living God. (Number 21)

The parable then turns to those who receive the invitation and accept it thankfully. These guests did not expect an invitation, but still they are appreciative enough to drop whatever they are doing and share in the feast offered by the host. In the end, the feast is enjoyed even by people who are usually excluded from such gatherings. With this parable, Jesus shows that God's invitation to fullness of life is offered to all. All are eligible, and all are free to accept or reject God's offer.

Grateful acceptance of God's invitation to a full and abundant life is the first step toward fulfilling God's intention for creation. Those who accept are ready to cooperate with God in bringing about the conditions necessary for creation to survive and flourish. They are ready to build a world in which justice governs all their relationships within the creation community.

Justice and Rights

We have seen that acts of justice create the conditions in which all of God's creation can enjoy well-being. Later chapters of this text explore some of those conditions and the ways people help create them. But before moving on, it is important to understand the concept of rights. Knowing about rights can help us determine what is just in a particular situation.

9. Make two lists—one of survival rights and one of thrival rights. Choose one right from each list and write down the ways each is met in your community. If either is not met, write down possible reasons.

Rights Flow from Worth

As discussed earlier, a primary biblical lesson about justice is that God declared that all creation is good. In other words, in God's eyes all creation has value and worth. Creation has worth simply because it is God's handiwork. Its worth does not depend on how humans judge it.

From this basic worth, rights flow. **Rights** are those conditions or things that any part of creation needs in order to fully *be* what God created it to be. And as we also saw in the Book of Genesis, God does not want creation to exist in a minimal fashion. God wants all of creation to do more than just survive, but to thrive and flourish as well.

With this is mind, consider these two types, or categories, of rights: **Survival rights** are those that entitle living things to the basic needs for survival. For human beings, such needs are food, shelter, and basic health care. **"Thrival" rights** refer to having a claim on those things needed to foster full potential. For humans, these include education, meaningful work, and time for recreation. Both categories of rights must receive our attention for true justice to occur.

If rights are to be meaningful, they must be respected. Human beings have an obligation to respect the survival and thrival rights of all creation. This obligation requires that we not interfere with the rights of others and that we actively promote the fulfillment of rights.

For Review

- What is the essence of living the Christian faith?
- What did Jesus teach about the Kingdom of God?
- Define the concept of rights.
- Explain the difference between survival rights and thrival rights.

An Invitation to Explore

The Christian understanding is that God desires a world in which all aspects of life are guided by justice. In its broadest sense, **justice** means creating the conditions that enable each member of the community, and the community as a whole, to not only survive but flourish. This is done by respecting and promoting the rights of all members of the

Faith-Based Principles to Guide Us

Christians turn to a number of general insights gleaned from the Scriptures and from the faith community's lived experience to help discern what a justice-based world should look like. The following list summarizes some of the most important of these faith-based principles. In subsequent chapters of the text, these principles will be more fully described.

Inclusive: The community God desires is inclusive. No member is a stranger, an outsider, or unimportant.

Responsible: In the just community, everyone is their neighbor's keeper. This refers especially to looking out for members of the community who are more vulnerable and less able to stand up for their rights.

Grateful: The community governed by justice recognizes that its very existence is a gift from God. The community conducts its life with gratitude and humility.

Earth-conscious: In the just community, people know that their well-being is closely tied to that of the earth. The earth's continued well-being must be part of the community's justice concerns.

Renewing: Life in the justice-based community revolves around a respectful observance of the Sabbath, the principle by which time is set aside for rest and rejuvenation.

Peace-seeking through justice: Peace—the state in which the community is able to resolve its conflicts creatively and to the benefit of all—flows from keeping justice at the forefront of all of the community's actions.

Changing: The community centered around justice recognizes that change is a built-in part of life. Working for justice in this climate means the community must continually adapt itself to new challenges.

Hopeful: The community governed by justice is hope-filled. It places its trust in the liberating, transforming love of God and truly believes that love is more powerful than sin.

Believing: The community believes God's promise to people who seek justice in the world: *I will be with you and love you always. My ways will be your ways, for I will write them upon your heart. Together we can create this community of justice!*

creation community. Justice must govern all activities of the community, including personal relationships; economic, social, and political structures; and the management of natural resources.

The remainder of this course focuses on some of the major concerns and activities of a community guided by justice, by God's desire that creation should flourish. A specific concern or activity of justice is highlighted in each chapter, including a discussion of the practical issues involved and how Christians can respond.

You are invited to explore this Christian vision of what the world could be and can be with God's guiding hand. Consider the hope and power of this vision, and decide for yourself if this is the kind of world you would like to be a part of.

2 Respecting Human Dignity

I *think everyone has some good in them, if you can find it. I don't think there's anybody that's born bad or born cruel. If you dig deep down enough, there's something in everybody. My dad says I dream too much. But I think there's a good in people. I can't say: "Oh, that is a bum." I just can't do that. I'm always looking and hoping there's something there. I can't write 'em off. (A high school student, quoted in Terkel,* American Dreams: Lost and Found, *pages 448–449)*

1. Think of someone who has hurt you. Are you able to see any good in him or her? In a paragraph, explain the reason for your response.

Respect: For Goodness' Sake

Seeing the good in others and refusing to write them off point to a major ingredient in the Christian vision of justice: the belief that all of God's creation has goodness and dignity. The **goodness of creation** has its source in the goodness of God, the creator. God is good, so all that proceeds from God is also good: "God saw everything that he had made, and indeed, it was very good" (Genesis 1:31).

Taking a Second Look

Recognizing the goodness of creation is at the heart of **respect**. We all have an idea of what respect is. We have heard, "Respect your elders," "Respect yourself," and similar references to respect throughout our lives. From statements like these, we gather that respectful behavior means treating others and ourselves with courtesy and sometimes even honor.

That is an important way to understand respect, but when we consider respect as an element of Christian justice, we must take our understanding further. The root meaning of the word *respect* is "to take a second look." To be truly respectful, we must look beyond outer appearances and see our neighbors and our world in the light of the goodness inherent in all God's creation.

A New Focus

Some children in Los Angeles received an opportunity to "take a second look" at the world around them. Through photography, they began to see goodness and beauty where they had not seen it before.

In 1983, Jana Taylor founded the Los Angeles–based American Child Foundation, a nonprofit organization that introduces photography and other arts to poor and orphaned children. The children Taylor works with are between eleven and fourteen years of age. Some of them are the children of homeless people, some live at an area mission camp, and others live in single rooms in family hotels or apartments. According to Taylor, exposing a child who lives in dismal and often chaotic surroundings to the expressiveness of art can have a dramatically positive impact.

Taylor says, "I want to awaken consciousness; inspire these children on a creative level. Many of these children have been abandoned, literally left on someone's doorstep. It is important that they be loved, moved, and inspired. They must know that they have an inner worth that is vibrant and wonderful."

On the first day of class, she asks the kids, "What is beautiful in your home?" The typical response is, "Nothing." But by the end of the six-week class, Taylor receives a totally different response to the question. "They told me they found beauty in the way 'light hits the kitchen table,' 'dirt reshapes the pattern on the floor,' and 'birds sing in the trees outside the window.' They saw beauty in simple things."

Through photography, Jana Taylor's students begin to see goodness and beauty where they have not seen it before.

The children take photographs of familiar subjects and begin to see them in new ways. Elisa Sanchez said, "I can see things I never saw before. I also found ugly can be turned into beautiful your way." Rafael Hous discovered, "Photography is real nice because you get to see things a better way. The camera can help take you beyond what you see in front of you—see beauty in a piece of wood or even in the trash." Ralph Flores learned a lesson about life. "I see life as something that's important rather than just something to run through. It's important that we stop and see what's there rather than run away from it."

"The message of my photography and my teaching," says Jana Taylor, "is that life is good, even though many of the children got a shaky start, and goodness is the foundation of everything." (Based on Wood, "Poor No More")

Worth Given by God

With the help of their cameras, the young people in Jana Taylor's classes begin to see more clearly the goodness within themselves, others, and their surroundings. This is in harmony with the teaching of the Christian tradition: Goodness, given by God, is at the core of all people and creation. Respect is the recognition of that goodness.

All of God's creation has value and worth because it is good. This worth does not depend on the standards that humans use for judging value. In God's scheme, each and every part of creation is precious and valuable. All that God has made receives God's unconditional, freely given love so that it may exist fully as God intended. Christian justice requires that we respect the worth of creation. Such respect is grounded in God's intention that creation should survive and flourish.

Justice: Respect in Action

When an attitude of respect is expressed in actions, justice occurs. The well-known proverb "Actions speak louder than words" sheds light on many situations in which people's actions contradict their apparent attitude. A politician, for example, may express respect and compassion for the unemployed in words, but if his or her actions cause further unemployment, we can doubt the sincerity of the words and attitude. In the Sermon on the Mount, Jesus compared attitude and action to a tree (attitude) and its fruit (action):

2. Is there beauty in your surroundings? Survey them as if you were looking through the lens of a camera—or actually do so if you have a camera available. Write a paragraph about what you saw and whether it appeared to you as beautiful.

Just as the fruit of a tree demonstrates the health of the tree, human actions demonstrate human attitudes.

"Every good tree bears good fruit, but the bad tree bears bad fruit. A good tree cannot bear bad fruit, nor can a bad tree bear good fruit. Every tree that does not bear good fruit is cut down and thrown into the fire. Thus you will know them by their fruits." (Matthew 7:17–20)

An attitude of respect can be cultivated and developed. As we have seen, taking a second look is the first step in developing respectful actions. Actions that demonstrate respect bring to life the attitude of respect and have an impact in all areas of life. They are essential for the work of justice—for ending conflicts nonviolently, eliminating prejudice, creating a more inclusive economy, or bringing an end to environmental destruction. In other words, the Christian vision of justice can be realized only when respect, based in the God-given goodness of creation, is active in human life.

3. Write about a situation in which you were able to see the worth of someone or something on God's terms instead of on human terms.

For Review

- What is the source of the goodness of creation?
- Summarize Jana Taylor's goals for teaching photography to poor children.
- How does respect lead to justice?

Respecting the Dignity of the Human Person

This text has said that *all* creation has goodness and worth simply because it is created and loved by God. This is a fundamental biblical teaching. The Bible also teaches that God created human beings in a way that distinguishes them from nonhuman creation. What is that difference?

Created in God's Image

The difference between humanity and the rest of God's creation is that humankind is created in the **image of God.** Every person thus has immense **human dignity.** As the Creation story in Genesis expresses it:

Then God said, "Let us make humankind in our image, according to our likeness. . . ."

Every person, created in the image of God, has immense human dignity.

So God created humankind in his image,
in the image of God he created them;
male and female he created them.

(1:26–27)

The idea that human beings are created in God's image is an important one to understand. It sheds light on a basic demand of justice—that all persons deserve respect.

Reflections of God

A helpful way to grasp the idea of being created in God's image is to think about the meaning of the word *image*. An image is a reflection of something else. Looking into a pool of calm water, you see an image or reflection of yourself. You and your image are closely related—you are the source of the image and it looks like you—but you and your image are not the same thing. Similarly, as an image of God, you are like God but you are not actually God.

The notion of the human person as an image of God suggests some marvelous implications. God created human beings to do something of incomparable importance in the world: to reflect God. Creating human beings is one way God chose to be present in the world. When we act truly human, we reflect to one another and to all the world the loving goodness and power of our Creator. In other words, our loving actions, actions that flow from the core of our being and display our concern for others, demonstrate most fully that we are images of God.

To help us in fulfilling our task as images of God, God equipped human beings with abilities and skills that are unique to us among creatures. We have a basic capacity to love, along with abilities to think, reason, imagine, and remember. We are conscious of ourselves as individuals, as members of communities, and as persons with a spiritual life. Each and every person has been given these qualities, and it is through them that humankind expresses its dignity as the image of God on earth.

A Permanent Dignity

Human status as God's image gives all people a dignity that cannot be taken away, even by their own wrongful actions. All people have the God-given right to express themselves as reflections of God and to have their dignity be respected. At the **Second Vatican Council**, a worldwide gathering of Catholic bishops in the 1960s, the Catholic church

A mirror image is similar to its original, but not the same. As an image of God, a human person is like God, reflects God, but is not actually God.

4. Choose a human ability such as thinking, reasoning, imagining, or remembering. Write a paragraph on how that ability helps a person be an image of God to others.

5. List five actions or circumstances that you feel assault human dignity. Decide which of the five is most serious, and explain why you think so.

All human beings deserve respect, simply because all have been created in God's image—even those who have committed crimes.

saw the issue of respect for human dignity as an important matter that deeply influences all areas of human activity:

> The Council lays stress on respect for the human person: everyone should look upon his neighbor (without any exception) as another self, bearing in mind above all his life and the means necessary for living it in a dignified way. (*The Church in the Modern World*, number 27)

Our dignity as creatures made in God's image ultimately cannot be destroyed or taken away, but it can be violated, disregarded, and disrespected. Our dignity is assaulted by any action or circumstance that prevents us from expressing our true nature as images of God. The Scriptures and the Tradition of the church clearly see such assaults as violations of God's intention for creation.

For Review

- What Christian belief is the basis for understanding the dignity and worth of human beings?
- What abilities distinguish human beings from the rest of creation?
- Can basic human dignity be destroyed or taken away? Explain.

Respect Is a Right for Everyone, Even Criminals

Throughout history, Christians and others have often been willing to ignore human dignity and treat people with great disrespect. This can happen in almost any area of life, and later in this chapter several examples are presented. But first, let's take a detailed look at a significant example of respect: how respect applies to the treatment of those who have committed crimes and are imprisoned in correctional institutions.

As discussed previously, all human beings deserve respect, simply because all have been created in God's image. Still, many people hold the opinion that those in prison do not deserve respect. "They are in there to suffer, so let them," says a man from Chicago. A woman in New Jersey agrees:

"Prisoners should have no rights when they go to jail" (quoted in Moore, "Sounding Board").

These attitudes do not acknowledge the basic human dignity of prisoners. Other people wonder, though, "If prisoners' dignity is not respected, will they ever become productive members of society?"

An American Prison: A Look Inside

Perhaps the first step toward respecting the dignity of prisoners is the recognition that they are individuals with their own identities. A look inside a typical American prison, one in Lebanon, Ohio, gives us some insight. Its population is as varied as that of a small community in the United States:

> The inmates come from every walk of life. Some were reared in prosperous, upper-middle-class surroundings, while others have spent their lives in abject poverty. Some are talented and educated, while others get by on their wits or through brute strength. Some are serving their first sentence, while others are repeat offenders who have spent most of their adult lives behind bars. (Wojda et al., *Behind Bars,* page 79)

Keeping that variety and individuality of prisoners in mind, let's go on to see how the Catholic church views prisoners.

The Church's View of Prisoners and Prisons

The Catholic church has a long tradition of respecting the dignity of those who are in prison. It is a tradition that goes back to the life of Jesus and the Hebrew Scriptures.

The Teachings of Jesus

Jesus gave his followers a direct command to act justly toward all who are in need, including those in prison:

> "Then the king will say to those at his right hand, 'Come . . . inherit the kingdom prepared for you from the foundation of the world; for . . . I was sick and you took care of me, I was in prison and you visited me.' Then the righteous will answer him, 'Lord, . . . when was it that we saw you sick or in prison and visited you?' And the king will answer them, 'Truly I tell you, just as you did it to one of the least of these who are members of my family, you did it to me.'" (Matthew 25:34–40)

6. Before reading any further, write down your response to this statement: *Even criminals have a basic dignity that must be respected.*

The Social Teachings of the Church

The Catholic church's social teachings, which have grown from the Scriptures, provide guidance concerning the Christian attitude toward prisoners. The U.S. Catholic bishops acknowledge the important purposes of prisons: They are places where people make amends for crime. They protect society from some of its dangerous members. The threat of prison is meant to discourage people from committing crimes. The most important purpose of prisons, though, is **rehabilitation**—the reorienting and re-educating of those who have committed crimes, so that they will lead a lawful and productive life.

The church insists that rehabilitation can happen only if the rights of prisoners are taken into consideration. The most important right of prisoners is that of respect for their human dignity. The bishops of Tennessee express this teaching quite plainly:

> Let there be no mistake: Justice demands protection of the common good and strict accountability from those who harm others. But we Christians must also remember that even the murderer does not forfeit the God-given right to be called "neighbor." ("Violence and Capital Punishment")

Christian teaching is firm: Respect for human dignity is a right due to *all* people, even criminals. All are deserving of this respect. It is not something that Christians are free to give to some people and deny to others.

U.S. Prisons: Vengeance or Rehabilitation?

It is important to examine the prisons of the United States through the lens of a Christian understanding of justice. The United States has the highest rate of incarceration in the world. For each 100,000 in the U.S. population, more than 450 people are in prison—far more than in any other nation. How these prisoners are dealt with is of interest to people who are concerned with justice. In the prisons of the United States, the incarceration experience varies widely. In some cases it appears that the justice system is punishing criminals with **vengeance**—"getting even" with them. In others, the goal of punishment is rehabilitation.

Vengeance

Although U.S. laws contain strong mandates to respect the rights of prisoners, there is widespread evidence that

7. Do you agree with the U.S. Catholic bishops that rehabilitation is the most important purpose of prisons? Write a paragraph explaining why or why not.

A Christian Cry for Compassion and Forgiveness

A priest who has ministered to jail and prison inmates full-time for sixteen years pleads for a more compassionate attitude toward people who have broken the law, an attitude that is more in line with the teachings of Christ and the Christian tradition:

> The images of God whom we incarcerate are just like you and me, not only in the unity of the Creator but as persons gifted in countless ways and degrees. They share with us the capacity to love and an innate longing for the good, the true, and the beautiful.
>
> Contrary to popular opinion, persons who commit crimes want what everyone else wants: spouses who respect them, jobs that provide sufficient income to support their families, and living space that allows dignity and the freedom to expand. Perhaps you see "them" as statistics, but I see the unique character and personality of each prisoner. No matter what the offense has been, each person remains an individual capable of depths of feeling and understanding and reveals and shares strengths of spirit and wit, humor, sadness, weakness, shame, and joy. Most suffer intensely for the suffering they have caused in their victims, the victims' families, and their own families and friends. No matter how serious the offense, God's love is always present and bursting through. (Moore, "Sounding Board")

many state and federal prisons fail to live up to the ideals expressed even in the U.S. Constitution, let alone in Catholic social teaching. Those in prison are perhaps the best witnesses. A death row inmate in Virginia is working to make prisons into places where true rehabilitation can take place. Through his efforts, he has become aware of many violations of human dignity in prisons:

- rampant guard violence against prisoners
- mentally ill prisoners chained to steel bunks

- prisoners forced to lie in their own excrement
- prisoners denied proper medical care
- prisoners locked down under long-term isolation for minor rule infractions (or just on the whim of a guard)
- prisoners subjected to body cavity searches for no apparent reason other than to harass them
- attorneys for prisoners harassed and denied access to their clients
- visitors harassed and intimidated to discourage them from visiting their family members who are prisoners

(Summarized from Giarratano,
"Prison Reform Viewed from Inside")

This list represents the extreme of assaults on prisoners' dignity that can happen in prisons. Such assaults make rehabilitation unlikely, if not impossible. But not all prisons operate in this way. The next example shows an alternative approach to prisoners that has been fostered by one man, a warden.

8. Have you ever gotten even with someone? Were you satisfied by the experience, or have you had second thoughts about your actions? Reflect on this in a paragraph.

Rehabilitation

John Whitley took over as the warden of the Louisiana State Penitentiary in 1990. At the time, this maximum-security prison was plagued by violence, and known as the bloodiest prison in the nation. A mood of hopelessness prevailed among the 5,186 inmates.

During his first two-and-a-half years as warden, John Whitley turned the prison around. His tactic: to trust his own personal sense of decency and fairness. The result: the stabbings, hangings, and escape attempts are down considerably; the sense of hopelessness that dominated the prison has been lifted.

Whitley has proven himself to be a straight-up guy through a long series of interactions and dealings with the prisoners that have built trust. One incident was especially significant to prisoners. Whitley had directed the prison's metal shop, staffed by inmates, to build the table that would be used in executions by lethal injection. Understandably, inmates then refused to go to work, and Whitley saw his error. He publicly admitted his mistake, which indicated to the prisoners that he was a different kind of warden. Patrick DeVille, on death row, says, "He admitted he was wrong. Wardens just don't do that."

The inmates feel that Whitley actually cares about them as human beings. Nathan Arnold, who is serving a life sentence for murder, says, "He's made a lot of difference. People have started feeling like people again." Curtis Kyles, a prisoner on death row, echoed the sentiment: "The warden's pretty cool people. He sees people as individuals, not throwaways." Whitley makes himself available to the inmates on a regular, informal basis. He listens and asks questions. Says Whitley, "Even if it's a small problem, it may be the biggest problem they have. You don't just blow anyone off." (Based on Smolowe, "Bringing Decency into Hell")

> **9.** A situation in which Warden John Whitley publicly admitted to a mistake showed his respect for prisoners. Describe in writing a time you had to admit you were wrong. Did your admission demonstrate respect for others (parents, friends, teachers)?

John Whitley's respect for the dignity of prisoners is most apparent in his attitude about rehabilitation. According to Whitley, a prison system cannot rehabilitate inmates; prisoners must rehabilitate themselves. "All we can do is provide the opportunity," he says. Respecting prisoners' basic dignity is a key part of empowering them to bring about their own rehabilitation. Whitley's example demonstrates that respecting human dignity in prison is not an impossible task. It is simply a matter of having the desire and courage to do so.

An American Prison: Taking a Second Look

Here is another example of a respectful attitude toward prisoners, this time by an outsider to the prison system.

Grace Wojda, a photographer, was assigned to take pictures inside the Lebanon, Ohio, prison described earlier. She was moved by the face-to-face contact with the inmates. Her work as a photographer and her compassion as a human being led to a caring and respectful approach to the prisoners. Her experience seemed like that of someone photographing her neighbors:

"During each of my visits, I asked the officers and inmates to avoid discussing the kind of crime anyone had committed. I didn't want to know what anyone was in for or how long of a sentence he was serving.

"As a photographer, I had to stay totally neutral. My job was to capture the images of the prison as objectively as I could. I wanted to produce a straight documentary, without taking sides.

"But as a mother, I could not help but think that at one time all of these men were somebody's children, innocent and uncorrupted and with a bright future in front of them. And I could not help but ask myself what went wrong that they ended up here." (Wojda et al., *Behind Bars,* page 80)

Like the young photographers described earlier in this chapter, Wojda took a second look. As a result, she respected

When Grace Wojda photographs prisoners, she keeps in mind that "at one time all of these men were somebody's children, innocent and uncorrupted."

Respect Beyond the Prison Walls

The Christian responsibility to see that prisoners are treated in ways that respect their dignity and foster their rehabilitation does not end when those persons leave prison. It carries over into the released prisoners' transition back into society. Many examples of this kind of work for justice could be described. These are just a few:

- A church in Norman, Oklahoma, buses soon-to-be-released prisoners to church services within the community. This helps them prepare for their re-entry into society.
- Wheaton College, a Christian college in Oklahoma, has a private scholarship geared toward enabling ex-prisoners to attain a college degree.
- In California, the Match-Two Prisoner Outreach Program, run by Christians, matches volunteers one-on-one with prisoners who have a year left on their sentence. The volunteer becomes the prisoner's friend and mentor. Becoming friends leads to a caring friendship on the outside. Once released, the former prisoners have a friend who wants them to succeed.
- In Milwaukee, Wisconsin, Project RETURN offers a variety of supports to prisoners who are in a transitional phase between their time of incarceration and their full re-entry into society. Project RETURN staff for example, find jobs for former prisoners and help them get into schools. The project's goal is to see that the ex-prisoner's return to community, family, and friends is positive and permanent. A recent college graduate who volunteers with the project sees respect as a basic ingredient for success: "If you want people to behave in a way that is acceptable, you have to treat them with a certain amount of dignity or they're just going to get turned off to the world in general. They really appreciate having someone in the outside world who cares about them."

the goodness within each inmate, regardless of his crimes and failings. Her experience can give us on the outside of prisons some insight into how to regard all prisoners.

10. If your local church asked for volunteers to work with prisoners who are about to be released into the community, would you be interested in signing up? Write the reasons for your answer.

For Review

- What are the sources of the Christian teaching that prisoners deserve respect?
- According to the U.S. Catholic bishops, what is the most important purpose of prisons?
- Name three ways in which the dignity of prisoners has been violated.
- According to John Whitley, what is the key to successful rehabilitation?

Some Dimensions of Respect

The need for respect cuts across all levels of human relations with one another and with the environment. We have seen that respectful treatment of prisoners can have a positive influence on rehabilitation. The following examples illustrate that the value of respect can be seen in many other aspects of life as well.

Respecting Life: The "Seamless Garment" Approach

Cardinal Joseph Bernardin, of Chicago, calls the church's approach to the issue of respect for life a **"seamless garment."** The approach is so named to recall the garment that Jesus wears in John's Gospel account of the Crucifixion. The seamless garment approach is also known as the **consistent ethic of life.** This particularly Catholic viewpoint holds that respect for the life of the unborn, expressed in the church's firm **opposition to abortion,** must be extended beyond birth—indeed, "from the womb to the tomb":

> If one contends, as we do, that the right of every fetus to be born should be protected . . . , then our moral, political and economic responsibilities do not stop at the moment of birth. Those who defend the right to life of the weakest among us must be equally visible in support of the quality of life of the powerless among us: the old and the young, the hungry and the homeless, the undocumented immigrant and the unemployed worker. . . . Consistency means we cannot have it both ways: We cannot urge a compassionate society and vigorous public policy to protect the rights of the unborn and then argue that compassion and significant public programs on behalf of the needy undermine the moral fiber of the society or are beyond the proper scope of governmental responsibility. ("Cardinal Bernardin's Call for a Consistent Ethic of Life")

The seamless garment teaching covers attitudes about war, health care, employment, and many other issues of social and personal well-being. Cardinal Bernardin's stirring

In a peaceful act of protest, Fr. Daniel Berrigan is about to be arrested for illegally entering a military facility. On the previous day, Berrigan was arrested for a similar protest at an abortion clinic.

words remind us that the call to respect human dignity is a basic element of justice. Justice will not be done where respect for the dignity of human life in all its forms is not shown.

Capital Punishment: The Ultimate Disrespect

The National Coalition to Abolish the Death Penalty reports that in 1993 there were 2,676 inmates on death row, that is, awaiting **capital punishment.** Some of the most vocal opponents of the death penalty, amazingly, are family members of murder victims. Groups like Murder Victims' Families for Reconciliation (MVFR) have been organized to try to abolish the death penalty in the United States, which is one of only two Western industrialized nations that still allow the death penalty.

Groups like MVFR believe that "capital punishment is an expensive, ineffective and barbaric response to violent crime. It does not help families or nations to heal." They also recognize

> a depressing pattern coursing through death row. The inmates are generally indigent and represented by overworked court-appointed attorneys. They have been on death row for six years or more and most had codefendants who testified against them in exchange for a lesser sentence. They are victims of child abuse; many are suffering from mental illness; many are measurably retarded. There's a good chance that many were sentenced because of race and an equally good chance that they could be innocent. (Unsworth, "Victims' Families: 'End the Death Penalty'")

The MVFR's opposition to the death penalty is founded on principles that go deeper than statistics. A woman whose young daughter was brutally raped and murdered believes that "in God's eyes, the man who killed our daughter was just as precious as Susie." She goes on to say, "To kill someone in her name is to violate her. I honor her life and memorialize her far better by insisting that all life is sacred and worthy of preservation" (Unsworth).

The U.S. Catholic bishops would agree. In their *Statement on Capital Punishment,* they teach that abolition of the death penalty would do the following:

- send "a message that we can break the cycle of violence, that we need not take life for life"

11. Write a one-page essay explaining how you think the seamless garment approach applies to one of these issues: war, health care, abortion, employment, hunger, or education.

12. Write a paragraph agreeing or disagreeing with this statement: *Sending a murderer to the electric chair or to death by lethal injection continues society's cycle of violence.*

- display "our belief in the unique worth and dignity of each person from the moment of conception, a creature made in the image and likeness of God"
- testify "to our conviction . . . that God is indeed the Lord of life"
- be in harmony "with the example of Jesus, who both taught and practiced the forgiveness of injustice"

(Pages 7–8)

The issue of capital punishment is emotional and controversial. Debate on the death penalty is complete only when it considers the need to respect human dignity.

People with Disabilities: Access to Respect

People with disabilities are full members of the human race, created in the image of God. Only in recent years, however, has American society in general begun to respect disabled people's right to have access to transportation, restaurants, movie theaters, schools, churches, and so on. Geeta Dardick tells a story about her husband, Sam, a highly educated, responsible citizen and father, and a paraplegic. In a California restaurant, Sam had to crawl into the bathroom because the bathroom door was not wide enough to accommodate his wheelchair. Because of this experience, Dardick became involved in the campaign to gain greater **access for people with disabilities.**

Years of struggle by people like the Dardicks led to success. In 1990 the United States Congress passed the Americans with Disabilities Act (ADA), making the issue of access for people with disabilities a matter of law. When the ADA is fully implemented and enforced, fewer people with disabilities will be faced with lack of access to work, school, worship, and entertainment.

Drug Abuse: A Lack of Self-respect

Drug addicts who have overcome their drug abuse often look back and see their **addiction** as a sign of their lack of **self-respect** and pride. An example is Bill Giddens, who as a heroin addict was "a one-man crime wave: in two years he had robbed more than 200 people." He eventually became an inmate at the Phoenix House Drug Treatment Unit, part of the state prison system in Marcy, New York.

Phoenix House recognizes that to treat addiction, "one must change a person's values, thinking, moods, behavior and spirituality." The program also tries to see that addicts "embrace responsibility, honesty and caring for others." Of the treatment, Bill Giddens said, "This is the place where you get your pride and quality." Released from treatment, Giddens has a job as an assistant in a recreation program. By reclaiming his self-respect, Bill Giddens has proven that even his own wrongful actions did not take away his dignity (Quoted in Kerr, "The Detoxing of Prisoner 88A0802").

13. Think of something you have done that displayed a lack of respect for yourself. Write a letter to yourself (no one else will read it) about how that experience can help you learn to respect yourself more.

Respecting Women: Improving Wages

Traditionally, women have been paid less than men in similar jobs. This **wage gap** has improved in recent years; but still, in 1991, women earned on the average only seventy cents for every dollar paid to men in the same or similar occupations. Even for professional women the gap is quite wide, and in some cases it is growing. For instance, a female lawyer can expect to earn just seventy-five cents for every dollar earned by a male lawyer. Female physicians fare even worse: only fifty-four cents for each dollar.

This kind of injustice has many possible consequences. For example, more women than men live in poverty. And many of these women have dependent children who, as a result of their poverty, lack proper nourishment and educational opportunities. Another example: Women caught in abusive relationships with men oftentimes feel forced to stay in the situation because they don't have the earning power to survive. Pay scale injustices lead to problems in families

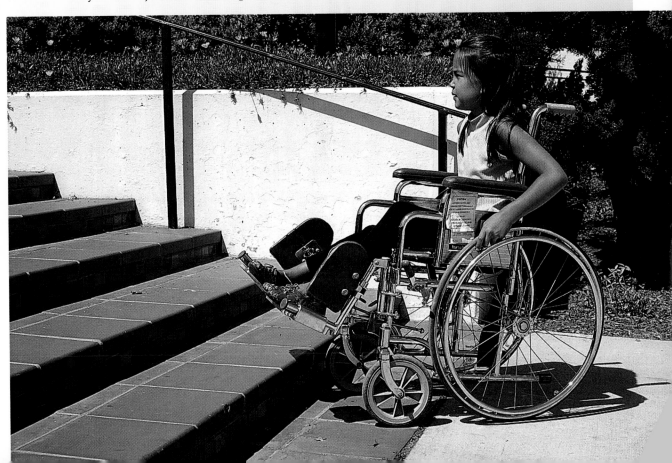

People with disabilities often face lack of access to work, school, worship, and entertainment.

and society that could be addressed by simple respect and fairness.

Respecting Intelligence: The Case of Advertising

Our lives are surrounded by **advertising.** Television, magazines, and radio fill each day with the sights and sounds of products and services that someone wants us to buy. The announcer of a televised sporting event cannot even give the score without mentioning the brand name of a product. But advertisements, a key part of a consumeristic society, often fail to respect the intelligence of the individual. Rather than simply providing information about a product, much advertising presumes to know our needs better than we ourselves do. Ads try to convince us that we are not good enough unless we purchase a particular product. They substitute their slogans and jingles for our own decision-making skills.

The failure of much of advertising to respect individual intelligence can have harmful, even shocking, effects in society. People become identified by what they own rather than by who they are or what they think. Violent crimes have been committed by young people who feel they must have a popular but high-priced brand of shoe or jacket. Commercial broadcasting, of course, is dependent on funds provided by businesses. And even museums, schools, and public broadcasting stations are increasingly funded by businesses. The responsibility of these institutions to the community as a whole can be undermined by the pressures of a commercial sponsor.

When our intelligence is not respected by advertising, we must give ourselves and our community the respect we deserve. We can do this by thinking for ourselves and making our own decisions about what products we need.

For Review

- Briefly explain "the consistent ethic of life."
- How many Western industrialized nations allow capital punishment?
- What is the purpose of the Americans with Disabilities Act?
- What is the average difference between wages paid to women and wages paid to men in similar jobs?

Respect: Basic to All Just Relationships

We have been examining many areas of human relationships and have seen that two basic truths are the foundation for justice in relationships:

- All people have a basic goodness and dignity because they have been created in the image of God.
- This human dignity must be acknowledged and respected.

Assaults on human dignity can occur in a great many ways—inhumane prison conditions, hunger and poverty, political and economic oppression, and even the small, everyday behaviors we use to hurt one another. All these assaults block the victims' abilities to fully express themselves as images of God. Justice demands that the dignity of every person be respected simply because it is God-given.

The dignity of every person, in every culture, must be respected because it is God-given. Members of the A-Khaw tribe in Thailand are seen here in traditional dress.

3 Tapping into Power

This is our generation. We need to take a stand," declared student Leisha Weeks to a packed auditorium at Brevard High School in North Carolina. Then, facing the members of the board of education, she pleaded, "Please listen to the students of Transylvania County. We need Mal Crite to teach us."

Weeks's compelling testimony was one of eleven offered on behalf of Marion "Mal" Crite. Crite, a young former Brevard High School and North Carolina State University star athlete, had been hired by the school superintendent six weeks earlier as home-school coordinator for "at risk" students.

One after another, pastors, parents, community leaders, counselors, and friends rose to speak on behalf of Crite's integrity and compassion for youth. Referring to his conversion to Christ following a drug conviction nine months before, they spoke of forgiveness and the grace of God. And they stated their belief that Crite's profile in Brevard—as well as the turnaround he made in his life—uniquely positioned him to serve the students.

Only three people spoke against Crite, on the grounds that he was on probation; two had never met him. The audience sat in stunned silence as the school board voted three to one to fire him.

The day after Crite's firing, seventy black high school students and a score of their friends walked out of classes, claiming that the firing was racially motivated. School principal James Williams called Rev. Frederick Gordon, pastor of Bethel "A" Baptist Church, to the school. Gordon in turn called all the black pastors in the county and asked them to meet him there.

The student protest was peaceful. But when the pastors left the campus, Williams called in the police, who arrived in full force with a police dog. Despite what appeared to be a provocation on the part of the school administration, the students remained calm. After school hours, they moved to Bethel "A" for prayer and planning, where they were joined by a hundred parents and other concerned Brevard residents.

The students' first demand was met the next day, when school board members returned to the school at the students' insistence for an emergency meeting.

With the firing of Mal Crite as a catalyst, issues that had been simmering at the high school for years came to the surface. One by one, with a compelling display of clarity, dignity, and self-control under pressure, the students addressed the school board. Parents and Reverend Gordon beamed with pride, but remained in the background as the students controlled the meeting.

The students presented a list of demands, including hiring black teachers at the high school; offering a black history course; implementing strict policies regarding racial slurs and demeaning behavior by staff and students; requiring training among

1. Before reading further, write a brief definition of human power. Is it something you are born with, or is it something you obtain? Can human power be lost or taken away? Does God have a place in your definition of human power?

staff to minimize prejudice; and hiring a home-school coordinator, preferably Mal Crite. In the ensuing weeks, the adults followed the lead of the students, meeting at the church to organize themselves, adding demands, and putting into place an implementation team to follow through with the board of education.

Selena Robinson, a grandmother and community leader, reflected: "Stick together and you can get some things accomplished. And always keep God in front." (Adapted from Hollyday, "Civil Rights, 1990s Style")

Discover the Power Within

The students of Brevard High School felt that the school board's power was being used to do something wrong. Rather than allow it, they chose to make themselves heard. They drew on their own power as individuals and as a community. They used their power in a way that showed respect for all who were involved. The final outcomes of their actions would take months or even years to develop, but they demonstrated the positive value of using power responsibly.

What Is Human Power?

The Christian understanding of human power sees God as the source of power, and human freedom as the most important factor in how it is used. **Power** is the God-given capacity of everyone to affect their own life, the lives of others, and the world around them either positively or negatively.

The outcome of using power—whether the effects are positive or negative—is based on the choices of the person. The power God gives to human beings is tied to our freedom to choose either the way of God, which is love, or the way of sin, which is total self-interest.

Let's consider two different ways of looking at power.

Power-Over Model

A common way of understanding power in Western society is to think of it as a limited commodity. For example, power is thought of like oil: The supply is limited. There is only so much to go around. As a result, power is seen as something that some people—the powerful—have and other people—the powerless—do not.

Looking at power this way leads to a society where those who do not have power are subjected to the decisions of those who do. The powerless see power as something outside themselves, in the hands of someone else—a school principal, the police, people in "authority positions." It is as if

God is the source of human power—the capacity to affect one's own life, the lives of others, and the world.

those with power have climbed a ladder, and from the top of the ladder they have power over all that is below them. This understanding of power is referred to as the **"power-over" model.**

The trouble with power-over is that it is usually an abuse of the human capacity for power. The interests of those who hold the power dominate those who do not. In the opening story of this chapter, the board of education at Brevard High School was operating from a power-over understanding. The board members disregarded the needs of those who would be most influenced by their decision, and their own concerns dominated.

The irony of the power-over model is that it ultimately harms not only the powerless but the powerful as well. Though the powerful in this model might advance in control, influence, or wealth, they suffer the consequences of the division they create between themselves and those they dominate. The powerful, like everyone else, must live in a climate of fear and distrust. And they are cut off from experiencing the gifts and insights of those they dominate. Power-over relationships deprive the powerful, not just the powerless, of the well-being God wants for them.

Power-With Model

A model of power that is sensitive to the needs of the *whole* community is the **"power-with" model.** In this approach, power is seen as something within every person. And each person can freely choose to use it *with* and *for* others to bring about good in the world. The power-with model does not entrust power to a single person or group at the top of a ladder. Rather, power is entrusted to all members of the community, who use it together for the good of the community.

Power-Over: A Global Case of Abuse

Ruling classes throughout history have used slavery, torture, high taxation, corruption, unemployment, and other unjust practices directed toward poor people to support their own privileges, interests, and status. In our own day, a similar situation can be found in the relationship between the majority of countries in the Northern Hemisphere and those in the Southern Hemisphere.

Since the time Columbus and his successors claimed the "New World" for Europe, the wealth of the northern countries has been built on the exploitation of countries in Africa, in southern Asia, and in Central and South America. This abusive relationship continues today. For example:

- Many southern countries are so indebted to countries in the north that they must put more effort and resources into raising crops for export to pay off debt than into feeding their own people.

Above, right: Much of the hunger that affects children in countries like Somalia is caused by the unjust practices of wealthy nations.

2. Certain countries are sometimes referred to as "superpowers." The United States is a superpower in terms of military and economic strength, and Japan and Germany are superpowers in terms of economic strength. Answer in writing: *What policies would a superpower country have if it were to act in a power-over way? in a power-with way?*

The Brevard High School students who challenged the board of education were using the power-with model. They did not try to take control of the school. Rather, they gathered their own power resources as individuals and as a group. They considered the needs of their community and confronted the board in a dignified manner. Not satisfied with being subjected to the power-over operation of the board, the students offered the opportunity for a power-with exchange, for the benefit of the entire community.

Community Power, God's Power

Human power, the God-given capacity to affect things, to make a difference, exists in each person. But this power can be misused in such a way that God's intention for creation is violated. The proper, just use of power seeks to fulfill God's intention that creation should survive and thrive. Selena Robinson's comment in the story of Brevard High School offers some insight into the proper use of power: "Stick together and you can get some things accomplished. And always keep God in front," she said.

Join Together

When power is viewed according to the power-over model, as a limited commodity, it becomes something to be hoarded. The fear is that if power is shared with others, some of it will be lost. Many people respond to this fear by trying

- Multinational corporations from northern countries like to build factories in less-developed countries in the Southern Hemisphere to take advantage of extremely low wages and weak or nonexistent environmental protection laws.

By looking out for their own interests and abusing their power, wealthy countries in the north have created great poverty and oppression in the south.

In his encyclical letter *On Social Concern,* **Pope John Paul II** recognizes that the responsibility for this situation lies with those who abuse power. The pope's letter is paraphrased here in a popular translation by Fr. Joseph Donders:

Responsibility for the deterioration
from bad to worse in so many underdeveloped
regions rests on both the developing nations,
especially on the part of those
holding economic and political power,
and on the more developed nations
which have not made a sufficiently great effort.

One must denounce
the economic, financial and social
mechanisms and structures
which are manipulated
by the rich and powerful,
for their own benefit at the expense of
the poor. (Number 16)

to get far enough up the ladder that they do not have to worry about losing power.

On the other hand, people who operate from a power-with model recognize that their power is within them; they are not afraid to form a circle of power that includes many other people. They know that their ability to make things happen is magnified when they come together and share their concerns and work as a unified force. When power is shared, it multiplies and enhances each person's individual power.

The people who testified on behalf of Mal Crite at the school board meeting were, as individuals, tapping into their own personal power. Coming together as they did expanded their circle of power, and they were able to be more effective at the next meeting. The school board had to listen to them and take their concerns seriously. The students also set a wonderful example for their parents and others in the community, which expanded their power even more. The entire community learned a valuable lesson about using power to make justice happen.

Keep God in Front

The Brevard students planned and prayed about their actions at a local church. By basing their actions in community prayer and reflection, they "kept God in front." They

Salvadoran citizens celebrate in a march for unity.

3. Write a description of a person you know of who is willing to share his or her power. Then describe someone you know of who sees power as a limited commodity to be hoarded.

By recognizing that our power comes from God, we open ourselves to using power in a just way, with God as our guide.

4. Write a one-page essay agreeing or disagreeing with this statement: *Because God is the giver of the gift of human power, ultimately no person can take it away from another.*

recognized that their power came from God. To use their power in a just and positive way, they let God be their guide.

As a gift of God, power is similar to God's gift of human dignity. The power that is within each person can be violated and negated, but ultimately no person can take power away from another. The students took steps to prevent the violation of their own power to make a difference.

The students at Brevard High School tapped into the God-given power within themselves as individuals and as a community. By choosing to follow the power-with model in order to bring about good effects in their community, they used their power for justice, not simply to control others or the situation.

For Review

- In your own words, define *power*.
- What is the relationship between freedom and power?
- Identify and briefly explain two models of power.

Jesus and Power

The use of power can either fulfill or violate God's intention for creation. To discover how God wants human power to be used, Christians turn to the example and teachings of Jesus.

"To Bring Good News"

The fourth chapter of Luke's Gospel offers a clear picture of the power Jesus based his ministry on. The chapter begins, however, by showing us that Jesus rejected power that did not serve God's intention.

The Temptations: Jesus Rejects Power-Over

In Luke's account, following the baptism of Jesus by John, Jesus goes to the wilderness, "led by the Spirit." In the wilderness, he fasts for forty days and is tempted by the devil. The **temptations** involve power, but not the kind of power Jesus will use in his ministry. These are temptations to accept power-over. (See Luke 4:1–13.)

Because he is fasting, Jesus is hungry. The devil says to him, "'If you are the Son of God, command this stone to become a loaf of bread'" (4:3). But Jesus rejects the temptation to take **power over nature** simply to prove his identity. Later in his ministry, when he heals the sick, Jesus does take power over nature out of compassion for those who suffer, not to prove himself as a wonder-worker and impress others.

In the second temptation, the devil claims to have authority over all the world's kingdoms. If Jesus will worship the devil, **power over all the kingdoms** will be given to Jesus. Again Jesus rejects power-over, reminding the devil that he worships and serves only God. Taking power over kingdoms will not help fulfill God's intention, because the Kingdom Jesus proclaims has nothing to do with conventional power and politics.

Finally the devil takes Jesus to the top of the Temple and tempts him to take **power over God:** "'If you are the Son of God, throw yourself down from here'" (4–9). The angels of God, says the devil, will protect Jesus from harm. But Jesus rejects the temptation, responding matter-of-factly, "'It is said, "Do not put the Lord your God to the test"'" (4:12).

By resisting these temptations, Jesus demonstrates that his ministry will not be characterized by power-over. When he proclaims the Kingdom of God, the power Jesus displays is clearly not one of controlling others but of sharing power with those who respond to his call.

The Announcement of His Ministry: Jesus Accepts Power-With

The temptation story in Luke is immediately followed by this one, in which Jesus begins his public ministry:

> When he came to Nazareth, where he had been brought up, he went to the synagogue on the sabbath day, as was his custom. He stood up to read, and the scroll of the prophet Isaiah was given to him. He unrolled the scroll and found the place where it was written:
>   "The Spirit of the Lord is upon me,
>   because he has anointed me
>   to bring good news to the poor.
>   He has sent me to proclaim release to the captives
>   and recovery of sight to the blind,
>   to let the oppressed go free,
>   to proclaim the year of the Lord's favor."
> And he rolled up the scroll, gave it back to the attendant, and sat down. The eyes of all in the synagogue were fixed on him. Then he began to say to them, "Today this scripture has been fulfilled in your hearing." (Luke 4:16–21)

By quoting Isaiah, Jesus publicly announces that he intends to use his God-given power to have a positive effect on others. His energies will be directed toward power-with, power that liberates and heals. Jesus sees his power as a gift to be used *with* and *for* others, not over them. It is power that brings about justice.

Jesus challenges the powerful figures of his time—the oppressors, the hypocritical religious leaders who lay heavy legalistic burdens on the people, the rich who do not share their goods with the poor. But in these instances, he is not challenging them out of a desire to control them but out of love. He wants to liberate them from the narrow, stunted lives they are living.

Empowerment: Jesus Heals

The **healings** performed by Jesus show the way Jesus used power. Consider this example:

> As he went, the crowds pressed in on him. Now there was a woman who had been suffering from hemorrhages for twelve years; and though she had spent all she had on physicians, no one could cure her. She came up behind him and touched the fringe of his clothes, and immediately her hemorrhage stopped. Then Jesus asked, "Who touched me?" When all denied it, Peter said,

The Gospels show us that Jesus heals by sharing power. In this seventeenth-century painting by Nicolas Poussin, Jesus heals a blind man in Jericho.

"Master, the crowds surround you and press in on you." But Jesus said, "Someone touched me; for I noticed that power had gone out from me." When the woman saw that she could not remain hidden, she came trembling; and falling down before him, she declared in the presence of all the people why she had touched him, and how she had been immediately healed. He said to her, "Daughter, your faith has made you well; go in peace." (Luke 8:42–48)

In the story, Jesus acknowledges that he has power, but his power alone does not heal the woman. "Your faith has made you well," Jesus tells her. The healing takes place when Jesus' power becomes connected with the woman's faith.

A similar pattern occurs throughout the Gospels. Those who are sick come to Jesus. He does not seek them out, desiring to use power over them. He uses his power with and for them, easing their pain. Those who are healed are often sent back to their homes and towns, strengthened and renewed by their experience with Jesus, to proclaim what God has done for them. Jesus offers **empowerment** to people; their power grows, rather than diminishes, because of their contact with him.

The story of the woman with the hemorrhage also points out Jesus' special care for those who are on the margins of society. In Jesus' time, this woman has several marks against her. First, she is a woman, and therefore a second-class

5. Spend a few minutes reflecting on Jesus' announcement that he came to preach good news to the poor, release the captives, recover the sight of the blind, and free the oppressed. Does this message of liberation and healing speak to any aspect of your own life? Write a short response.

Jesus' care for those on the margins of society is a model for our behavior toward marginalized people like Brazil's poor children.

The Power of the Poor: A Base Community Reflects on the Scriptures

Solentiname is a group of islands in Lake Nicaragua in Central America. There, for several years the *campesinos,* or peasants, in a **Christian base community** celebrated Mass and shared their faith with the priest and poet Ernesto Cardenal. It was a time of immense suffering by Nicaragua's poor people, as the society's structures were stacked against the masses of peasants. The structures of privilege, land ownership, and power were kept in place by the notoriously ruthless dictator Anastasio Somoza.

After sharing the Gospel at Mass, the small community of Solentiname would talk about the passage that had been proclaimed. Reflecting on the Scriptures together was a crucial way for these poor people to discover their own power in an oppressive, unjust society. This excerpt is from their dialog about Mark 4:35–41, the passage in which Jesus is in a boat with his fearful disciples, and he calms a storm on the Sea of Galilee.

Felipe: Faith is the faith that many young people have today. It's faith in change, in the revolution. It's faith that the world can be changed by love, that evil can become good, that those angry waves can be calmed.

Alejandro: But here in Solentiname, right here and now. If some lady's child is sick with malaria, we're not going to tell her to have faith in God and the child won't die. Faith in God is also faith in people united in a community, and that faith *can* cure the child.

Alejandro's mother: The greatest evils of humanity are due to lack of love, and God doesn't solve them personally. He does it through love among people. We used to be content with faith in a Jesus in heaven, who isn't the one who's in the storm, the one who is here with us in the person of the other, in so-and-so, in what's-her-name, the Jesus who's with the people, even though he's asleep.

Ernesto: We also see many miracles or signs—*miracle* means "sign"—that Jesus has performed throughout history, the transformations that his word has brought about. And still we often doubt that the world can be transformed, that the winds and the waves of history can be calmed.

Oscar: Everything is in getting together. Together we can work a lot of miracles.

Another: Many misfortunes are due to the people themselves, even shipwrecks, like the wreck of the *Maria Guadalupe* that sank because the captain had it overloaded. Not to speak of the sicknesses

citizen. Second, her illness makes her "ritually unclean," which means she cannot enter the Temple and participate in her community's worship. Third, she is poor; all her money has been spent on finding a cure. She is an outcast from society. Society's power over her has violated her dignity and prevented her from living fully as an image of God. Jesus, however, recognizes her dignity, shares power with her, and she is restored to fullness.

Power and Poverty

The Gospels are filled with stories in which Jesus reaches out to people who are considered powerless: beggars, prostitutes, that can be cured and many other setbacks that we shouldn't blame on God but on people.

Tomas, deliberately: On everybody. Because the fact is that if we don't speak, nobody can understand. Only when the people insist can things be understood. That's why it must be us.

Adan: I think that now a lot of people don't believe anything. Maybe even most people. Even the most religious people, they don't believe either. They are absolute unbelievers. I've seen it. They say you can't make any changes here. And many talk against it. They have no faith.

Oscar: This change in people is made by people themselves.

Elvis: Then we're going to have a society the way the lake got that time with Jesus. The wind calmed down and everything was absolutely quiet.

Tomas: The fear ended and they felt liberated.

Bosco: We are now traveling in that boat. The oppressions, that's the overturn, right? But we've got to feel safe, because Jesus is in the boat with us, even though he's asleep in the stern.

Tomas: Our boat is filling with water and we can't bail it out. But then we have to call out to Jesus, and that means getting together. If we all agree on doing something, it'll get done quickly, no matter what it is, because he'll be right in the middle of us to make the miracle.

Felipe: The storm is the attacks of the enemies of this Gospel message. And we shouldn't be afraid. We must have faith, as Jesus said that time to the men who were in a boat with him.

Olivia: He travels with us in the community. The boat is the community.

(Adapted from Cardenal, *The Gospel in Solentiname*, vol. 2, pages 184–189)

Above: "The boat is the community," and with faith it can endure the storm, as depicted in this painting by Solentiname artist Ignacio Fletes.

physically or mentally ill people, foreigners. He takes the side of anyone his society rejects, victimizes, or neglects. In the Scriptures, these people are referred to as "the poor."

That Jesus would align himself with the poor and in favor of justice was completely consistent with his Jewish tradition. Throughout the Hebrew Scriptures, there is an unmistakable connection between doing real justice and having concern for the poor. Real justice in the Scriptures involves actions such as freeing slaves, stopping oppression, feeding the hungry, housing the homeless, and clothing the naked. In fact, according to Jewish Law, the truest measure of a just community is how it cares for its most vulnerable members. When a community neglects the well-being of

6. Using the standard of Jewish Law that the truest measure of a just community is how it cares for its most vulnerable members, examine one of your own local communities—your school, neighborhood, or city. Can it be called a just community? Why or why not? Write down your answer.

orphans, widows, beggars, and strangers, the whole community's well-being is damaged.

Jesus' focus on the poor influenced the way Jesus understood and used power. He made a strong connection between power and poverty. As a result, a Christian understanding of power must always take this connection into account.

Poverty is usually associated with a lack of material things: money, food, clothing, shelter, and so on. Material poverty is an important justice issue that must be addressed by Christians everywhere. But poverty must also be understood in a broader sense. **Poverty** is a state in which the ability of individuals or groups to use power to bring about good for themselves, their families, and their community is weakened or blocked. In other words, poverty prevents us from acting as images of God, as fully human.

Poverty and the Abuse of Power

Poverty is caused by the abuse of power. Material poverty does not exist because people are lazy or unmotivated. It exists because some people who have power use it in ways that undermine the power of others. For example, if those in power cut the funding of a school lunch program so that more can be spent on military weapons, children of poor

Material poverty exists because some people who have power use it to undermine the power of others. Fighting in Afghanistan has left many, like this woman, poor and destitute.

families will go hungry. In a similar way, if a young boy is punished for crying because "real men don't cry," he may become a man who experiences emotional poverty. The power of what he has been taught could block his own power to experience the full range of human emotion.

Pictures of Poverty

If we understand poverty as something that prevents us from being fully human, we see that a person's power can be undermined or blocked in many ways. Consider these different kinds of poverty and their effects:

- Material poverty can be seen in hunger, crime, and homelessness. These assault full humanness in obvious ways.
- Low self-esteem is an experience of poverty as well; it can lead to behaviors that show a lack self-respect, such as drug abuse.
- Many people are denied the experience of full humanness because they are on the margins of society, rejected by most of society or excluded from it altogether because of some supposed defect.
- Greed, too, is a form of poverty. It diminishes a person's or organization's self-perception; worth is thought of in terms of money and possessions rather than as derived from being made in God's image.
- Those who are vain and self-centered also live diminished lives, because they fail to care about the needs of others.
- People who seem to have an abundance of privilege and power often live narrow lives, never really grasping the significance of being fully human.

Perhaps we have never thought of some of the above as examples of poverty, but in a broad sense they are.

Liberation for All

The Gospels show that Jesus definitely took the side of those who were materially poor, outcast, and in need of healing. But his ministry and message were directed to all people. Whatever the cause of our poverty, whether it is emotional, material, or spiritual, Jesus offers to share his liberating, healing message with anyone who will receive him.

To those who experience any kind of poverty, Jesus offers a message of solidarity and empowerment. He offers a share of power that does justice. To those who abuse power, Jesus issues a challenge. He challenges them to choose the path of love and justice so that they, too, can experience the liberation of a fully human life as a creature made in God's image.

The teaching and example of Jesus demonstrate the way God intends human power to be used. Jesus' example proves

7. Poverty prevents us from acting as images of God. Write a paragraph discussing a time when someone abused power in such a way that you could not be fully human.

8. Jesus proclaimed liberation for all. Make a list of the kinds of poverty you would like to be liberated from—those things that keep you from experiencing your full human potential.

A Peasant and a Bishop Stand Up to Unjust Systems

Rigoberta Menchú of Guatemala

The winner of the 1992 Nobel Peace Prize is a thirty-three-year-old **indigenous** (native) woman from Guatemala. **Rigoberta Menchú** is known for her work defending the human rights of her country's native Indians. After receiving the Nobel Prize, Menchú returned to her homeland to celebrate with tens of thousands of Guatemalans. But she had spent most of the previous decade living in exile, fearing she would not be safe in Guatemala.

Rigoberta Menchú was born in a small village in the Guatemalan highlands. She began working in the coffee and sugarcane fields as a small child. In her teens, she became a leader in her community as

it struggled for the most basic of human rights.

Menchú fled Guatemala in 1981 after many of her family members were killed. Soldiers killed her father when he and other indigenous people peacefully occupied the Spanish embassy in Guatemala City. This action protested army occupation of their villages. Four siblings were killed and her mother was raped and tortured to death by the military.

When she received news of the peace award, Menchú said, "It's not enough to speak out against war; the causes of war must be eliminated. That is, we must end unjust distribution of wealth. I blame the first world for having taken our riches for so many years."

She says the honor she received recognizes the struggle

of many who have dared to speak the truth. "We have broken the silence around Guatemala. Now I would like to see Guatemala at peace, with indigenous and nonindigenous people living side-by-side. I think it would be the most beautiful thing. Maybe I won't

---

9. Answer the following question in one page. Use examples from your own experience to illustrate your reasoning. *Do power-with actions do more than power-over actions to create the Kingdom of God?*

that although power can be abused and cause injustice, power itself is something good. It is intended to be used with and for others, to liberate, to heal, to create well-being. Power is meant to do justice.

For Review

- What kind of power did Jesus reject? What kind of power did he base his ministry on?
- In his ministry, what did Jesus seek to do with his power?
- Describe the connection between Jesus' ministry and his Jewish tradition.
- Define *poverty.* In Luke's Gospel, how does Jesus respond to poverty?

live to see it, but maybe others after me will."

Of one thing Rigoberta Menchú is certain: "We indigenous people, not just the Guatemalan people, deserve this prize. It is a gift of life, a gift for history, and a gift of our time." (Based on Resource Center of the Americas, *Rigoberta Menchú,* page 14)

Bishop Willy Romelus of Haiti

For decades, Haiti's people have suffered in every way imaginable—from hunger, torture, terror, and the crucifixion of their hope. At last in 1990 they found hope in their first democratically elected president, Fr. Jean-Bertrand Aristide. But when a military coup removed him in 1991, the rule of terror was back— until Aristide was allowed to return in October 1994.

During the three years of the coup, **Bishop Willy Romelus**, one of Haiti's ten Catholic bishops, was a rare voice in defense of the victims of persecution. He consistently denounced the coup and the military's violent reprisals against any person who supported President Aristide. The bishop's outspokenness made him vulnerable to attack. For denouncing such acts, Bishop Romelus also suffered reprisals: verbal harassment, death threats, late-night searches of his home by soldiers, graffiti that defamed his name all over town, and an organized attempt on his life.

His position put him in danger, but Bishop Romelus firmly believes that he has been placed there by the Holy Spirit. He insists that people who have found strength in God don't get discouraged

easily. Said the bishop: "We are looking for a way out of our problems, but we are limited in the means we can take with our own hands. So we must trust in God to deliver us. Changing Haiti is not in my hands. It is in God's hands, but God uses human beings to change things." (Based on Puleo, "A Bishop Who Hears the Cry of Haiti's Poor")

Tap into Your Own Power

We are all gifted with power. Even those who think they are powerless *do* have power, the capacity to make a difference. But they may need to discover that power and work with it.

Tapping into our power to create justice and well-being for everyone and our world takes commitment, courage, and a clear focus. But sometimes it is hard to know where to begin; so many situations need the influence of positive power. To use our power well, we must begin by recognizing what we are concerned with. Then we must determine where the use of our power will be most effective.

Start Where You Have the Most Influence

Our power is most effective when we use it where it can make the most difference.

Identify Your Circle of Concern

The first step in determining where our power will be most influential is to recognize our **"circle of concern."** This circle can be very large. It includes all those matters in life that concern us in a general way—our health, friends, family, work, school, the environment, world hunger, and so forth.

Identify Your Circle of Influence

When we examine our circle of concern, we see that it probably contains some things we have little or no influence on. At the same time, we see that it contains many things we actually can influence. Within our circle of concern, the things we *can* affect make up our **"circle of influence."**

Our circle of influence is the ideal starting point for tapping into our power. From there we can influence more and more of our circle of concern. Often, however, people try to use power by focusing from the start on the items in their wider circle of concern. They neglect the things they can really influence, which leaves them feeling scattered and in-effective. They have good intentions, but are not making the best use of their power.

On the other hand, negative use of power often arises when a person's circle of concern is actually smaller than his or her circle of influence. What the person cares about is smaller than what he or she can influence. For example, someone whose overriding concern is to live in a quiet neighborhood may successfully use power to have a railroad line rerouted. But suppose this action influences another neighborhood by making it necessary to demolish an apartment building there, leaving others without homes. Obviously, the influential person's circle of concern was too small. The person had only narrow self-interest as an area of concern.

For most of us, our circle of concern is bigger than our circle of influence. The best way to address our larger concerns is to start with the items that we can truly influence; that means starting with our own behavior. From there we can begin to influence the actions of others. In the process, our circle of influence begins to expand, along with the effectiveness of our power.

Power in the Real World

Taking a look at some real-life examples will show us both negative and positive uses of power. Exposing the bad and shedding light on the good can help us examine the ways we use our gift of power. Do our choices and actions promote justice, or do they block it?

Your circle of concern may be as large as the environment, but to make an impact it is best to begin where you have influence, for instance, by talking with your government representatives.

Circles of Concern, Circles of Influence

1. Our circle of concern is usually much larger than our circle of influence:

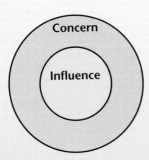

2. Effective use of power focuses on our circle of influence, which grows as we use our power:

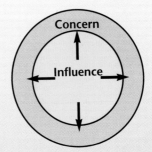

3. Ineffective use of power results from trying to affect our circle of concern instead of our circle of influence. This makes our circle of influence shrink, rather than grow:

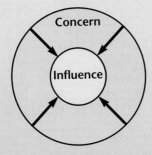

4. For some very powerful but self-centered people, their circle of concern is smaller than their circle of influence:

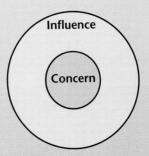

(Covey, *The Seven Habits of Highly Effective People*, pages 82–85)

Teachers in Norway Confront the Nazis: Nonviolent Resistance

Our first example shows the dramatic contrast between power used for good and power used for evil. The Nazi regime, led by Adolph Hitler in Germany, tried to impose fascism throughout Europe during World War II. In the process, more than six million Jews and five million non-Jews were executed in concentration camps. In this true story, the violence of Nazism is met with **nonviolent resistance**. This is a story of the power of words and integrity:

> Hitler's armies conquered Norway in June 1940 after two months of armed resistance. Nazi decrees disbanded Norway's parliament, outlawed all but fascist political parties, and installed Vidkun Quisling, a Norwegian fascist, as the head of state. Quisling abolished the constitution and all elections.

10. Make a diagram of your circle of concern and your circle of influence, filling in the first circle with things that concern you and the second circle with things that you can influence. Choose one item from your circle of concern and describe a strategy for affecting it.

Quisling's goal was to transform Norway into a fascist "corporative state," as Mussolini had done in Italy. He selected the country's teachers, the molders of the minds of youth, as his first recruits for the new order. During late 1940 and early 1941, Quisling issued a series of decrees: his portrait must be hung in all schools; the curriculum must be revised along fascist lines; and teachers must give students a sympathetic view of the fascist regime. He also ordered students to join a fascist youth movement and teachers to join a union headed by the military police.

Nazi storm troopers, marching through Nuremberg, Germany, personified the negative power resisted by Norway's teachers.

The teachers refused. They agreed on common guidelines: do not obey government orders that conflict with conscience; do not teach Nazi propaganda; do not cooperate with fascist organizations. Resistance leaders met in Oslo and issued a declaration, which they distributed widely. It said that Quisling's orders went against conscience and therefore should not be obeyed.

Within weeks, twelve thousand of Norway's 14,000 teachers had signed the declaration and refused to join the new union. Massive numbers of students refused to join the youth movement. Over 200,000 parents and all of Norway's Lutheran bishops wrote letters of protest to Quisling. When the few fascist teachers attempted to hold classes, students refused to attend.

In exasperation, the government closed the schools. Teachers responded by holding classes in their own homes. Thirteen hundred teachers were arrested and sent to Gestapo-run concentration camps in Norway's frigid north.

Months later, when the schools reopened, the remaining teachers still refused to join the fascist union. They read a statement to their students that said: "The teacher's vocation is not only to give children knowledge; teachers must also teach their pupils to believe in and uphold truth and justice. Therefore, teachers cannot, without betraying their calling, teach anything that violates their conscience. That, I promise you, I shall not do."

The Gestapo spread a rumor that if the teachers did not give in, their arrested colleagues would be killed. After a tremendous struggle of conscience, the teachers decided to continue the resistance. In response, Quisling sent the arrested teachers to a concentration camp farther north, above the Arctic Circle, where they had to do forced labor. As the trainloads of teachers passed through the mountains, children stood at the stations and sang patriotic songs to encourage them. Five hundred teachers were shipped north on a ship designed for ninety-six passengers. Two teachers died in the freezing camps.

Quisling believed that these harsh measures would intimidate the teachers, but they refused to back down. Their courage inspired the nation. Finally, in November 1942 Quisling released the arrested teachers, who returned home to triumphal processions. Quisling showed his exasperation in an enraged speech to teachers in which he said, "You teachers have destroyed everything for me." (Adapted from Sider and Taylor, *Nuclear Holocaust and Christian Hope*, pages 238–241)

The teachers' power: The teachers in Norway had a large circle of concern. It included their students, and their own personal integrity and that of their country. Their actions, though, remained within their circle of influence. They were teachers, and their best line of action was to refuse to teach anything that violated their own dignity and that of their students and nation. The way they used their power expanded their circle of influence, affecting even the ability of a vicious military government to achieve its goals.

The response of the overwhelming majority of Norway's people, led by their teachers, illustrates a courageous way of using power. The teachers used power the way God intended it to be used—to bring about justice and well-being for their whole society.

11. Make a diagram of the Norwegian teachers' circles of concern and influence. Can you think of additional strategies they might have used to resist the Nazis?

Right over might: By rejecting and refusing to cooperate with actions and ideas that went against their sense of what was right, Norway's teachers tapped into the very core of their power. Furthermore, they bonded together and encouraged—rather than bullied—thousands of others to join them.

Each attempt by Quisling's government to exert power over the teachers was met by an act that simply but firmly reinforced their original stand. When the schools were shut down, the teachers held classes in their homes; when teachers were arrested, they were cheered by their students.

Norway's teachers and their supporters used their God-given gift of power in liberating, life-promoting ways. Their example enriches their nation and the world. The Nazis abused their gift of power, turning it into an oppressive weapon of death. Yet in spite of the terror the Nazis inflicted on the people of Norway, fascism ultimately could not prevail over the determination for truth and justice.

Power in the Marketplace: A Boycott

The story of the successful boycott of the General Electric Corporation in the early 1990s demonstrates how power can be used for good or for bad in the marketplace. A **boycott** is an organized, large-scale refusal to buy certain products. Here is an account from a young woman who was dedicated to the goals of the boycott:

> I was working part-time at a hardware store in my hometown in Wisconsin when I first learned about the power of boycotts. The owner decided not to sell any products made by General Electric. No light bulbs, toasters, irons, nothing. He explained to us that he was angry because GE was one of the biggest manufacturers of nuclear weapons in the United States, and he didn't want to support that business by selling their "peaceful" products. "Plenty of companies make light bulbs and household appliances," he told us, "but they don't endanger life on the planet."

I started following the controversy. I got so interested that I joined INFACT, an organization that promoted the boycott of GE products all over the country. In the first few years, we tried to educate the public about GE. Very few people knew about the company's weapons business. In response, GE increased its advertising. They ran ads about bringing "good things to life," completely ignoring the fact that they were into building weapons of death.

We also educated doctors and medical facilities about GE. It didn't make sense to buy high-tech, life-saving equipment from a company that was building nuclear arms. Many customers went to other companies, and GE lost millions of dollars in sales.

Then in 1992, INFACT received an Oscar, the Academy Award, for a documentary film about GE. The film showed GE commercials along with interviews of people who had been harmed by radiation and other poisons in GE's weapons factories. About one billion people watched the Academy Awards on TV, and they learned about the boycott that night.

About a year later, I was finishing my final term paper before receiving my degree in marketing. My paper was about boycotts, and I was able to add this information: The seven-year-long boycott was over. In April 1993, GE sold its nuclear weapons division to another company. The weapons are still out there—there's still work to be done. But U.S. consumers used their power and caused a corporate giant to listen.

Uncovering a lie: The General Electric Corporation used its power in a negative way. It tried to deceive the public with its ad campaign about bringing "good things to life," when in fact a major portion of its business was in the making of nuclear weapons. The boycott and public education campaign uncovered this deception. The organizers educated consumers about what they were buying and who they were buying it from. Thus they enabled consumers to work in their own circle of influence—what they buy. By using power in this way, consumers affected their circle of concern, a circle that took in the safety of the earth and all its inhabitants.

Power Closer to Home: Assertiveness

In our personal lives, power can also be used in positive or negative ways. In this story, a student has to determine how best to use his personal power when he is faced by a difficult situation:

Consumers can affect major corporations simply by choosing which products to buy.

12. Have you ever participated in a product boycott such as the one against General Electric? What factors would be important in deciding whether to participate in a boycott? Write a brief response.

The summer he turned sixteen, Ray got a job making deliveries for a carryout restaurant. Several other high school students worked there, along with two guys who had just graduated. They had been working there for over a year when Ray started.

At first, these two guys just ignored Ray. But after a couple of weeks, they started pulling pranks on him. They would switch orders on him so that he delivered the wrong food to people. Or they would hide the car keys, and then after Ray had frantically searched for several minutes, they would slip them into an obvious spot, making Ray look like a fool in front of the manager.

One time the guys damaged a tire on the car so that it would go flat while Ray was out on deliveries. Stopping to put on the spare made him a half hour late. Customers complained, and Ray was in deep trouble with the manager. But he was afraid to say anything about the pranks. He didn't want the two guys to get even meaner.

Finally, things came to a head. Two more angry customers called when Ray's deliveries were wrong. At the end of the night, the manager took Ray aside, gave him his paycheck, and fired him. Ray started to protest, wanting to say it wasn't his fault, but no words came out. He stared at the floor, grabbed his jacket, and left.

Ray was fuming. His anger grew as he got closer to home. He parked the car, but didn't get out. He just sat there and talked out loud.

"Why should I get fired just because of those two jerks? It'll be hard to find a new job now. And I need to save money for college. What should I do?"

When he calmed down, Ray decided to call the manager and tell the truth. He would apologize for not saying anything sooner. But he would also point out that firing him was not fair because the other two guys set him up. He deserved another chance to prove himself. Even if he didn't get the job back, Ray knew he would feel better if he stood up for himself and made his case.

Influence from within: Ray learned that he did not have to let the circumstances of his life run over him, resigning himself to them as if he had no other choice. Even though his circle of influence was quite small in this situation, he discovered that he could tap into his gift of power. He started with himself and his own response to a difficult experience in his life. Ray decided to act with **assertiveness**, to tactfully but confidently speak up for himself.

Our God-given capacity for power is meant to be used positively in all areas of our life. Everything we are involved in, from the simplest situation to the most complex, is an opportunity to use our power for good.

13. Write about an incident in your life when you were able to tap into your power and have a positive effect. If a similar situation arose today, how would you respond?

For Review

- What is the difference between a circle of concern and a circle of influence?
- Explain the best way to have an effect on your circle of concern.
- How did the teachers in Norway affect their circle of concern?
- How did consumers affect General Electric's manufacturing of nuclear weapons?
- How did Ray use his power in the difficult situation with his employer?

In God's Hands

When people tap into their gift of power and use it to promote justice, the results can be remarkable. It is also true that when power is used for good, there is risk or struggle. The struggle for justice can sometimes last for years and even decades before success or victory can actually be claimed.

Tapping into our power for the sake of justice is risky, scary business. But the previous examples show that the outcomes—even if they only amount to preserving personal integrity—are well worth the risks.

When we seek to use our power for good, we are never alone. Whether we find ourselves standing up with others to the oppressive actions of a corrupt government or focusing on our circle of influence to improve our personal relationships, God is with us in our efforts. God is the source of our power, and ultimately, power's use for the sake of justice is in God's hands. As Bishop Willy Romelus of Haiti has said, "It is in God's hands, but God uses human beings to change things."

4 Making Neighbors Out of Strangers

Marla and Jennifer had been best friends since third grade. Jennifer had been the new kid in town, and didn't know anyone. Marla seemed to have lots of friends, but even so she came over to Jennifer right away and said hi. That was all it took. They'd been best friends ever since, sleeping over at each other's houses, sharing secrets, you name it. They were inseparable—"the twins," their parents joked, because they were almost always together.

But high school suddenly made things different. Marla and Jennifer were part of just a handful of kids from their grade school who went on to high school together. At first Jennifer was delighted. She and Marla could still see each other every day! But then one day somebody said to her, "You don't want to be seen with that crip, do you?"

Jennifer was stunned. Sure, Marla used a wheelchair to get around, but she was so—normal, you just never thought about it. Still, the comment struck a nerve. Jennifer did want to be popular. Would her friendship with Marla stand in the way?

On Marla's part, as Jennifer's coolness toward her became apparent, she felt confused and hurt. Marla's mom even noticed the change in the girls' relationship. She asked if anything was wrong.

Marla's feelings spilled out. "Ever since we started high school, Jennifer's been acting like she doesn't know me. I say hi in the hall and she just ignores me. When I call her on the phone, she acts like she's too busy to talk to me. She says she's not mad at me. I guess I believe her. I haven't seen her enough to make her mad at me, but something's wrong, I just don't know what. Why won't she talk to me?"

When Jennifer was new in town, a total stranger, she was welcomed by Marla. But when the girls reached high school, Jennifer treated Marla like a stranger. All of a sudden, due to peer pressure, she saw Marla as different, odd, because she used a wheelchair. Jennifer went through some anxiety as a result of this, and did choose to exclude Marla from her circle of friends.

If a community intends to be just, it ought to be concerned whenever anyone is excluded from participation. A justice perspective shows us that when "the stranger" is pushed out or left out, the whole community's well-being is assaulted, along with the excluded person's dignity. Participation in community is a basic human right.

Participation in Community

Our Social Nature

Exclusion harms persons and groups because it violates a basic aspect of what it means to be human: human beings are social creatures. None of us can survive and thrive apart from other human beings. Because of our **social nature**, we need and desire friendship, love, and contact with others in general. Our social nature also accounts for the existence of communities. We do not live simply as individuals but as members of communities. A **community** is a group that shares a bond of some kind. It may be based on common characteristics, circumstances, interests, or a combination of these elements.

Each of us belongs to more than one community at a time. We belong to some by choice, as with an activity group at school or the political party we favor. Our membership in other communities is less intentional, based as it is on circumstances such as our family, our race, and our neighborhood. Still, every single moment of our life is lived in community. Nothing that we do happens outside of a community—even if it is none other than the large community we call humanity. Community places us in communion with others, which is essential to human life.

1. In writing, describe one of the communities in which you take part. Does it have a strong sense of purpose, or is it less intentional? How is participation encouraged?

What's Wrong with This Picture?

More than likely, each of us has had some experience of being excluded from a community. See if this scenario is familiar:

> Don goes to a party with a couple of his friends. As soon as they walk into the room, Don realizes that the only people he knows are the two he came with. Don's friends know a lot of other people there, but before he knows it, they have gone off, talking and laughing with their other friends.
>
> Now, Don is not the type of person who easily strikes up a conversation. He's wondering why he even agreed to come. Left to fend for himself, Don does what he usually does in these situations—he heads for the food. With his plate in one hand and a can of soda pop in the other, Don seeks out a corner to lean into, hoping that someone will come talk to him.

If he doesn't make a stronger effort, Don will spend the whole evening on the fringes, observing the fun but not participating in it. If that is the case, both Don and other people at the party will lose out. Don's chance to gain new friendships and more confidence in his social skills will not materialize. Other people will miss out on discovering what a nice, fun guy Don is under his shyness, or what they have in common with him.

This small example at the level of an individual in a group illustrates why it is wrong to exclude people: it hurts the individual and the whole group as well. If we consider exclusion at a broader level, we will see that it causes serious harm to individuals, groups, and whole societies.

The Christian Vision: An Inclusive Community

The Christian understanding of justice recognizes our human need to be social, to be part of our communities. Jesus, in his ministry, reached out to people from all levels and sectors of society. He invited especially those who had been rejected to be his neighbors and participate in the Good News that he preached. He instructed his followers to take the Good News "'to the ends of the earth'" (Acts 1:8), not just to a select group of the population. The early Christian communities, depicted in the Acts of the Apostles, are models of participation:

> Now the whole group of those who believed were of one heart and soul, and no one claimed private ownership of any possessions, but everything they owned was held in common. . . . There was not a needy person among them, for as many as owned lands or houses sold them and brought the proceeds of what was sold. They laid it at the apostles' feet, and it was distributed to each as any had need. (Acts 4:32–35)

Such a community could not survive without the participation of all members.

Because we need communities to maintain our well-being, participation in them is a basic human right. In *Economic Justice for All*, the U.S. Catholic bishops emphasize the **right to participation** and the wrongness of **marginalization**, which is the forcing of people to the margins of a society or community:

> *Basic justice demands the establishment of minimum levels of participation in the life of the human community for all persons.* The ultimate injustice

2. Think of a time you were excluded from a community. Reflect on how you felt at the time. Did you feel hurt or violated, or did you feel that exclusion was justified? Write down your thoughts.

Exclusion is harmful to the individuals who are excluded and to the group they are excluded from as well.

is for a person or group to be treated actively or abandoned passively as if they were nonmembers of the human race. To treat people this way is effectively to say that they simply do not count as human beings. This can take many forms, all of which can be described as varieties of marginalization, or exclusion from social life. (Number 77)

The bishops also recognize that **social patterns**—established, taken-for-granted ways of doing things—have developed, patterns that automatically exclude certain people or groups from community participation. The bishops insist that this is wrong and that such patterns of exclusion and powerlessness must be overcome if a society is to be just.

What Does Participation Require?

The right to participation requires that several principles be followed in the life of a community or society. When these requirements are not met, real participation and real justice cannot happen. The dignity of a member or group within the community is violated, and the well-being of the community as a whole suffers.

1. Participation requires that all have access to opportunities and the freedom to choose which opportunities to act on. When people or groups are denied opportunities because they are, for example, poor or disabled, the

In April 1994, black South Africans were allowed to vote in national elections for the first time. Nelson Mandela, a black leader, was elected president.

requirements for participation are not met. Communities must take steps to ensure that all members can exercise their right to participate, for their own benefit and that of the community.

2. **Participation requires that all have access to the benefits and resources of the community.** When people or groups are denied access to the community's benefits and resources, their ability to survive and thrive is threatened. When members are threatened, the community as a whole is threatened as well. Communities, and society at large, have a duty to organize structures and institutions that promote the well-being of all members.

3. **Participation requires that all be allowed to contribute toward the well-being of the whole community in meaningful ways.** Each member of a community has something to contribute. When the gifts of all members and groups are not recognized, for instance, because some are considered too young or too old, everyone loses out—the excluded persons and the whole community. The community loses because it has denied itself the gifts of some of its members.

4. **Participation requires that no member of the community be forced to remain on the edges of the community, unable to fully contribute and receive.** Marginalization often leads to the exploitation of those in the margins. For example, they may be offered no choice but low-paying jobs that no one else in the community will take. Or they may be blamed for problems that are rampant throughout society—such as drug abuse, crime, or the breakdown of the family.

Marginalization, once again, violates the dignity of some members of society while preventing the talents and gifts of the marginalized from enriching the community.

3. In a paragraph, describe a social pattern that marginalizes certain people or groups in your school or community.

Saint Paul Teaches About Community

Saint Paul recognized how important it is for everyone in a community to participate. In his first letter to the Corinthians, he says that the Christian community consists of many members who have a variety of gifts:

> Now there are varieties of gifts, but the same Spirit; and there are varieties of services, but the same Lord; and there are varieties of activities, but it is the same God who activates all of them in everyone. To each is given the manifestation of the Spirit for the common good. (1 Corinthians 12:4–7)

Each member of a community can participate in a number of ways. Men, for example, can nurture children as well as contribute to family finances.

4. Write down some of the gifts that you have to offer. Explain in writing how you could share one of those gifts with a community you are a part of. Do you ever feel limited by how that group expects you to participate?

Paul goes on to compare the community, with its variety of gifted members, to the human body. The body has many parts—a hand has a different function than an eye, and the feet cannot take the place of the ears—but it works together as one. In the body and the community, "If one member suffers, all suffer together with it; if one member is honored, all rejoice together with it" (1 Corinthians 12:26).

The different members of a community, like the parts of the body, are all vital to the community's well-being. The comparison between the Christian community and the human body sheds light on any human community. Christian justice rejects the notion that some members' contributions have less value than others, and can therefore be disposed of.

Unlike the parts of the body, each member of a human community can participate in a number of ways. We are not restricted to just one function or gift.

- Older people can shape society and its institutions by using their vote and sharing their experience—they should not be made to feel that retirement excludes them from public life and democratic processes.
- Young people have things to contribute to—and not just receive from—a top quality educational system.
- Many prominent professional athletes have changed careers and made important contributions as lawyers, doctors, judges, and legislators.
- Men can nurture children and run households as well as contribute to the finances of their family.
- Women can be political and business leaders as well as mothers.

The basic human right of participation in community should be encouraged and celebrated. Saint Paul appreciated its value in the Christian community of his day. Justice demands that we recognize and promote its value in the human community as a whole.

For Review

- Define the word *community*.
- Whom did Jesus reach out to in his ministry?
- Why is participation in community a basic human right?
- Summarize the requirements for participation.
- What analogy did Saint Paul use to teach about community?

The Anatomy of Exclusion

In spite of the fact that justice demands participation for all, the opportunity to participate is often denied. Here are just a few of the types of reasons—or excuses—offered by those who deny the participation rights of others:

- "If blacks move into our neighborhood, our property values will go down."
- "We have to keep our membership dues high. We have an image to maintain, and some people just don't fit in."
- "We can't have gays and lesbians in the military; it'll jeopardize morale."
- "I wouldn't travel in the Middle East. I'm afraid I'd be taken hostage by some Muslim fundamentalist group."
- "We can't have a woman president. She'd let her emotions make decisions for her."
- "We need a mandatory retirement age. In our competitive industry, we can't risk having someone on staff who forgets things all the time."
- "We had to move. The city was being overrun by all those boat people."
- "We can't hire an epileptic. Our schedule is too tight to have it interrupted all the time by someone having fits."

All sorts of excuses are given for excluding people from community. Race, social class, religion, gender, age, sexual orientation, ethnic or cultural background, disability, and other distinguishing characteristics have all been used as excuses for exclusion. These differences among people are used to make the case that some people "just don't belong." Or they are used to "prove" that some people, by nature, are "just not fit" to play certain roles within the community. Excuses for exclusion try to claim that something about "those" people makes them unacceptable or inferior. The Christian vision of justice challenges us to see through the arrogance and insecurities that give rise to these excuses and to find none of them acceptable.

When we consider the excuses given for excluding people, we come to the complex issues of stereotypes, prejudice, and discrimination.

5. Write a list of three or more excuses for exclusion that you have heard in your daily life or on television, in magazines, books, and so on. In a paragraph, describe how these excuses make you feel.

Stereotype: A Harmful Assumption

The way we treat others is based on our attitudes toward them. But our attitudes are built on knowledge, and when that knowledge is incomplete, it is likely that our attitudes will not be accurate. An image or assumption about a person or a group, if based on faulty or incomplete knowledge, is a **stereotype**.

Stereotypes can be positive ("older persons are wise") or negative ("people on welfare are lazy"). Either way, stereotypes are too broad. It is impossible for stereotypical characteristics to apply to all members of a group. Basing our attitudes toward others on stereotypes demonstrates disrespect for the uniqueness of persons or groups.

Direct Experience, Faulty Logic

Many stereotypes develop from direct experience of others. But the conclusions represented by these stereotypes are the result of faulty logic. In the following list of examples, the conclusions, which are stereotypes, do not necessarily follow from the observations:

- Three high school juniors were caught cheating on the SATs; therefore all high school students are dishonest.
- Several members of the chess club are Asian Americans; therefore all Asian Americans are brainy.
- That math teacher goes over material too fast; therefore there are no good math teachers.
- The fastest running back on the football team is African American; therefore blacks are always the best athletes.

It is rather obvious that those conclusions represent faulty logic, and few of us would agree with them. However, just such logic is the basis for comments like the following, which also show stereotyped thinking:

- "When high school kids come into my store, I watch them like a hawk. Otherwise, they'll rob me blind."
- "Mary's boyfriend is an Asian American; he probably works for a computer company."
- "My math teacher last year was so bad that I don't even pay attention to the one I have this year."
- "Our football team has eight black players, so I can't understand how they lost so many games."

6. Reflect on a community or group you do not belong to. What do you assume about its members? Do you think your assumptions are accurate, or are they possibly stereotypical? Put your thoughts in writing.

Learned from Our Surroundings

Stereotypes often come from direct experience that is misunderstood, but this is not their only source. Many stereotypes are actually learned from the people around us, such as parents, friends, and teachers. Television, movies, and books also pass on stereotypes to us, as do social institutions like churches and schools. Whatever the source, justice demands that we examine our assumptions about other members of society. Are our assumptions accurate? Or are they stereotypes, based on faulty logic?

Stereotypes and Participation

Stereotyping is an everyday occurrence. Many stereotypes, especially positive ones (like "blacks are great athletes"), seem harmless. So it is easy to lose sight of how much they limit the right of some individuals and groups to participate in community as they choose.

Stereotypes such as "welfare recipients are lazy" or "homeless people are drug addicts" keep us from seeing the facts about the situations of these groups and individuals. Stereotypes like these provide the fuel for deep-seated negative attitudes toward homeless people and those on welfare. In turn, efforts to include them more fully in the life of our communities are obstructed, and their right to participate is violated.

Stereotypes prevent us from seeing the facts about various groups and individuals. Black and white Americans challenged stereotypes in this 1968 protest in Memphis, Tennessee.

Prejudice: A Hostile Attitude

We have seen that stereotypes are images or assumptions about others that are based on faulty logic. When stereotypes become part of the way we think, our attitudes and behaviors are affected. We can develop **prejudice**, an attitude of hostility directed at whole groups of people.

Prejudice involves prejudgment—making a judgment about something before all the facts are known, or without considering the facts. The hostility of prejudice blinds one to the facts and creates a kind of poison in relationships. A person who exhibits prejudice may do so in speech or in action.

An Example: Racism in the United States

Prejudice can be connected to any of the many issues that make people different from one another—gender, age, class, religion, and so on. But one of the most explosive, widespread, and deep-seated forms of prejudice in the United States is **racism** (hostility based on race), especially against African Americans. White racism against blacks is a strong reminder of the history of slavery in America.

The following account by a young black man is about living in a society where he is not welcomed because of his race. It has even more to teach us when we keep in mind that his ancestors were kidnapped, sold as property, and forced into hard labor without any recognition of their human dignity.

> Cops hassle me, but I'm too educated now. When I was young, I used to get a lot of grief from the cops. In this white suburb, when I was riding my bike, I'd get stopped by the cops. They thought I stole the bike. I was scared of cops. I don't know one black person who has never had an encounter with cops.
>
> One day, I'm running to catch the El [elevated train]. This is the third time I got stopped by the cops that year, okay? Once they searched my laundry because they thought I stuffed a stereo in there. This time I'm running for an appointment with my barber. I realize I don't have any money. So I stop by my bank on the way. I take out sixty dollars. I take a short-cut through the alley, counting my money. A cop car pulls up. They slam me against the wall, throw me in the car, no *Miranda* rights or anything.
>
> I had a book under my arm. I think it was Salinger. I'm well-dressed. He said, "You stole this woman's purse." I said I didn't steal any purse. They take me to this lady's apartment building a few blocks away. They parade me in front of her window. She's three stories up. I look up. "Don't look at her!" I try to explain. "Shut up, you got no rights, kid." They really let me have it the whole time. I happened to look up a second and saw an old woman in her seventies with glasses. The window was dirty. I'm this black kid, three stories down, and she's going to identify me. I can't believe this. They had me walking back and forth. Fortunately, I was wearing glasses, too. She said it wasn't me because the guy who robbed her wasn't wearing glasses. They gave me my book back and said, "Get out of here." (Quoted in Terkel, *Race*, pages 402–403)

This young man's experience is a clear case of being victimized by prejudice. He was a black person in a white neighborhood, and he had money; therefore, the police reasoned, he must have stolen it. Individual attitudes of prejudice are just the beginning, however. Attitudes can build until the structures of society encourage prejudice.

From Individuals to Structures

In the latter half of the twentieth century, the attitudes of whites toward blacks in the United States have grown toward more racial tolerance. In surveys conducted during the past thirty years, a growing number of white Americans have affirmed that African Americans should have the same chance as white people to find employment.

Such indications of racial tolerance at the level of personal attitudes are encouraging, but they do not show us the whole picture of racism. What they miss are the forms of racial prejudice that are less visible. These are the forms of prejudice that exist within the structures of society, in the very institutions society sets up to maintain itself. These structural barriers make it difficult for black Americans to participate fully in society, despite increased tolerance among whites.

Though more enlightened in its attitudes than in previous decades, the white majority is fairly resistant to real change because it does not favor creating policies to improve the existing structures. This is seen in resistance to fair housing programs, school desegregation plans, affirmative action programs, and other policies that would directly affect the structures of society.

Individuals' feelings and actions toward persons of different races are powerful, and in fact, deep change for the good can happen only when people are transformed within themselves and act out of a new heart. But acting out of a new heart also must include efforts to find structural solutions to structural problems or there will not be significant change toward racial justice.

The call for structural changes is an essential part of the message offered by the U.S. Catholic bishops in their 1979 pastoral letter on racism, *Brothers and Sisters to Us:*

> Racism is not merely one sin among many; it is
> a radical evil that divides the human family and

7. In writing, describe an incident in which you saw someone treated badly due to prejudice. Or write a fictional account of being treated badly yourself because of some distinguishing characteristic you have (for example, your race or the color of your hair).

Racism, say the U.S. bishops, is a "radical evil that divides the human family."

Practical Guidelines from *Brothers and Sisters to Us*

In their pastoral letter on race, *Brothers and Sisters to Us,* the Catholic bishops of the United States make suggestions for a Christian response to what they call the radical evil of racism. They address individual Christians, the church community, and society at large (pages 10–14).

Guidelines for Individuals

- If our personal attitudes are affected by racial bias, "we are called to conversion and renewal in love and justice."
- "We should try to influence the attitudes of others by expressly rejecting racial stereotypes, racial slurs, and racial jokes."
- We should make an effort to learn "more about how social structures inhibit the economic, educational, and social advancement of the poor" and commit ourselves to action for justice.

Guidelines for the Church

- The church should try to achieve racial balance in church institutions and programs, ensuring that "minority representation goes beyond mere tokenism and involves authentic sharing in responsibility and decision making."
- The church should foster greater racial and minority diversity in its hierarchy.
- Policies of Catholic institutions (schools, universities, social-service agencies, and hospitals) should be reviewed to ensure that the rights of racial minorities are respected.

Guidelines for Society

- Our society must strive for authentic full employment, decent working conditions, adequate income, housing, education, and health care for everyone.
- Government must be held accountable for providing the services essential to everyone.
- The private sector of the economy has a responsibility to work with racial communities to ensure they receive their fair share of the wealth they help to generate.
- In relations with other nations, racial differences should not interfere with our dealing peacefully and justly with them.
- The wealthiest nations of the world have a duty to share wealth with nations in need.
- In the global economy, the private sector has a responsibility "to promote racial justice, not subordination and exploitation, to promote genuine development in poor societies, not mere consumerism and materialism."

8. Imagine a situation in which your personal behavior could influence an entire group to move away from being prejudiced. Write up the situation as if it actually happened.

denies the new creation of a redeemed world. To struggle against it demands an equally radical transformation, in our own minds and hearts as well as in the structure of our society. (Page 10)

A Wide-ranging Problem

To demonstrate and define prejudice, this chapter has used the issue of race as an example. Keep in mind, however, that prejudice is more than just a racial issue. It operates in the areas of religion, gender, ethnicity, economic class, age, sexual orientation, disability, and so on. For example, Catholics have often been the target of prejudiced actions in the history of the United States. The Jewish people have suffered through centuries of prejudice known as **anti-Semitism,** most horribly in the Holocaust (also called *Shoah* by Jews) during World War II. In recent years, people of the Islamic faith have increasingly become the targets of religious prejudice in the United States. But regardless of which group is focused on, prejudice always interferes with people's basic right to participate in the life of the community.

Discrimination: An Injurious Action

The ability to discriminate is a natural and important human ability. To discriminate means to perceive the differences among various things. Without this ability, we could not tell green from red at a traffic light, or we might not perceive the difference between good advice and bad advice, or have a preference for oranges over apples.

Justice, however, is concerned with the kind of discrimination that goes beyond simple perception of differences. **Discrimination** in this sense means using the differences among human beings as reasons to actively deny individuals or groups their right to participate in community.

Discrimination can operate in two ways: directly and indirectly.

Direct Discrimination: Immediate Effects

Direct discrimination refers to unequal treatment, exclusion, or negative judgments directed toward persons or groups based directly on a factor such as race, religion, or ethnic background. Direct discrimination can be committed by way of personal acts but also through social, political, and economic structures.

Personal examples: Here are some examples of direct discrimination experienced at the personal level:

- Ahmed says, "On my cross-country trip, a motel clerk out in the middle of nowhere charged me double the real price for a room. He probably figured I was a rich Arab oil sheikh or something."

- "I live in a small city and work on a factory line," says a middle-aged woman. "When the city council announced they were looking for volunteers to join a fair-housing study committee, I wrote to them expressing my interest. I never heard from them. Every person who was asked to join the committee had college degrees and powerful jobs. I guess I just wasn't 'good enough' for them."

- Jack recalls, "After I got a low grade on a test, my science teacher called me into his office and said, 'Your brother was a straight-A student at this school, one of my best students ever. You better work harder. I expect a lot more from you.'"

Social-structural examples: Direct discrimination committed through social structures is common in history and in the present day:

- The enslavement of African Americans was legal in the United States until 1865, when the Thirteenth Amendment to the Constitution finally abolished it. A few years later, the Fifteenth Amendment gave black males the right to participate politically by voting.
- It was not until 1920, with the passage of the Nineteenth Amendment, that the participation rights of women in the United States were recognized with the right to vote.
- In Hitler's Germany, a series of laws directly discriminated against Jews in almost every facet of life. The final outcome was that six million Jews were killed in Nazi concentration camps.
- Until the 1990s, South Africa's system of racial segregation, **apartheid,** kept power from the black majority by denying participation rights of all kinds.
- The policy of "ethnic cleansing" perpetrated against Muslims in the former Yugoslavian republic of Bosnia deprives them of their homes, livelihoods, and even their lives.

Indirect Discrimination: Ripple Effects

Indirect discrimination refers to the negative ripple effects that follow acts of direct discrimination. It can have a wide impact. As a result, indirect discrimination is difficult to trace because, as these examples show, the sequence of events can be extremely complex:

- People with disabilities tend to have lower incomes than other people with comparable education. The direct reason they are paid less is not that they are disabled. Their

In Hitler's Germany, a series of laws directly discriminated against Jews. A Nazi boycott of Jewish shops in Berlin was one of the early steps taken by the government toward the eventual execution of millions of Jews.

lower earning power is the result of earlier direct acts of discrimination, such as being denied access to workplaces and technology.

- Public schools receive their funds from local taxes. Poor areas, which receive revenues from a low tax base, usually have schools that are less up-to-date, with fewer teachers and more overcrowded classes than wealthy and middle-class areas. The result is a poorer quality of education, leaving many students without opportunities for further training and education. The poverty that may have had its source in direct discrimination is perpetuated through generations by this indirect form of discrimination.

Indirect discrimination demonstrates the ongoing influence of direct discrimination. Every direct act of discrimination, no matter how small it may seem, has the potential for creating ripples in society at large. Stereotypes and prejudice, which begin with individuals, have strong but negative power that gradually works its way into the fabric of society.

9. Write an analogy from the physical world that helps you understand how direct and indirect discrimination work. For example, if the power fails at a power plant (direct effect), the electricity in the entire region will be turned off (indirect effect).

Breaking the Cycle of Exclusion

Discriminatory actions, prejudicial attitudes, and stereotyped images all work together to form a cycle of exclusion. This cycle consists of barriers that interfere with rightful participation in community. Justice seeks to break the cycle—to tear down the barriers, open the doors, and create inclusive communities that promote the well-being of all.

To launch the ways of justice, we must search our heart, weeding out whatever may cause us to exclude others. With this start, we can help make a clear path toward participation for everyone. Seekers of justice must respond to the challenge Jesus gives us: See the stranger as your neighbor.

For Review

- What is a stereotype? Give three examples.
- What is prejudice?
- How do the U.S. Catholic bishops describe racism, and how do they say we must struggle against it?
- Name three areas of differences among people that are often the bases for prejudice.
- In a justice sense, what is discrimination?
- Describe the two ways that discrimination can operate.

Jesus' Challenge: Even the Stranger Is Your Neighbor

This discussion so far has focused on how people treat those who are different from themselves, on whether and how groups and individuals are excluded from social life. This concern was a major theme of Jesus' life and ministry.

An expert in Jewish Law once asked Jesus, "'What must I do to inherit eternal life?'" Jesus responded by asking the expert what answer was written in the Law. The expert said, "'You shall love the Lord your God with all your heart, and with all your soul, and with all your strength, and with all your mind; and your neighbor as yourself'" (Luke 10:25–27), and Jesus praised him for his answer. The **Great Commandment**, love of God and love of neighbor, is at the heart of the Jewish faith tradition in which Jesus was raised. Following the Great Commandment is a key to justice. For Jesus, however, *who* one's neighbor is becomes a crucial question.

In this fourteenth-century painting by the Italian artist Duccio, Jesus teaches his disciples: Even the stranger is your neighbor.

Who Is My Neighbor?

The term *neighbor* refers to those who are "nigh," or near, to us. This can refer to physical nearness, such as the neighbor across the street. It can also refer to people we have something in common with. Often, however, we are tempted to think of "something in common" in narrow ways, such as having the same skin color, a similar income level, the same faith, or the same degree of education. But if we examine the life of Jesus, we see that he understood the Great Commandment much more broadly. For Jesus, **neighbor** referred to anyone who deserved his love—even those who might be considered enemies (Luke 6:27). Jesus' neighbors were *all the members of the human race.*

Jesus Embraces Humanity

Jesus was often in trouble with the authorities because he associated with the "wrong" kind of people: "Now all the tax collectors and sinners were coming near to listen to [Jesus]. And the Pharisees and the scribes were grumbling and saying, 'This fellow welcomes sinners and eats with them'" (Luke 15:1–2).

When he called his first disciples, Jesus did not try to find them in the schools and synagogues. Instead he went to the Lake of Gennesaret, where he encountered fishermen like Peter, whose first response to Jesus was, "'Go away from me, Lord, for I am a sinful man!'" (Luke 5:8). Still, Jesus called Peter and his companions to be his neighbors and to follow him.

The healings performed by Jesus also demonstrate his full embrace of humanity. Those suffering from leprosy were especially singled out as outcasts in Jesus' day. To even touch a leper would cause "ritual impurity," but Jesus could not turn away from such a neighbor:

> Once, when he was in one of the cities, there was a man covered with leprosy. When he saw Jesus, he bowed with his face to the ground and begged him, "Lord, if you choose, you can make me clean." Then Jesus stretched out his hand, touched him, and said, "I do choose. Be made clean." (Luke 5:12–13)

The greatest example of Jesus' embrace of humanity is his death. He willingly shed his blood for the forgiveness of the sins of all. He excluded no one.

The Good Samaritan

Jesus responded to the direct question, "Who is my neighbor?" by telling the parable, or story, of the good Samaritan (Luke 10:30–37). He challenged his listeners to expand their limited notions about who their neighbors were. Jews did not have much respect for the people of Samaria, and even disdained them. So Jesus' listeners would have been shocked that the Samaritan man in his story understood the Great Commandment better than the priest and the Levite did: All people, even strangers and those who are different from us, are to be treated as neighbors.

Molly Roscoe, a Catholic high school student from Billings, Montana, captures the essence of the story of the good Samaritan in her updated retelling:

> A delivery man was out making his usual rounds. He had one extra trip to make to a section of town he was unfamiliar with. He took a wrong turn and ended up in a very bad neighborhood. He stopped at a convenience store to ask directions, but before he got to the door, three men approached him and held him at gunpoint. They then proceeded to beat him terribly, and took his wallet, plus all of his valuable belongings.
>
> There lay the man, bloody, beaten to a pulp on the sidewalk—he was barely conscious. Then a priest came walking by. "Thank God," thought the wounded man,

10. Think of someone you have encountered who is often excluded from social activities. Write a story in which Jesus encounters that person.

The story of the good Samaritan challenges us to reach out to all who are in need, like this homeless Vietnam war veteran.

"help has arrived." But much to his surprise, the priest walked right by him, pretending to be in deep thought. A short time later, a woman approached the man. She was carrying a large box that contained numerous loaves of bread. She held the box up high so as to obstruct her line of vision when she passed the man. Apparently concentrating on not falling over, she made her way to the soup kitchen half a block away and went inside. At this point, the man began to think that he would be lying in the cold on the sidewalk until nightfall.

Finally, the man made out another figure walking toward him. This person was pushing a shopping cart filled to the brim with pop cans and a blanket. He had on a pair of well-worn shoes and a thin jacket—clothes hardly fit for the cold winter weather. He immediately paid attention to the beaten man lying helpless on the sidewalk.

Removing his coat and taking the blanket from his cart, he placed the two items over the beaten man. He then proceeded to pick up the feeble man and carry him down the street—toward the soup kitchen, where a clinic was located nearby.

Entering the clinic, he handed the nurse all the money he had, which totaled around three hundred dollars. This was money he had been saving for a long time; he had been hoping to move into a cheap apartment soon. He told the nurse he would cover the cost, and with that he left.

The injured man was immediately attended to, and then he rested for a few hours. He woke to find a doctor sitting at his bedside. "Well, it wasn't as bad as it could've been—you have a few cracked ribs, and we had to give you a good number of stitches," said the doctor.

"How much is all this going to cost me?" questioned the man. The doctor then explained that the majority of his bill had been covered by the man's friend. Then the man recalled what had taken place—of the three people who had come upon him, the "friend" was the one who had seemed most unlikely to help. But he had given all he had to show mercy for a man in need.

A Lesson from Saint Paul

Saint Paul continued Jesus' teaching that all people, especially those we consider strangers, are to be seen as neighbors. In his letter to the Christian community in Galatia, Paul wrote, "There is no longer Jew or Greek, there is no longer slave or free, there is no longer male and female; for all of you are one in Christ Jesus" (Galatians 3:28).

11. Think about your classmates and make a list of the differences you see among them. Then answer the following questions in writing: *How do the differences make each person special? How do the differences combine to make the class as a whole special?*

Paul is saying that the differences among people are not as important as unity in Christ, as common membership in the human community. He is encouraging the Galatians to see *beyond* the differences, rather than ignore what distinguishes them from one another, and to base their relationships with one another on their faith in Jesus.

The Creator God did not make a world full of such wonderful diversity only for it to be ignored or scorned. Making neighbors out of strangers does not mean we stop seeing all the things that distinguish persons and groups from one another. But it does mean we welcome and celebrate diversity as the gift it is, rather than see it as an obstacle to good relationships.

Making neighbors out of strangers means we must always look for what lies underneath the diversity among people: our common humanity. To create communities in which all people are able to participate, we must celebrate diversity while acknowledging our common humanity.

Getting to the Heart

To eliminate the complex evils of stereotyping, prejudice, and discrimination from all levels of the human community is a daunting task. To change exclusive communities into inclusive ones, we must address the root causes of exclusion. In his encyclical *On Social Concern*, Pope John Paul II explains that such change is **conversion**, or a "change of heart." Quoting the words of Ezekiel the prophet, he says that we need to appeal to God, who can transform a "heart of stone" into a "heart of flesh" (Ezekiel 36:26).

Searching Our Heart

All of us have a responsibility to our communities to examine our own heart and attitudes, to become aware of how we contribute to the exclusion of others. Awareness can then blossom into corrective action. Here are some areas to search in our heart:

We need to examine our attitudes and gut feelings about difference and diversity. When we are around people who are unlike us, how do we feel deep down? Is our behavior different from when we are around people who are more like us, with whom we may feel more comfortable?

To address the root causes of exclusion requires conversion, a change of heart.

12. Read over the four areas we need to search in our heart. Write a paragraph reflecting on each one.

We need to look at our level of self-acceptance. People who have a hard time accepting themselves often fail to accept others. They make a show out of what is "wrong" with others in order to hide what they feel is wrong with themselves.

We need to examine what lies beneath any hatred or ill feeling we have toward a person or a group. Do we fear that they will harm us in some way? Do our fears have any basis in reality or are they irrational? Or have we already experienced a harm of some kind and not yet forgiven the one who hurt us? Are we taking out our anger toward that person or group on others?

We need to examine our fundamental approach to life. Do we put most of our efforts into serving our own needs? Do we have any concern about other people or about contributing to the common good of our communities? To what extent are we guilty of the sins of greed and apathy?

Fruits of the Search Within

If we are honest with ourselves—and actually recognize and act on the areas we need to change—the fruits of our inward look at attitudes and beliefs can be great.

Winifred Honeywell is a white woman who has lived and raised her family in an interracial neighborhood since 1965. Many incidents during those years helped her continually transform her thinking about her neighbors. She recalls a time she hesitated to answer her front door when an African American stranger knocked:

> After peeping through the door at this huge truck driver (his cement truck was parked at the curb), I realized he was carrying our toddler, Robert. When I opened the door, he grinned and said, "Looks like this one might be yours; I found him on the curb of the side street."
>
> At such times I felt ashamed and guilty about my reactions; yet I also realized that the kind of irrational fear I was experiencing is what prejudice is all about. It makes no sense, but prejudice . . . is a fact of the inner self that must be faced if there is to be growth. And I discovered for myself that it was through acting time and again against such feelings that my attitudes changed. ("Rainbow Coalitions")

Honeywell learned over and over that she had to face her own prejudice in order to grow out of it, to change her heart.

Choosing Transformation

The marriage of "conquest and conversion" that occurred when the Europeans laid claim to the "New World" is described by church historian Jay Dolan:

> There is no denying that the Spanish were greedy; that they robbed, pillaged, and eventually annihilated millions of Indians in South and North America. They were conquistadors, crusaders armed with Toledo steel and mounted on Spanish horses. Theirs was a crusade, made all the more just, precisely because it was conducted on behalf of the Church. Indeed, the Spanish conquest was the last great crusade to abolish "paganism." . . . Such holy wars are the worst possible kind. But it was the sixteenth century, and conquest and conversion in the name of God and king was the way the Spanish set out to "Christianize and civilize" the people of the New World. (*The American Catholic Experience*, page 16)

Bartolomé de Las Casas, a Spanish Dominican priest in the Americas during the years of the conquest, became an ardent defender of the Indians. Arguing against the enslavement and cruel treatment that the Indians suffered, he wrote of the conquerors:

> No sooner did the Spaniards know [the Indians] than like the cruelest wolves, tigers and lions, starving for many days, they leaped upon them. And nothing different have they done for forty years up to this time, and even today they still do the same. All they do is to tear them to pieces, kill them, distress them, afflict them, torture them, and destroy them by strange and new and never-before known or seen forms of cruelty. (Quoted in Dussel, "1492: The Discovery of an Invasion")

Indigenous peoples of the Americas and their mixed-blood descendants (many of whom are Hispanics today) were burdened by a terrible legacy of cruelty. Although many of them received the gift of Christian faith, unfortunately it was mixed with subjugation.

Yet this history of domination of one culture by another does not need to continue. Our society can choose transformation. Writer Barry Lopez expresses what this transformation can be:

> This violent corruption needn't define us. Looking back on the Spanish incursion, we can take the measure of the horror and assert that we will not be bound by it. We can say, yes, this happened, and we are ashamed. We repudiate the greed. We recognize and condemn the evil. And we see how the harm has been perpetuated. But, five hundred years later, we intend to mean something else in the world. (*The Rediscovery of North America*, page 11)

Searching the Heart of Society

Groups, communities, and societies have a responsibility to look into their hearts as well, if they truly desire real justice.

The five hundredth anniversary of Christopher Columbus's arrival in the "New World" provided our society an opportunity to search its heart. In the years leading up to the quincentenary in 1992, American society took an inward look. The meaning of the historical event, especially its devastating impact on native peoples, was re-evaluated. A significant step toward justice was taken by acknowledging the role of the indigenous peoples of the Americas in the history of the American continents. Much remains to be done, but this re-evaluation opens the doors of participation for these peoples and begins to recognize their contributions to the world community.

The Catholic bishops of the United States join in the spirit of inclusion. In a letter entitled *Heritage and Hope*, written for the quincentenary, they offer an apology to Native Americans for the church's role in perpetuating the injustice:

> As Church, we often have been unconscious and insensitive to the mistreatment of our Native American brothers and sisters and have at times reflected the racism of the dominant culture of which we have been a part. In this quincentennial year, we extend our apology to the native peoples and pledge ourselves to work with them to ensure their rights, their religious freedom, and the preservation of their cultural heritage. (Page 2)

Working to Create Inclusive Communities

Creating inclusive communities, communities that encourage and promote the participation of all, takes work. Such communities emerge from efforts made on two levels: the societal level and the personal level.

The struggle to create inclusive communities often requires great sacrifices, such as those made by these African American protesters in Birmingham, Alabama, in 1963.

Societal Efforts

The work of creating inclusive communities can take a number of forms. Governments play a key role in this work when they enact legislation that promotes participation and justice. For instance:

- The U.S. Civil Rights Act, passed in 1964, seeks to put an end to discrimination based on race, color, religion, or national origin. It does so by guaranteeing voting rights, prohibiting segregation, and banning discrimination in trade unions, schools, and most businesses.
- The Americans with Disabilities Act of 1990 addresses the rights of disabled Americans to participate in society, by seeking to guarantee their access to schools, workplaces, and so on.

Sometimes the work of creating inclusive communities requires that we stand up publicly against prejudice and discrimination. For example, in December 1992, a half-million people in a dozen German cities marched in protest. They were outraged by violence committed by neo-Nazis, whose goal is to restrict immigration into Germany in order to promote a "pure" white race.

Exclusion happens at the global level, too. The participation of developing countries in the world economy is hampered by their huge debts to rich nations. These debts prevent the poorer countries from providing for the basic needs of their own citizens. Major societal efforts are needed to bring about change in this regard, as the Catholic bishops of the United States note in their statement *Relieving Third World Debt:*

> Constructive and courageous actions by corporations, banks, labor unions, governments, multilateral agencies, and other major actors in the international economy will be needed if real progress is to be made in alleviating poverty and promoting social justice. (Number 48)

Personal Efforts

Efforts by individuals are also required if inclusive communities are to be created. These actions can be more powerful than they might seem at first, for they offer the world a glimpse of what it means to celebrate diversity and acknowledge our common humanity with others. The smallest actions of individuals who treat their neighbors the way Jesus did can have a wide influence. The personal vision and behavior of individuals can begin to transform structures that seem unchangeable. Here are some examples of individuals and groups making a difference:

A 1991 racist neo-Nazi rally in Dresden, Germany, was countered by a rally for unity the following year in Berlin.

Diversity on a team: Coach Bill McGregor of DeMatha Catholic High School in Virginia sees team sports as an area in which students can learn the value of diversity. He says, "We have three team rules: Do what's right. . . . Do your best. . . . Treat others the way you want to be treated." DeMatha's student population is diverse, and many white students here make close contact with minority students for the first time. One white athlete, new to the school, saw blacks and whites sitting side-by-side in the lunchroom. "It was a new thing for me," he says. "I didn't know what to expect." But he adds that in time, "My attitudes adjusted. Everybody can be friends and help each other." (Based on Asayesh, "Huddle Up!")

Getting to know migrant families: Catholic teenagers in the area of New Ulm, Minnesota, are involved in an exchange program called Crossroads, run by their diocese. Mexican American families of migrant workers who spend the summer working in Minnesota are matched with teenagers from the diocese. They meet in the summer, then correspond for several months after the migrant families return to Texas. The following February, the Minnesota teenagers travel to Texas, where they live with their Mexican American families for a week. The program enables the teenagers to understand Mexican culture and to diminish prejudice.

A Mexican American woman looking forward to hosting a student said, "It's a good idea so they can know how we feel about the prejudice here. I'm going to treat [the student] just like a daughter." A seventeen-year-old girl decided to participate because of the experiences of past participants. "It made them look inside of people instead of just seeing the outside cover or the color of their skin," she said. "It's being part of another family who invites you into their home and takes you in." (Based on Smith, "Migrant Workers, Minnesota Teens Form a North-South Bond")

13. Describe in writing any efforts you have been involved in to create a more inclusive community. Or write a proposal for an effort you could make toward inclusiveness, at either the societal or the personal level.

Friendships in school: A tenth grader in Connecticut offered these comments about overcoming racial and ethnic discrimination: "Well, I think people should get to know each other. In my high school, I think I'm very fortunate. We have every race, religion, ethnic group, everything. I think that people should not be afraid; just saying 'hi' can't be too hard to do. My generation and the way we feel are going to be the future, and if people want to stop racial and ethnic conflicts it has to start now with us" (Hawkins, "The Importance of Being Curious").

In all of these examples, individuals are working to further the cause of justice and participation. They are using their personal power, however limited, to influence the quality of the communities in which they participate. They are loving their neighbors as themselves.

For Review

- What is the Great Commandment?
- How did Jesus understand the term *neighbor?*
- Name three ways in which Jesus embraced humanity.
- According to Saint Paul, what is more important than the differences among people?
- What is conversion?
- To whom did the U.S. Catholic bishops apologize in *Heritage and Hope?*
- Give an example of efforts to create inclusive communities at the societal level and at the personal level.

Making Neighbors, Every Day

Jesus challenges us to regard every person as our neighbor—as someone who deserves our respect, compassion, understanding, and fair treatment. Each day presents us with many opportunities to be a neighbor to the stranger. The key is to be aware of those opportunities and to make the most of them. Making neighbors out of strangers, on an everyday basis, builds the foundation on which inclusive communities can be built. Individuals and communities working together ensure that every person's right to participate is respected.

14. Write a letter or prayer to Jesus responding to his challenge to follow the Great Commandment and make neighbors out of strangers.

5 Waging Peace

The King of Benares and the King of Kosala once met on the road. Each sat erect in his chariot, taking the middle of the road. Each refused to make way for the other.

The charioteer of the King of Benares thought to solve this dilemma by letting the older of the two pass first. But on inquiry he found both to be of the same age.

Next he inquired about the extent of their kingdoms. Both ruled kingdoms of three hundred leagues. In wealth and family they were also matched.

At last he thought, "I will make way for the most righteous." And he asked, "What kind of righteousness has this king of yours?"

The charioteer of the King of Kosala proclaimed his king's virtues thus:

"The strong he overthrows by strength.
The mild by mildness.
The good he conquers by goodness,
and the wicked by wickedness too.
Such is the nature of this king!
Move out of the way, O charioteer!"

But the charioteer of the King of Benares was not impressed.

"If these are his virtues, what are his faults?" And he began to recite the virtues of the King of Benares.

"Anger he conquers by calmness,
and by goodness the wicked.
The stingy he conquers by gifts,
and by truth the speaker of lies.
Such is the nature of this king!
Move out of the way, O charioteer!"

And when the King of Kosala heard this, he and his charioteer came down from their chariot and made way for the King of Benares. (MacDonald, Peace Tales, pages 70–71)

The two kings in this folktale from India represent two quite different approaches to dealing with others and handling conflict. When we look at the world around us, we probably see more of the King of Kosala's approach: Respond in kind, with actions and attitudes similar to those being directed at us. This seems to be common sense.

In the story, the King of Benares, however, resists the tendency to respond in kind when someone acts badly toward him. Because his ethic is to overcome evil with good, he is finally acknowledged to be the more righteous of the two kings.

This little tale has a lot to teach us about waging peace and dealing with conflict in a violent world. Let's step back first, though, and consider conflict and violence as they are experienced today.

Understanding Conflict and Violence

Conflict is inevitable, even in the most peaceful of societies. Whenever we are faced with conflict in the human community, we have two main choices for finding a resolution: we can resolve conflict with violence, or we can resolve it through peaceful, creative means. In a truly just community, conflicts are resolved without resorting to violence.

Conflict: Not Necessarily a Bad Thing

When differences cause competition or opposition between persons, groups, cultures, or nations, there is **conflict.** Conflicts may arise due to differing ideas, goals, needs, interests, and so forth. Some conflicts grow simply from the nature of relationships. Each partner in a relationship naturally brings needs and desires to the relationship. Conflict results when these needs and desires are not shared by, or agreeable to, all the partners. Conflict can occur quite innocently with no connection to the motives of the people involved, and such conflicts and differences are inevitable. But conflict can also develop on purpose, due to the selfish motives of a partner, and then it is sinful.

Inevitable Conflicts

Here is an example of a natural, **inevitable conflict:** Two new roommates discover that one is afraid of the dark and needs to sleep with a night-light on, while the other sleeps lightly and is disturbed by light and noise. They simply have incompatible needs.

People can also reasonably hold different opinions on how to reach a shared goal. For example, one student may find that cramming for an exam results in a satisfactory grade, while another prefers to study for short periods each day in the weeks leading up to the exam. If these two students try to study together, they will most likely experience a conflict. Of course, there is no single right way to sleep or study, so such conflicts are inevitable. They are part of the nature of human life and can be resolved with dignity and respect.

Sinful Conflicts

Sinful conflicts result from sinful actions, in which people or groups pursue their own selfish interests with little or no concern for the needs and desires of others. A conflict of this type can arise if a landlord regularly raises rents but fails to provide tenants with a building in good, safe condition. Wars and fighting among ethnic groups often emerge from the selfish motives of one or more sides, such as a desire to control resources. Unlike the conflicts that naturally arise in relationships, selfish conflicts are not inevitable. They arise because someone or some group has sinful motives.

Conflict in a Peaceful World

Justice demands that conflicts rooted in sin should be eliminated. But even in a world filled with peace and governed by justice, natural conflicts will remain. They are part of our nature and help us to grow and change. Good and just relationships require give-and-take by everyone in the relationship. Conflicts in a just world are resolved in positive, constructive, and creative ways, for the greater good of all.

Seeing conflicts of all kinds as opportunities for creative growth gives us a fresh understanding of peace. **Peace** is not a static state of no conflict. Rather, it is a dynamic way of relating, by which people resolve conflicts with creativity, motivated by whatever is best for all, and without the need for violence.

Violence: Harm and Destruction

Violence refers to harming or destroying the well-being or existence of a person, group, or community. The harm is not restricted to physical action; it can also be psychological, or some combination of both. Violence touches every level of human relationships, from the personal to the global, including our treatment of the earth.

Violence Today

The following are some examples of violence:

- Violence against women is a serious worldwide problem. Female infanticide (killing baby girls because they are unwanted), coerced abortion, and mass rape amid armed conflict are among the atrocities, not to mention the violence of discrimination against women seeking fair treatment in health care, education, and employment.

1. Write a paragraph describing an inevitable conflict you have experienced. Write a second paragraph about a sinful conflict you have experienced. In a final paragraph, compare and contrast the experiences.

Worldwide sales of arms spur on the use of violence in regional conflicts like the civil war in El Salvador, which ended in 1992.

- In the United States, violence in schools is becoming commonplace. Much of this violence reflects a widespread cynicism among young people who feel they have no future.
- Worldwide sale of arms and war technologies spurs on the use of violence in regional conflicts and increases the danger of nuclear war.
- A child in the United States who watches two to four hours of commercial television each day is exposed to 8,000 TV murders and 100,000 other acts of violence by the age of twelve. Scientific research has shown a direct link between screen violence and criminal violence.
- Violence of some sort occurs in one out of four marriages in the United States. Repeat occurrences of violence happen in one of every fourteen marriages.
- In 1993, over forty armed conflicts within and among nations were being waged throughout the world.
- In the United States, at least 2.2 million people are the victims of violent injury every year. Homicide is the second leading cause of death among young people.
- Millions of people do violence to themselves by abusing drugs, alcohol, and tobacco.
- Environmental violence is seen in the destruction of ecological communities and habitats such as rain forests, and in agricultural techniques that destroy rather than replenish farmland.

Institutional Violence

Violence can occur on a person-to-person level, as in a case of murder, and it can occur on a nation-to-nation level, as in a war. Understanding violence more broadly requires that we also look at injustice itself as a form of violence. In this regard, injustice is known as **institutional violence**.

2. Of the examples in this list, which one or two concern you most? Explain why in writing.

A Bosnian woman mourns her son, killed during fighting in Sarajevo.

Institutional violence is much like indirect discrimination—it is woven into the fabric of society. Institutions such as governments, businesses, schools, police forces, or churches engage in institutional violence when their policies and practices deprive individuals and groups of their basic needs, their dignity, or their right to have some control over their lives.

Institutional violence has a much different appearance than our standard picture of violence. It is less visible, and, like indirect discrimination, its effects can be hard to trace. In an act of person-to-person violence, it is often obvious who is guilty—but not so with institutional violence.

The effects of racism, sexism, poverty, and militarism are general examples of institutional violence. For example, if government economic policies assume that a certain amount of unemployment is inescapable, and therefore acceptable, this threatens people's basic right to employment. All people need jobs to earn the money necessary for housing, food, clothing, health care, and education. Providing for oneself and one's family is also critical to self-esteem and a sense of hope. Basing economic policies on the assumption that a certain amount of unemployment is acceptable is a way of dismissing the rights and needs of people and causing them harm. It is a form of institutional violence.

The Spiral of Violence

Whether of a person-to-person or an institutional nature, violence is rarely isolated. An act of violence almost invariably gives rise to another act of violence, then another, and so on. **Dom Helder Camara**, a retired Brazilian archbishop, recognized this sequence and called it the **"spiral of violence."**

The spiral of violence is made up of three strands. The first strand, **violence number 1**, is institutional, caused by basic injustice. When the victims of this violence respond with violence, the second strand of the spiral, **violence number 2**, forms. At this point, the authorities try to restore order by force, thus creating the third strand, **violence number 3**. The spiral then usually becomes self-perpetuating.

The spiral of violence can be seen on many levels. It is apparent in situations of domestic and neighborhood violence, as well as in the violence used by a repressive government against its citizens.

3. In writing, agree or disagree with this statement: *The effects of basic injustice, such as racism, sexism, and poverty, should be thought of as violence.*

Family members gather to commemorate the killings of leaders of the political opposition in Chile, which were rampant in the 1970s and 1980s. Such killings perpetuate the spiral of violence.

The Spiral of Violence

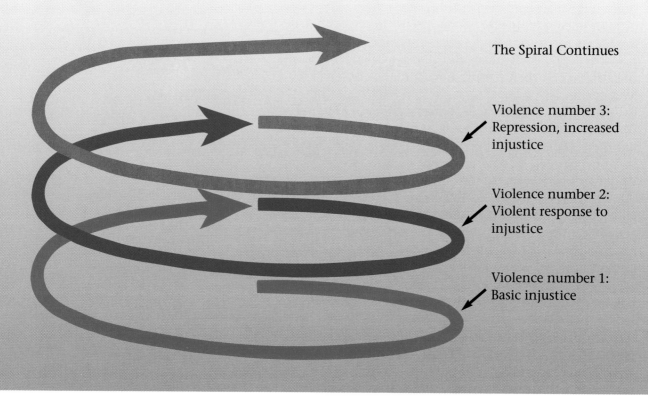

The Spiral Continues

Violence number 3:
Repression, increased
injustice

Violence number 2:
Violent response to
injustice

Violence number 1:
Basic injustice

The Spiral in Action

The spiral of violence occurs in many developing nations. It is common that the citizens of these nations suffer many basic injustices. Those in power do all they can to prevent the masses of the population from taking power. Land ownership is generally restricted to an elite few, unemployment is often high, and wages for those with jobs are usually not high enough to avoid poverty. Educational opportunities are out of reach for the majority. Indigenous populations are often marginalized. Injustices like these are violence number 1 in the spiral.

Prevented from using their power, the victims of this violence eventually rebel, in the form of general strikes, riots, crime, terrorism—violence number 2. Sometimes their resistance takes a nonviolent form, but oppressive regimes often see any act of resistance as a form of violence.

The result of this is violence number 3, when the oppressive government responds with more violence. Recent examples of violence number 3 range from censorship and harassment by police to military and death squad action aimed at civilians. Entire village populations may be slaughtered if they are suspected of harboring resisters.

The spiral of violence can also be seen in developed nations like the United States. It occurs when the victims of basic injustices like poverty and joblessness rebel against unjust structures. Such rebellion may not be aimed directly at the structures, but may take the form of increased crime, drug abuse, and other destructive behaviors. Again, society's institutions respond with force, like increasing police action in troubled areas, imposing harsher prison sentences, and building more prisons to contain criminals.

In both of these examples of the spiral, it is clear that violence does not provide a solution. It does not lead to peace. Violence merely adds injustice to a situation that is already unjust. Catholic social teaching tells us that the way to bring about peace is to work for justice. For justice to come about, the spiral of violence must be interrupted.

4. Give a written example of the spiral of violence in action. This example can be either fact or fiction.

Is Violence Inevitable?

Interrupting the spiral of violence is a difficult challenge. Violence is so common that many people simply accept it as a part of life. They see violence as something that cannot be eliminated, and they build up their defenses against it with more prisons, more guns, and deadlier bombs. The spiral continues.

A young man from Minneapolis displays a resigned attitude about violence in his answer to the question, Why does violence exist?

Violence is so common that many people simply accept it as a part of life and build up their defenses against it.

My philosophy is that violence exists because that's how God wanted it to be. As long as there's going to be people on the earth, there's going to be violence because a lot of people of different races don't get along. Like some of the Jews don't get along with the whites; the blacks don't get along with the whites. And that's how it's always going to be. (From City Quest, "Increase the Peace," a radio documentary)

This young person's attitude is disturbing and tragic, but his comments also show how deep-seated sin is in human experience. His view is tragic because he does not understand God's intention for the well-being of creation, and because he focuses on sin as the most basic characteristic of human activity. He ignores other human capacities—our God-given capacities for love, goodness, forgiveness, and reconciliation—and is left with an attitude of resignation: Violence will always be there.

The Spiral Can Be Broken

Not all people who face violence on a daily basis believe that violence is inevitable. Instead of responding to basic injustice with violence, some people are trying another way. They seek to correct the injustices that begin the spiral of violence.

Here is one example: A group of people came together in the spring of 1993 to find ways to stop the spiral of violence that they were experiencing. Members of urban gangs from twenty-six cities organized the first National Urban Peace and Justice Summit, which took place in Kansas City, Missouri. Many of the participants had lost friends or family members because of gang violence; others had taken part in gang violence themselves. But they came together to try to stop the violence.

Explaining the need for the summit, one of the organizers said, "'Our barrios are suffering. We come here for peace. We're tired of seeing our mothers come to the graveyard.'" For one teenage gang member, there was a basic reason for the summit: "'We would rather live than die; it's as simple as that'" (quoted in Wallis, "A Time to Heal, a Time to Build").

The participants recognized that gang violence was just one type of violence that needed to be addressed by the summit. The violence of basic injustice also had to be dealt with, as a young man explained: "'I have to go to school without books. That's violence. I watch TV programs which degrade my people. That's violence. I never see anyone in power who looks like me. That's violence.'"

At the National Urban Peace and Justice Summit, gang members talked with children about the problems of gang life.

Rev. Ben Chavis, a leader in the African American community, also emphasized basic injustice in his opening speech to the summit:

> "Ending gang violence is only the first step and not the last step. If we just end gang violence, but let racism, poverty, drugs, unemployment, and exploitation stay in our communities, we have not done our job."

The summit participants saw that the spiral of violence must be interrupted. Gang violence, which pulls communities further apart, cannot be the answer. Although they could not deny the influence of violence in their lives, the summit participants chose to take steps to break the spiral. They chose not to respond in kind, fighting injustice or institutional violence with more violence. They chose instead the way of overcoming evil with goodness.

5. Imagine you are a speaker at a summit meeting of gang members. What will you say to them? Write a short speech.

For Review

- What is conflict?
- What is the difference between an inevitable conflict and a sinful conflict?
- Define *peace*.
- What is violence?
- What is institutional violence?
- Describe what happens in the spiral of violence.

Responding to Violence

Anyone faced with violence is also faced with a choice: Do I respond with violence, or do I seek an alternative response? To respond with violence is, as stated at the beginning of this chapter, the "commonsense" choice. We must question whether it is a *just* choice. And considering the spiral of violence, we can question whether it is even an *effective* choice.

Meeting Violence with Violence

Anyone who has been deeply angered or hurt by someone has probably felt the urge to lash back. For instance, our first thoughts when reading an article about a man who molested children might be, "He ought to be shot for what he did." To respond in kind—meeting violence with violence—is often our instinct.

A tragic example of this kind of logic can be seen in a study of young people and guns, conducted for the Harvard School of Public Health. In 1993, more than twenty-five hundred sixth through twelfth graders were surveyed. They represented urban, suburban, and rural schools, public and private, throughout the United States. The alarming findings of the study include these:

- Four percent of the students reported having taken a handgun to school within the last year.
- Fifteen percent had carried a handgun within the thirty days prior to answering the survey.
- Twenty-two percent—nearly one out of four students—said they would feel "safer" having a handgun on their person if they were going to be in a physical fight.

Young people today live in an increasingly hostile atmosphere at school, at home, and in the community. A significant number of young people believe that to protect themselves from violence they must respond in a way that matches the threat. If they are being threatened by guns, they need to protect themselves with guns.

These beliefs are not peculiar to young people; they are rooted in a culture that sees violence as a solution to violence.

The Way of Jesus: "Love Your Enemies"

The question for Christians in situations of violence is this: Is the "commonsense" way, responding in kind, the way of Jesus? Judging from Jesus' actions and teachings in the Gospels, the answer can only be *no*.

One out of four students surveyed in 1993 said they would feel safer in a physical fight if they had a handgun.

6. Do you think it is wise to try to solve violence with violent actions? Explain in a paragraph.

Overcome Evil with Good

The example of Jesus demonstrates that only goodness can truly and effectively neutralize evil. Jesus instructed his followers to do as he did, and what he did was the opposite of the common response to violence and injustice.

- Jesus said, "'To you that listen, Love your enemies, do good to those who hate you, bless those who curse you, pray for those who abuse you'" (Luke 6:27–28).
- In the face of opposition, Jesus encouraged his followers to "'be merciful, just as your Father is merciful'" (Luke 6:36). His followers should be like God, who is "'kind to the ungrateful and the wicked'" (6:35).
- On forgiveness, Jesus told Peter to forgive those who sin not just once but many times: "'Not seven times, but, I tell you, seventy-seven times'" (Matthew 18:22). While dying on the cross, Jesus asked God to forgive his executioners (Luke 23:34).

Clearly, Jesus believed in meeting evil with goodness. He did not accept the belief that conflicts should be resolved through violence. Saint Paul continued this line of teaching:

> Do not repay anyone evil for evil, but take thought for what is noble in the sight of all. If it is possible, so far as it depends on you, live peaceably with all. Beloved, never avenge yourselves, but leave room for the wrath of God; for it is written, "Vengeance is mine, I will repay, says the Lord." (Romans 12:17–19)

Many people of Jesus' time opposed his vision of a world liberated from sin and oppression, especially those who had a stake in the existing order of things. If Jesus had believed in the common way of responding to evil, he would have answered this opposition with force. He would have done everything he could to *make* people accept his vision—like attempt to overthrow the Romans and take political power. Instead, Jesus offered people a firsthand glimpse of his vision of a just world: he treated them with mercy, compassion, and loving service.

Jesus and Anger: Confronting Evil for Justice's Sake

Jesus taught forgiveness and love of enemies, but the Gospels also tell us of incidents in which Jesus expressed strong and even frightening anger. He was certainly not avoiding conflict when he addressed the scribes and Pharisees in this way:

> "Woe to you, scribes and Pharisees, hypocrites! For you clean the outside of the cup and of the plate, but inside

they are full of greed and self-indulgence. You blind Pharisee! First clean the inside of the cup, so that the outside also may become clean." (Matthew 23:25–26)

The Pharisees and scribes were religious leaders. Jesus felt that they had failed in their duty to serve God because they were serving their own greed. The anger that this inspired in Jesus energized him, enabling him to confront Jewish leaders and especially to teach them, and us, about the challenge of serving God.

In another famous incident, Jesus' anger led him to physically drive merchants and moneylenders from the Temple in Jerusalem. (See Matthew 21:12–13, Mark 11:15–17, Luke 19:45–46, and John 2:13–22.) Jesus knew they were violating the sacred Temple by engaging in unfair business practices. Scholars tell us that Temple merchants were likely to sell sacrificial animals at high prices, making it difficult or impossible for the poor people to participate in worship. Because they were abusing their right to sell in the Temple, Jesus forced them to leave, teaching an important lesson. Jesus' anger came from his passion to see truth and justice in all areas of life, and for the will of God to be done in the world. His was not anger born of greed or self-indulgence or a desire for power. It was anger for the sake of justice.

Christians, Violence, and the Gospel

Since the earliest days of the Christian church, faithful followers have sought to apply Jesus' teachings, including "love your enemies," to their everyday lives. The question of how Christians are to respond to violence and conflict has fo-

7. Write about a time that you responded with force or violence to someone else's force or violence. Then rewrite the situation, this time having Jesus take your place in the experience. How does Jesus respond?

Jesus' teaching "Love your enemies" applies to our everyday lives. Saint Mary's Catholic Church in Sarajevo was destroyed by artillery in fighting between Bosnians and Serbs.

cused around the issue of war. The principles expressed by Jesus, however, apply to all issues of violence and conflict resolution.

Pacifism

Pacifism, which means "making peace," is the oldest Christian approach to war and violence. This approach holds that violence is completely unacceptable in conflict resolution. For about the first three centuries of the church, most Christians felt that Christ's teachings about love were incompatible with killing and fighting in the army. **Clement of Alexandria**, an early church leader, described the Christian pacifist position in this way: "'If you enroll as one of God's people, heaven is your country and God your lawgiver. And what are His laws? You shall not kill, You shall love your neighbor as yourself. To him that strikes you on the one cheek, turn to him the other also'" (quoted in Forest, *Catholics and Conscientious Objection*). **Martin of Tours**, a fourth-century soldier who converted to Christianity, renounced his military profession, proclaiming, "'I am a soldier of Christ. It is not lawful for me to fight'" (quoted in *The Challenge of Peace*, number 114).

The pacifist position has its origins in the teachings of Jesus, but scriptural scholars cannot determine whether Jesus was an *absolute* pacifist. From the Gospels, we cannot tell with certainty whether Jesus would have rejected violence in all circumstances. His angry actions toward the merchants in the Temple lead some scholars to believe that Jesus did not reject all violence. It is also pointed out that Jesus allowed his disciples to carry swords on the night he was arrested, although he clearly discouraged use of them when the arrest actually occurred.

The overwhelming message from both Jesus and the Christian tradition, however, is that violence is ultimately not a morally justifiable means for dealing with conflict. Pacifists reject violence in all circumstances. They hold that fighting evil with evil, even for "good" reasons, simply generates more evil. As **Martin Luther King Jr.**, leader of the nonviolent civil rights movement in the United States, said:

> The ultimate weakness of violence is that it is a descending spiral, begetting the very thing it seeks to destroy. . . . Returning violence for violence multiplies violence, adding deeper darkness to a night already devoid of stars. Darkness cannot drive out darkness; only light can do that. Hate cannot drive out hate; only love can do that. (Quoted in Pax Christi USA, *Peacemaking*, volume 1, page 126)

Martin Luther King Jr., center, led a peaceful march in 1965 protesting racial imbalance in Boston schools. Working for justice, he emphasized "Hate cannot drive out hate; only love can do that."

Conscientious Objection: Refusing to Go to War

In *The Challenge of Peace,* the bishops of the United States stress the role of conscience in the promotion of peace. "The relationship of the authority of the state and the conscience of the individual on matters of war and peace takes a new urgency in the face of the destructive nature of modern war" (number 231). The bishops' letter continues:

> Catholic teaching does not question the right in principle of a government to require military service of its citizens provided the government shows it is necessary. A citizen may not casually disregard his country's conscientious decision to call its citizens to acts of "legitimate defense." (Number 232)

Still, the bishops emphasize that "no state may demand blind obedience" (number 233). If an individual, in good conscience, sees all wars as immoral, she or he may object to being forced to serve, or drafted, into the military. The legal term for such opposition is **conscientious objection,** and a person who applies for this status under U.S. law is called a **conscientious objector.**

The bishops go further. They also support **selective conscientious objection,** or "objection to participation in a *particular* war, either because of the ends being pursued or the means being used" (number 233, emphasis added). Current U.S. laws do not allow for this type of conscientious objection, which can be validly derived from just-war principles. The bishops insist that all conscientious objectors deserve respect and legal protection.

One Catholic conscientious objector who paid for his convictions with his life was **Franz Jägerstätter.** This Austrian peasant farmer, husband, and father was convinced that it was wrong to serve in Hitler's army. Against the advice of his pastor and those who loved him, he refused to serve. For this he was beheaded in 1943. Today he is called a martyr for following his conscience.

An individual's decision to seek conscientious objector status is a serious matter. Those who contemplate it are advised to seek guidance from a pastor or a spiritual director. The depth of examination of conscience that must go into this decision is implied in this statement by **Bishop Kenneth Untener** of Michigan:

> There are many ways to object, many kinds of objectors, [but with conscientious objection] we are talking about something that comes from love, not fear; something that comes from courage, not cowardice; from concern for our country and our world, not apathy; from a willingness to take on a difficult issue, not dodge it; from a desire to get involved, not cop out; from dedication to duty, not desertion; from prayer and conscientious belief and not from anything else. That, as you can see, is a very special kind of objection. (Quoted in *Catholic Trends*)

8. Martin Luther King Jr. said, "Hate cannot drive out hate; only love can do that." Do you agree with him? Why or why not? Write your answer in a paragraph.

Pacifist voices rejecting the use of violence have risen time and again throughout church history, but since the fourth century, pacifism has held a minority place within Christian discussions on war and the use of force.

The Just-War Theory

Christianity became legal in the Roman Empire in the year 313. When it became the *official* religion of the empire in 392, Christians had to rethink their position on war and military service. They were no longer a minor fringe group, but the majority religion. Many Christians felt a responsibility to protect the community, especially as the empire increasingly came under attack by nomadic peoples living just outside its borders. The pacifist approach of the early Christians was re-examined.

Two Christian leaders of the late fourth century, **Ambrose of Milan** and **Augustine of Hippo**, developed what has come to be known as the **just-war theory.** The theory sets criteria to determine whether a particular war is just or unjust. Augustine said, "'Love does not exclude wars of mercy waged by the good'" (quoted in Vanderhaar, *Nonviolence in Christian Tradition*, page 9). The just-war theory was developed further by later theologians like **Thomas Aquinas.** Gradually, seven criteria for justifying war developed.

The just-war theory does not completely reject war as a response to evil, but it does carry a strong presumption *against* war. According to the theory, all seven criteria *must* be met if a war is to be considered just. A summary of these criteria shows how difficult it is for a war to qualify as just:

The priority of Catholic teaching on war is summed up in the title of this painting by Nicaraguan artist Jose Salome Garcia: "The Most Beautiful Victory Will Be the War That We Avoid."

1. *Just cause:* War is permissible only to confront "a real and certain danger," to protect innocent life, to preserve conditions necessary for decent human existence, and to secure basic human rights. Wars of vengeance are not permissible.

2. *Competent authority:* War must be declared by those with responsibility for public order, not by private groups or individuals.

3. *Comparative justice:* No party in a dispute can assume that it has "absolute justice" on its side. Questions such as these must be answered: Which side is sufficiently "right"? Are the values at stake critical enough to override the presumption against war? Do the rights and values involved justify killing?

4. *Right intention:* War can be legitimately intended only for the reasons set forth above as a just cause. Once a conflict has begun, right intention means that peace and reconciliation must continue to be pursued, and unnecessarily destructive acts must be avoided.

5. *Last resort:* War *must* be a last resort. It can be justified only if all peaceful alternatives to war have been exhausted.

6. *Probability of success:* Irrational resort to force or hopeless resistance must be prevented when the outcome will clearly be disproportionate or futile. In other words, a

party that is far stronger than another must not resort to war with the weaker party, because the damage inflicted would be much too great. On the other hand, the weaker party must not engage the stronger in war, since the effort would be futile and destructive, with little or no probability of success.

7. *Proportionality:* The damage to be inflicted and the costs incurred by war must be proportionate to the good expected by taking up arms.

(Summarized from National Conference of Catholic Bishops, *The Challenge of Peace,* numbers 85–99)

In addition to these stringent conditions that must be met before war may be justly declared, two principles govern how the war itself must be conducted: **proportionality** and **discrimination.** Proportionality means that the harm done must not be greater than the harm that the war is supposed to correct. Discrimination means that innocent people (noncombatants) may not be targeted. Using these two principles, Vatican Council II condemned any act of massive destruction in war.

Is a Just War Possible Today?

The just-war theory has, by far, dominated the Christian response to war and violence over the centuries. However, the introduction of weapons of mass destruction in the twentieth century has made the issue much more complex. **Chemical, nuclear,** and **biological weapons,** by their nature, cannot meet the criteria of the just-war theory, especially proportionality and discrimination. Modern conventional weapons, too, have been developed to a degree that their destructive capabilities exceed the limits set by these criteria. These factors raise doubts as to whether a just war is even possible today. **Archbishop John Quinn** of San Francisco comments:

- "Engagements on the battlefield today have taken on a new horror and cost because of the modern technology of war. . . . In modern wars, tens of thousands are killed or wounded."

- "The advent of aerial warfare in the 20th century has led to military campaigns based on 'strategic bombing,' the effort to bomb an enemy's homeland in order to cripple his ability to wage war. The early targets of strategic bombing campaigns tend to be classic military targets. . . . But modern strategic bombing also includes a series of targets which are located in civilian areas."

- "The development of weapons of mass destruction—chemical, biological and nuclear—in the 20th century has greatly raised the stakes in any war by posing the threat that it may become a non-conventional war."

(Quoted in *Catholic Trends*)

The Value of the Just-War Theory

Doubts that a war can be just today lead some people to believe that the just-war theory is weak and obsolete. Others, however, insist that the theory is an important instrument for moral guidance. For example, by using the seven criteria of the just-war theory, the U.S. Catholic bishops, in their 1983 pastoral letter ***The Challenge of Peace: God's Promise and Our Response,*** concluded that a nuclear war could never be justified. However useful the theory may be, application of it cannot guarantee that a war will be avoided. After all, governments declare and fight wars, and no government is bound by law to satisfy the just-war criteria before engaging in war.

The Priority: Waging Peace

Whether we prefer the pacifist approach to conflict resolution or the just-war theory, it is clear that contemporary Catholic teaching is on the side of peace. In 1993, on the tenth anniversary of *The Challenge of Peace,* the U.S. bishops urged the world community to become more serious about finding ways to wage peace through nonviolent means. Pope John Paul II in his 1991 encyclical, ***On the Hundredth Anniversary of Rerum Novarum,*** also recognized that war—responding to violence with violence, even in pursuit of a greater good—simply does not make sense. Modern war is just too costly:

> [War] destroys the lives of innocent people, teaches how to kill, throws into upheaval even the lives of those who do the killing and leaves behind a trail of resentment and hatred, thus making it all the more difficult to find

9. Do you think it is possible to have a just war today? Write a brief essay on this question.

Pope John Paul II recognizes that war, even in the pursuit of a greater good, simply does not make sense.

If We Opt for Guns

Since the end of the cold war, the United States has cut back on military spending. However, a huge percentage of the federal budget—more than half in fiscal year 1995—still goes for the military or related purposes.

Archbishop Raymond Hunthausen, of Seattle, warned in 1991, following the war in the Persian Gulf, that dependence on militarism to deal with world conflicts will have dire consequences for U.S. citizens. Reflecting on the fact that military spending takes funds away from other important programs, Hunthausen said:

> It seems to me we've never truly been able to have both guns and butter. If we continue to opt for guns, I fear two dire consequences.
>
> 1. We will neglect pressing domestic problems such as poverty, crime, pollution, homelessness and unemployment. Isolation and alienation will increase, our social life will become sadder and meaner.
> 2. Opting for guns tempts us to use them. Weapons we built to deter nuclear attack were pressed into service in the [Persian Gulf war]. I fear that the weapons with which we won a quick and seemingly painless war will make going to war again all too easy. ("Waging Peace in a Decade of Power")

10. In writing, give an example of how a basic injustice was at the root of a violent conflict. Use an experience of your own or a situation you have learned about in the news.

a just solution of the very problems which provoked war. . . . Furthermore, it must not be forgotten that at the root of war there are usually real and serious grievances: injustices suffered, legitimate aspirations frustrated, poverty, and the exploitation of multitudes of desperate people who see no real possibility of improving their lot by peaceful means. (Number 52)

The challenge for Christian peacemakers is to address the roots of war without causing war. Peace must be waged by working nonviolently to end injustice. In the words of Pope Paul VI, "If you want peace, work for justice" (quoted in *Peacemaking,* volume 1, page 23).

For Review

- How does the way of Jesus differ from the "common-sense" way of responding to violence?
- Explain pacifism and its roots in the early church.
- What does the just-war theory try to determine? Explain three of the seven criteria of the theory.
- What is the priority of contemporary Catholic teaching on war?

Waging Peace Through Love

Just what does it mean to "wage peace"? How can this be done? Faced with a conflict, any person, group, or government must make choices. Different choices will have different effects. Some choices will resolve the conflict in a nonviolent fashion. Others will be part of a spiral of violence. But peace can be waged only through peaceful means.

Earlier in this chapter, we looked at the 1993 summit of gang members. A particular event at the summit symbolized what it means to wage peace through love. One summit participant had been involved with the gang called the Crips for over twenty years, engaging in drug selling and other destructive activities. He stood before the assembly and spoke about a member of the Bloods, a rival gang. The two had been trying to kill each other for more than a year.

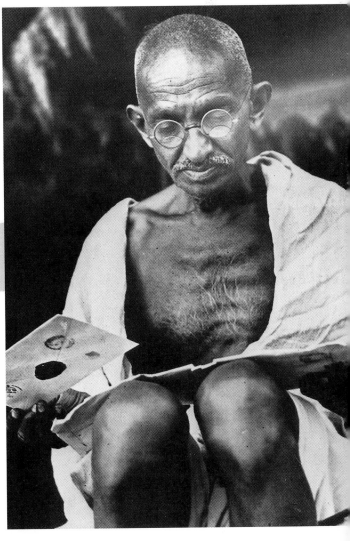

Mahatma Gandhi, of India, advocated active nonviolence as a method of promoting justice.

> I have something to say that is really moving me to tears. . . .
>
> I ran into a brother—that's right, Akili. The brother is standing here today. The brother is a Blood. Today I take my rag, and I say from now on there's a counterrevolution in progress. When you hear Crips and you hear Bloods, don't let it scare you because we have a counterrevolution. This is the brother I tried to kill. This day I love him. (Wallis, "A Time to Heal")

The two men embraced, choosing to overcome their history of conflict and violence with courageous and loving nonviolence. To take this step required that they deeply trust in the rightness and goodness of waging peace. Following the way of loving, nonviolent actions cannot promise that things will always turn out perfectly. It is not a guaranteed cure for all of the problems in the world. Still, it is the path Jesus challenged his followers to choose. Let's take a closer look at what loving, nonviolent actions are all about.

Tapping into the Power of Love

Active nonviolence is another term for pacifism. Far from being "passive," nonviolence in this sense reaches out and takes action. Pacifism in the Christian tradition takes seriously Jesus' command to love one's enemies. Truly nonviolent actions require an actively loving heart.

Love Your Enemies as Neighbors

With the command to love our enemies, Jesus indicated that enemies are to be regarded as neighbors. All of the elements of loving neighbors must be brought to situations of conflict and violence:

- We must have genuine concern for the well-being of our enemy.
- We must respect our opponent's human rights and dignity.
- We must believe in our enemy's innate goodness, even if it is hidden or distorted.
- We must believe in our enemy's capacity to change.
- We must reject the use of power to dominate others and impose our will.

A well-known advocate and teacher of nonviolence in the twentieth century was **Mohandas K. Gandhi** (also called Mahatma Gandhi), of India, who for decades led the movement to free India of British control. Influenced by Christ's teachings, the Hindu Gandhi taught by word and deed that the point of nonviolence is not to overcome the enemy but to make the enemy into a friend. Later, Rev. Martin Luther King Jr., leading the U.S. civil rights movement, followed the nonviolent way of both Jesus and Gandhi. King taught that loving one's enemies means not only refusing to harm them physically, but also refusing to hate them. For King, the power of active, loving nonviolence was that it breaks the spiral of violence.

11. Do you consider yourself to have any enemies, either on a personal level or as a citizen of a nation? If so, reflect in writing on how you view them. What insights might Jesus, Gandhi, and King offer you as a way to reconsider your enemies?

The struggle for justice in Poland's Solidarity movement during the 1980s required virtues such as courage, patience, and perseverance.

Jimmy Carter: Presidential Peacemaker

Jimmy Carter, former U.S. president, knows something about war and peace. In his book *Talking Peace,* he recalls, "As a submarine officer in the U.S. Navy and later as president of the United States, I learned firsthand about the terrible nature of war. This knowledge strengthens my personal commitment to work for the blessings of peace" (page xi).

When he left the presidency in 1981, Carter was not content to retire quietly. Instead, he founded the Carter Center in 1982. Here is the way the center sums up its mission:

The Carter Center is founded on the principle that everyone on earth should be able to live in peace. In pursuit of this goal, the center has earned an international reputation for bringing people and resources together to resolve conflict, foster democracy and development, and fight hunger, disease, and human rights abuses. (Page 29)

An important element of the Carter Center is the International Negotiation Network (INN), which studies conflicts and tries to find ways to end them. Jimmy Carter describes the INN's approach:

The INN attempts to link different peacemaking resources across the globe. Our organization also helps bring attention to conflicts that are not being addressed by world leaders and that may have been relatively ignored by the news media. Just as importantly, the INN helps spread the message that war is no longer an acceptable way of resolving a dispute.

Because of hatred and mistrust, disputing parties often find it very difficult to communicate constructive ideas or proposals. They may not even agree to meet each other face-to-face. A trusted third party can sometimes help by carrying ideas back and forth and by putting forward new proposals, step-by-step, until both sides accept them. This process of third-party negotiation is called mediation.

Agreement on every item, no matter how small or insignificant, must be voluntary and unanimous if an effective settlement is to be reached. If one side forces undesirable concessions on the other, then the cease-fire or peace is not likely to last. If both contenders, however, feel that they have gained more than they have lost from the process, the outcome is a *win-win* settlement—and peace may prove to be permanent. (Page 116)

Jimmy Carter believes that "the search for peace is worth the effort, no matter how formidable the obstacles might be" (page 119). The activities of the Carter Center are proof that by working hard and sharing resources, the human community can take steps toward peace without resorting to violence.

Not for the Fainthearted

Along with adopting an attitude of love, the person seeking to approach conflict with nonviolence must cultivate the virtues of courage, passion, patience, perseverance, and humility.

Courage: Nonviolence requires courage, an inner, spiritual strength that enables one to do what is good and loving in the face of harm or the threat of injury. Self-discipline, self-restraint, and a strong self-image are all part of this inner strength.

Passion: Nonviolence requires that one resist evil passionately, with all one's heart and soul and strength. Gandhi and King stood up to oppression with great passion, but they resisted with love, not hate.

Patience: Nonviolent conflict resolution requires patience. Real, substantial change does not happen overnight. For example, the nonviolent bus boycott that started the U.S. civil rights movement in 1956 lasted 381 days before African Americans were allowed to sit wherever they chose on buses. Today, several decades later, the struggle for full civil rights continues. It is not a struggle for those who give up easily.

Perseverance: Nonviolence requires perseverance in the face of suffering, hardship, and disappointment. Perseverance helps maintain a focus on the goal. It prevents retaliation and transforms suffering into a creative force.

Humility: Humility helps us recognize our limits and understand that no one person holds a monopoly on truth. Those who practice nonviolence must be humble enough to learn from their opponents and to modify their views for the sake of truth.

All of these virtues come into play in nonviolent conflict resolution on every level—interpersonal, community, national, or international.

Reconciliation: The Goal of Nonviolence

Rather than defeating the enemy, the goal of nonviolence is **reconciliation,** the restoration of harmony. Violence often seeks to humiliate or defeat the opponent. Nonviolence, on the other hand, aims to win the opponent over by awakening their moral sense of the good. Violence breeds bitterness, hatred, and brokenness. Nonviolence fosters reconciliation: healing, wholeness, and a just community.

Communities of Reconciliation

When people come together, share their concerns, and work as a unified force, good things can happen. The participants in the summit of gang members understood that the power of united action could bring healing and reconciliation to their communities. They made this clear in the motto of their gathering: "Apart We Can't Do It, but Together We Can."

In other words, to build community, people need to come together and *act* as a community. Individuals acting alone can only go so far. Communities, too, have a responsi-

12. Think about a person in your life whom you admire a great deal. Then complete each of these sentences:
- She or he displays courage when . . .
- She or he is passionate about . . .
- She or he shows patience by . . .
- She or he perseveres when . . .
- She or he exemplifies humility when . . .

bility to be peacemakers and reconcilers. They are especially vital in bringing resolution and reconciliation to conflicts *before* the situations have a chance to become violent. These are just a few examples of communities that attempt to deal with conflict creatively:

Preventing neighborhood violence: In San Francisco, the Community Board Program has trained more than sixteen hundred people to help resolve conflicts at the neighborhood level. Outreach workers educate people in the neighborhoods about the program's method for resolving disputes. Case developers work with the parties in disputes, helping them to identify the issues involved and to participate in a hearing with trained panelists. At the hearing, the conflict is defined, the parties are helped to understand each other and share responsibility for the conflict as well as its resolution, and an agreement is drawn up. This process helps to keep conflicts from escalating toward violence and community disintegration.

Using tribal traditions: In the Pacific Northwest, the Tribal Peacemaker system among Native Americans builds on their values and traditions for resolving conflicts. Parties involved in a dispute are brought together before a panel. Each tells his or her story. All must listen and show respect for the others. When all have had their say, the discussion turns to what actions need to be taken, and an agreement is reached. The process taps into traditional Native American values: the need for balance in relationships and the need for the whole community to participate in resolution. The process in some ways fulfills the roles that extended family members would have traditionally taken in resolving disputes. Most of all, it affirms that there cannot be peace for anyone if there is conflict among a few.

Learning from Buddhism: The Buddhist monastic tradition offers a method of conflict resolution that has evolved for twenty-five hundred years. A community with members in conflict begins by sitting silently together. The parties in conflict sit face-to-face, and after silence, each gives recollections of the conflict. They are expected not to be stubborn. Two elder, respected monks are appointed, one to represent each side of the conflict. The elder monks address the community in a manner that de-escalates the hard feelings of the monks who are in disagreement. Both monks must then publicly admit their shortcomings. The community then comes to a decision by consensus, which the

Participants in the National Urban Peace and Justice Summit understood the need for united action to heal their communities.

President Jimmy Carter brought together President Anwar Sadat, of Egypt, and Prime Minister Menachem Begin, of Israel, for a historic meeting to achieve peace in 1978.

13. Think of a conflict experienced by your family or a community you belong to. Choose the methods described here that could help resolve the conflict. In a paragraph, describe which methods you chose and how they could help.

conflicting members are bound to accept. (Their only option, if they reject the decision, is to leave the community.) This Buddhist approach requires that care and love come into the resolution process, and it has much to offer peacemakers in any tradition.

Waging Peace on a Global Scale

Waging peace on a community level probably seems like a simple task when compared with waging peace on a global scale. War is a common response to international conflict and threats from tyrannical leaders. Many people have come to believe that war is an unavoidable aspect of international relations. The nations of the world therefore devote tremendous amounts of mental and physical energy, as well as money, to preparing for war.

Nations that constantly ready themselves for war often fail to take advantage of resources and actions that can help to avoid war. Convinced that war is inevitable, nations fail to put their resources and energy into programs and styles of leadership that handle conflict without violence. The following are eight ways in which conflicts among nations can be solved or prevented without war or the threat of war.

1. **Address the background conditions that might lead to war.** Simply put, extinguish a small flame before it becomes a huge fire. Background conditions include the basic injustices that begin the spiral of violence: the large gap between rich and poor nations or groups, disputes over territory, and unresolved ethnic or national tensions.

2. **Stop the proliferation of weapons among all nations.** The massive buildup of military arms worldwide, especially in regions where tensions already exist, increases the likelihood that these weapons will be used. The alternative is for countries that manufacture and sell weapons to curb production and sales.

3. **Enforce embargoes and economic sanctions, and give them time to work.** Embargoes and economic sanctions are common tools nations use to pressure other nations to behave in a certain way. However, they are not always fully enforced or given the time needed to work. Embargoes and sanctions require patience. History has proven that when given enough time, embargoes and economic sanctions can be very effective alternatives to war.

4. **Scale military systems down to defensive levels only.** A military system geared solely to defend its own territory is typically smaller than one that can threaten aggression. With a smaller, defense-oriented military, nations are less tempted to be police for the world or to choose war as a method for looking out for their own economic interests.

5. **Practice diplomacy and negotiation.** Working out agreements and deals has solved many tense situations. To work, however, all sides must approach diplomatic negotiations with a willingness to give as well as take.

6. **Employ third- and fourth-party intermediaries.** To be successful, diplomatic negotiations often require third- and fourth-party intermediaries (those not involved in the dispute). Intermediaries can bring new insights or suggestions that those directly involved in the conflict cannot see.

7. **Allocate more authority and resources to international organizations such as the United Nations.** Programs of the United Nations such as UNICEF and refugee assistance have the potential to address crises that often spark conflicts. International organizations can also provide forums and resources for negotiation and diplomacy.

8. **Engage in nonviolent resistance and civilian-based defense.** This last alternative relies on people power rather than military power. Civilians can nonviolently assert their

will against oppressors or aggressors through collective resistance. Such resistance can be seen in nonviolent strikes, boycotts, the running of an alternative press, and mass civil disobedience. In recent years, collective resistance was a key strategy in overthrowing oppressive governments in the Philippines and Poland.

Waging peace is more difficult and challenging than waging war: it requires a greater investment of intellectual and emotional energy, and the rewards are not usually quick in coming. The news about waging peace is often less dramatic than the news of war. But the success stories of waging peace are stories of respect for human dignity and God's creation; they are stories of loving God, neighbor, and even enemy. The stories of war are stories of the degradation of human dignity and the environment, of returning violence for violence. Peace may be harder to wage than war, but the rewards have greater value.

As we cultivate a real yearning for peace, we will give more attention to war's alternatives. The more energy devoted to these and other alternatives, the more likely it is they will succeed.

For Review

- Name two well-known advocates of nonviolence in the twentieth century. What movements did they lead?
- Besides love of enemy, what are three virtues that should be cultivated in the heart of a peacemaker?
- Describe how the goal of a nonviolent approach to conflict differs from that of a violent approach.
- Describe three methods that can be employed to handle international conflicts without war.

Being Peace

In a world afflicted by violence, waging peace can often be frustrating and tiresome, even when people have joined together in the task. Creating and maintaining a sense of inner peace is crucial. Peacemakers need to learn how to *be* peace.

Thich Nhat Hanh is a Vietnamese poet and Zen Buddhist monk. His writings against war led to his being exiled from his native South Vietnam in 1966, at the height of the

---

14. Write an essay agreeing or disagreeing with this statement: *Waging peace is more difficult and challenging than waging war.*

Vietnam war. The following year, Martin Luther King Jr. nominated Nhat Hanh for the Nobel Peace Prize. Today, Nhat Hanh continues to live in exile in France. He travels and teaches all over the world about "being peace:"

Life is filled with suffering, but it is also filled with many wonders, like the blue sky, the sunshine, the eyes of a baby. To suffer is not enough. We must also be in touch with the wonders of life. They are within us and all around us, everywhere, any time.

If we are not happy, if we are not peaceful, we cannot share peace and happiness with others, even those we love, those who live under the same roof. If we are peaceful, if we are happy, we can smile and blossom like a flower, and everyone in our family, our entire society, will benefit from our peace. . . .

If a child smiles, if an adult smiles, that is very important. If in our daily life we can smile, if we can be peaceful and happy, not only we, but everyone will profit from it. This is the most basic kind of peace work. (*Being Peace*, pages 3–5)

Thich Nhat Hanh places a flower at the Vietnam Veterans Memorial in Washington, D.C., paying tribute to the thousands who died in the Vietnam war.

6 Living Simply

There once was a shoemaker who was a very happy man. While he fixed shoes he sang at the top of his lungs, and delighted passersby laughed and waved to him. People often stopped at his shop simply to share his happiness.

Another man in town was an unhappy banker. He never sang or laughed, and could hardly sleep. At first he was not charmed by the shoemaker's joy, but eventually he found it infectious. He decided to talk to the shoemaker about the secret behind his happiness.

They talked for some time, and the banker became quite curious about one subject. "Excuse me for asking," he said, "but—are you a wealthy man? How much money do you make in a year?"

The shoemaker thought for a moment. "I can't really tell you an exact amount. I work; some days people buy, some days they don't. But my family is hardly ever in need."

"That is delightfully simple," said the banker. "Because you have so generously shared your life story with me, I would like to ensure that your financial needs are met. Here is a gift of three hundred golden coins. Use them whenever you need to."

The shoemaker was overjoyed. He took the golden coins home and hid them under the floorboards of his house. From that point on, though, many things changed in his life. Concerned about the coins, he often left his shop to go home and check that no one had stolen them. He lost sleep at night worrying about the possibility that thieves might plot to steal the coins. His singing was not as cheerful as it had been. And when people dropped in to chat, he eyed them with suspicion.

Then one day the shoemaker took the golden coins and went to see the banker. "Your gift was generous, and I thank you," the shoemaker said. "But I cannot afford to own these golden coins. Please take them back, and I will again be able to enjoy singing and sleeping, and laughing with my friends. When I took these coins and hid them, it seems that my happiness was hidden away as well." (Adapted from a fable by Jean La Fontaine)

Living simply is about living happily. It is about making choices that deepen our joy in life because they focus on the essentials, not on illusions of what brings happiness.

The "big illusion" in our society is that having more—buying more, using more resources, piling up wealth and security—will make us happy. The shoemaker discovered this illusion for what it was before it destroyed him, and he returned to living a happy and simple life.

Living Crazily

Pursuing the big illusion requires people to live in complicated, stressful ways. Besides, consuming more resources such as energy, water, and food has a destructive effect on individuals, communities, nations, and the planet. Because it can be so destructive, this style of life—the opposite of living simply—might well be called **"living crazily."**

Let's look at an example of living crazily through the experience of a married couple over a twenty-year period.

A Family in Crisis

Jim and Joanne were in their mid-twenties when they married. He had just begun a career with an investment firm, and Joanne was a reporter with the local newspaper. With their combined incomes, they were able to buy a small house, though they would have liked a larger one.

After a couple of years, Jim was promoted. He was not thrilled with the work he was doing, but it was a step in the right direction. When Joanne became pregnant, she decided that she wanted to be a full-time mom. Even without her income, they would still be financially secure, so she quit her job when their son was born.

A few years passed. Just before their second child, a daughter, was born, Jim received another promotion and a substantial raise. The new job put much more pressure on him. He traveled a lot, and eating in hotels and restaurants caused him to gain weight. He saw less of his family, and when he was not traveling he had to bring work home. But he was becoming more and more important in the company, so he accepted this as the cost of advancement.

Jim found he needed an office at home and a more impressive place to entertain business associates, so he and Joanne decided to buy up, moving to a more expensive suburb, farther out from the city, even though the kids were upset about leaving their neighborhood and school.

The new house was larger than they needed and required lots of work to maintain. And now Jim had a long commute to work. It seemed to Jim and Joanne that all their spare hours were spent making the lawn perfect, painting, cleaning, and driving. Between the hectic demands of work and home maintenance, Jim felt guilty about not spending enough time with the kids, so he bought them just about anything they wanted—toys, games, gadgets, computers, a television for each bedroom. The kids used their new possessions to help attract new friends.

To help themselves out, Jim and Joanne hired a lawn service and a maid. They bought a vacation condo at the shore so they would have a place to get away from the pressure. Joanne had to go back to work to help pay the expenses. But she missed being a full-time mom, so her job was not as much fun as it used to be, and besides, the commute was so long. She gained weight and built up a lot of stress, which caused tension and anger at home, often making the kids retreat to their rooms.

Together Jim and Joanne joined a health club to try to work off their extra weight and stress. This took even more away from their time with the kids, whose grades started slipping at school. Joanne became depressed about her appearance. She felt she was no longer attractive to her husband and kept their intimacy to a minimum. Jim, in turn, felt rejected by Joanne, so he sought the companionship of a young woman from his office. Their affair made Jim deceive his wife and kids, and he spent more time away from them.

When Joanne found out about the affair, she filed for divorce. The divorce took two years, costing a great deal of money and emotional distress. Jim moved into a

1. Write about what you think went wrong in Jim and Joanne's marriage. Describe how each choice they made affected their sense of meaning in life and their family relationships.

condominium, spent his time at parties, and sought comfort in alcohol and shallow relationships. But he felt more lonely than he ever had before. He was picked up for drunk driving a few times, and finally the court ordered him to undergo treatment for alcoholism. Joanne spent several years and several thousand dollars in therapy, trying to get her life back on track. Their son and daughter were grown by now, and neither Jim nor Joanne felt like they really knew them anymore. As the years went by, they heard from their children less and less.

What Went Wrong?

Jim and Joanne began their married life with a lot going for them. They had enough income to take care of basic needs; they had secure jobs; they were committed to each other; they were open to starting a family. But something went wrong. As their responsibilities changed and grew, they tried to find fulfillment in things and experiences that just could not provide it. Their whole family suffered and grew apart because of the big illusion.

Possessed by Possessions

All of the good things Jim and Joanne brought to their marriage became overshadowed by an understanding of life in which what we own is more important than who we are. In this worldview, the prestige of our job seems to be more important than our relationships with family and neighbors. The condition of our house is given more importance than the condition of our emotions. We get our sense of identity from our possessions. We become trapped by **consumerism**, possessed by our possessions. Often our restless desire to consume is fueled by advertising that convinces us that we need something—a better car, a better body, a new experience—when perhaps we do not really need it.

Living crazily puts the focus on possessions rather than on our higher needs for meaning and a sense of belonging in family and community.

2. Have you ever felt that your material possessions were more important than family and friends? Write an imaginary dialog between you and your most precious possession, discussing what it means to you.

One-fifth of the world's population live in relative affluence, while another one-fifth live in extreme poverty.

A World in Crisis

Societies and nations can make the same kinds of mistakes as smaller communities and families. They can seek fulfillment in the wrong places, focusing on consuming material goods and using up the world's limited resources in the process. These mistakes are alarming and dangerous, threatening the future of life on earth. Here are some brief examples of the effects of living crazily on a global scale:

- About one-fifth of the world's population, or 1.1 billion people, live in relative affluence. And one-fifth of those people live in extreme luxury. Another one-fifth of the world's population live in extreme poverty.
- The richest one-fifth of the world's population earn 64 percent of the total world income—thirty-two times the income of the poorest one-fifth.
- The poorest one-fifth of the world's population are chronically hungry or starving. Most of the people who die from hunger-related causes are children.

A Choice for Community

The people of a remote tribal village bought a television set. For several weeks, everyone—young and old—sat in front of the set all day and night, watching all the different programs. But after two or three months they lost interest. They turned the set off and never used it again.

A visitor from a large city came to the village and asked one of the village leaders, "Why have you stopped watching television?"

"We have chosen to listen to our storytellers," he said.

"But doesn't the television know many more stories?" the visitor asked.

"Oh, yes," the leader replied, "but the storyteller knows *us*." (Based on White, *Stories for the Journey*, page 33)

How was the villagers' decision a choice in favor of community? How could this story apply to life in our society?

- Since 1950, the world's people have consumed as many goods and services as all previous generations combined.
- Overconsumption of resources threatens to exhaust or permanently damage the earth's forests, soil, water, and air.

The Control of Resources

The above examples all have something to do with the control of material resources, which is an economic issue. On a societal and global scale, billions of dollars can be at stake, and the issue of who controls the material resources needed for economic activity can become explosive. Control of resources can bring luxury to a minority of the earth's people, but it can also result in war, poverty, widespread starvation, environmental destruction, and a huge gap between rich and poor.

When societies consume too much and use resources irresponsibly, the results can be devastating. On the level of physical survival, we see severe hunger, poverty, and changes in world climate that threaten food production. On the level of culture and character, we see values such as integrity, good work, friendship, family, and community being sacrificed in the process of accumulating material wealth. These are all signs that people and whole societies have lost track of the real sources of fulfillment.

Societies Possessed by Possessions

As in the example of Jim, Joanne, and their family, the overconsuming societies of the world have been possessed by possessions. Societies measure their success by the size of their economy and how much it grows each year. There is an ever increasing demand for more resources to fuel **economic growth.**

3. Find a newspaper or magazine article about a conflict in which the control of resources is at stake. Summarize the conflict in writing and then tell your class about it.

Those who live in poverty, lacking life's basic necessities, are tragic victims of a system that puts economic growth ahead of the dignity of people and creation. Other examples may seem less dramatic, but they arise from the same value:

- A company closes a factory in the United States so that it can take advantage of cheaper labor in a developing nation. The company is putting economic progress before human dignity.
- To lower costs and thereby increase profits, a lumber company clear-cuts entire forests rather than selectively harvesting timber. But its method violates the integrity of the forest and endangers the future supply of lumber.

The bishops of the United States, in their introduction to *Economic Justice for All,* teach that from the viewpoint of faith and justice, an economy's success must be evaluated by more than its growth: "Our faith calls us to measure this economy, not only by what it produces, but also by how it touches human life and whether it protects or undermines the dignity of the human person" (number 1).

When a society is possessed by possessions, human and environmental concerns take a back seat to growth, acquisition, and profits. The society's economy fails to serve the needs of its members; instead, the members must serve the needs of the economy.

4. Recall a time that you felt valued or devalued because of what you *produce* rather than who you *are.* Write about your feelings in the situation.

For Review

- How can our society's big illusion keep us from true fulfillment?
- Write a brief explanation of consumerism.
- Name three possible results of the struggle to control resources.
- According to the U.S. Catholic bishops, what factors must be considered in evaluating the success of an economy?

Faith and Economics

Whether we choose to live simply or crazily is more than a personal matter. We have seen that the way we live, as individuals and as a society, has a great deal to do with economics. For most people, the word *economics* probably conjures

The word *economy* probably conjures up images of business and the stock market. But the root meaning of economy is "household management."

5. Think about the way your family household is managed. What lessons from your household could help the global household? List and explain them.

up images of statistics, graphs, stock market ups and downs, and other abstract mathematical notions.

We can simplify the concept of economics if we look at the roots of the word. The word *economy* comes from a Greek word meaning "household management." Basically, **economics** is the way we live or manage our lives and households. Jim's and Joanne's choices were about economics, as are the management choices made by businesses, societies, and nations. Small-scale, large-scale, or both, we are all involved in economics.

A Global Household

When we think of economic choices as ways of "managing a household," by extension we can think of the world as a **"global household."** It needs to be properly managed, just like a family household does. This notion of a global household makes economics more personal; it highlights three important, but often ignored, aspects of economics:

- *Care:* Household members care about one another. They share a close bond and know that their success or failure is related to how they treat one another. Thinking about the world economy as global household management brings a quality of personal concern to our understanding.
- *Interconnectedness:* Activities in a household are interconnected. What each household member does affects all the other members as well, in either a positive or a negative way. The same is true with the world's economic activity; choices made in one part of the world affect every other part of the world.
- *Relationships:* Managing a household involves more than money management; it also involves the relationships within the home and whether these relationships support everyone's well-being in the home. Economics on a global scale, too, is about relationships that contribute to the whole earth's well-being; it is not simply about the flow of money and markets.

What's Faith Got to Do with It?

When we understand that economics is really about our connections with all members of the world household—the human and creation family—we can see that the concerns of economics are very much the concerns of Christian faith.

However, many people are uncomfortable seeing religion linked to "public concerns" like politics and the economy. When bishops issue a document such as *Economic Justice for All,* a common response from some people is that the bish-

Economic Justice for All: Six Principles

The U.S. Catholic bishops issued a pastoral letter entitled *Economic Justice for All* in 1986. They took guidance from the Scriptures and the Catholic tradition of social teaching to articulate their vision of a just economy in the United States.

The following six principles form the heart of the bishops' message on economic justice:

1. Every economic decision and institution must be judged in light of whether it protects or undermines the dignity of the human person. The economy should serve people and not the other way around.

2. Human dignity can be realized and protected only in community. The obligation to "love our neighbor" has an individual dimension, but it also requires a broader social commitment to the common good.

3. All people have a right to participate in the economic life of society. It is wrong for a person or group to be unfairly excluded or unable to participate or contribute to the economy.

4. All members of society have a special obligation to the poor and vulnerable. As followers of Christ, we are challenged to make a fundamental "option for the poor"—to speak for the voiceless, to defend the defenseless.

5. Human rights are the minimum conditions for life in community. In Catholic teaching, human rights include not only civil and political rights (freedom of speech, worship, etc.) but also economic rights. As Pope John XXIII declared, all people have a right to life, food, clothing, shelter, rest, medical care, education and employment.

6. Society as a whole, acting through public and private institutions, has the moral responsibility to enhance human dignity and protect human rights. In addition to the clear responsibility of private institutions, government has an essential responsibility in this area.

(Catholic Update)

ops have no business discussing economic matters—they should only concern themselves with "matters of faith."

The Scriptures and church Tradition, however, support the opposite view. Faith and public aspects of life are not separated in the Bible. In the Hebrew Scriptures, the Creation story contains elements having to do with the economy—the household management—of the whole creation, meaning *everything* in the world. The laws of the Covenant in Exodus, Leviticus, and Deuteronomy say a great deal about the economic life of the people of Israel. In the Christian Testament, the teachings of Jesus directly challenge and impact the economic practices of his, and our, times. The accounts of the early Christian communities give evidence of their strong interest in community economics or management.

Economics and matters of faith are so intertwined, in fact, that writer Wendell Berry suggests an alternative name for the Kingdom of God: **"The Great Economy."** The Kingdom of God is God's household of creation. God desires that

6. In your opinion, what is the relationship between "public concerns" and "matters of faith"? Are they two separate aspects of life, or are they intertwined? Write a page-long essay on your view.

this household be managed in a way that promotes the well-being of all members, which includes all of creation. When faith influences our economic action, the Kingdom of God becomes that much closer at hand.

Faith-Based Economic Principles

Economics is thus household management, and creation is the household of God. From the Hebrew and Christian Scriptures, we can discern three major principles to guide us in making responsible economic choices:
- Take care of all that God has made.
- Share the wealth of creation.
- Trust in God, not possessions.

Caring for Creation

The Scriptures show us that God has given human beings a special role in creation. Having created humankind in God's image, God calls us to be caretakers of the household of creation.

In a variety of situations, the role of caretaker comes with important responsibility. The caretaker of an estate, for example, must ensure that the buildings and grounds are secure and well maintained. Someone who cares for elderly or sick people is responsible for seeing that they receive proper nourishment, rest, and any needed medication. A caretaker provides service. A caretaker is a servant who is responsible, trusted, loving, and loved.

God has entrusted human beings, as caretakers of creation with nothing less than ensuring the well-being of creation and all its members. Fulfilling this responsibility is called **stewardship.**

In their pastoral letter titled *Stewardship: A Disciple's Response,* the U.S. Catholic bishops summarize the qualities of a steward:

Disciples
who practice stewardship
recognize God
as the origin of life,
the giver of freedom,
the source of all they have and are and will be.
They are deeply aware of the truth that
"The Lord's are the earth and its fullness;
the world and those who dwell in it" (Ps 24:1).
They know themselves to be recipients and caretakers
of God's many gifts.
They are grateful

Creation is the household of God, and faith guides us in making responsible choices about managing God's household.

for what they have received
and eager to cultivate their gifts
out of love for God
and one another.

(Page 1)

Those who practice stewardship know that the earth belongs to God, and they use their God-given power with that in mind. They share power with others rather than use it over them, following the example of Jesus. They understand that their responsibility to care for creation does not make them superior to creation, or give them the right to exploit it. They manage the household of creation in a way that brings glory to God the Creator.

7. Write a description of a person you know or have heard about who practices good stewardship. What are your feelings about this person? What have you learned from him or her?

Sharing the Wealth

To care properly for God's household, all must share equitably in the wealth of creation. It cannot be concentrated in the hands of just a few members of the household. Sharing the wealth requires that those who have resources be kind, compassionate, and cooperative in distributing it fairly.

The Scriptures provide numerous examples of laws and practices designed to ensure the sharing of wealth. For example, in ancient Israel, widows were usually poor and could not afford more than one warm garment. So the Jewish Law declared, "You shall not take a widow's garment in pledge" (Deuteronomy 24:17). This forbade anyone from taking a widow's only source of warmth as a promise that she would pay a debt.

Similarly, the Jewish Law states, "When you gather the grapes of your vineyard, do not glean what is left; it shall be for the alien, the orphan, and the widow" (Deuteronomy 24:21). This way, some of the harvest would be left for those who had been marginalized. Catholic social teaching, as expressed by Pope Paul VI, echoes this demand for justice: "No one may appropriate surplus goods solely for his own private use when others lack the bare necessities of life" (*On the Development of Peoples*, number 23).

Jewish Law teaches that the harvest must be shared with those who have been marginalized.

The sharing called for by the Law goes beyond well-intentioned handouts. It is also meant to ensure that those who are poor will have *access* to their share of the earth's wealth: "If there is among you anyone in need, . . . do not be hard-hearted or tight-fisted toward your needy neighbor. You should rather open your hand, willingly lending enough to meet the need, whatever it may be" (Deuteronomy

15:7–8). This challenge is even stronger in light of a related law that tried to keep a cycle of poverty from beginning: "Every seventh year you shall grant a remission of debts" (Deuteronomy 15:1), which means all debts were canceled.

Jesus grew up learning these lessons on just economic relations from the Hebrew Scriptures, and he incorporated them into his community of disciples. He wanted his community to embody the economic values of the Kingdom of God. From John's Gospel we learn that Jesus and his followers shared a common purse (12:6), and that the common funds were managed so that provisions could be bought not only for their own community but also for the poor (13:29). The early Christian communities led by the Apostles also modeled themselves on economic practices like these so that no one among them would be in need (Acts 4:32–35).

Trusting in God, Not Possessions

To promote economic activity that is marked by justice, our trust and love must be in the right place. On this subject, Jesus reaffirmed what he had learned from the Hebrew Scriptures: "'"You shall love the Lord your God with all your heart, and with all your soul, and with all your mind, and with all your strength"'" (Mark 12:30). He made it clear that placing too much value on the things we own detracts from the value we place on God: "'Do not store up for yourselves treasures on earth . . . but store up for yourselves treasures in heaven. . . . For where your treasure is, there your heart will be also'" (Matthew 6:19–21).

The wealth and resources of the earth are not created as evil or bad. God the Creator declared that all of creation is good. But to give one's heart to God, a person must keep ma-

8. In a brief essay, react to this statement: *Those who have wealth ought to share what they have with those who are poor.*

Jesus taught that we should trust in God, not possessions. Jesus addresses his followers in this painting by Marina Silva, of Nicaragua.

terial things in proper perspective. We need the materials of the earth in order to survive and flourish; by themselves, though, they cannot fulfill our needs or promote well-being. To place our hopes on material things is the beginning of greed. "'Take care!'" Jesus emphasized. "'Be on your guard against all kinds of greed; for one's life does not consist in the abundance of possessions'" (Luke 12:15).

Jesus' teaching invites and challenges us to place radical trust in God's love for us. Loving God before possessions opens our heart to receiving all of God's gifts:

> "Therefore I tell you, do not worry about your life, what you will eat, or about your body, what you will wear. For life is more than food, and the body more than clothing. . . . Consider the lilies, how they grow: they neither toil nor spin; yet I tell you, even Solomon in all his glory was not clothed like one of these. But if God so clothes the grass of the field, which is alive today and tomorrow is thrown into the oven, how much more will he clothe you—you of little faith! And do not keep striving for what you are to eat and what you are to drink. . . . Instead, strive for [God's] kingdom, and these things will be given to you as well." (Luke 12:22–31)

Such a radical trust develops gradually over a long time, but as it grows it enables one to receive God's gifts in their fullness. As individuals and communities grow toward complete trust in God's love, managing God's household through justice becomes more and more possible.

9. In writing, describe an experience in which you or someone you know allowed a possession to have more importance than a relationship.

Serving the Common Good

According to the above faith principles, economics—household management—should benefit the entire creation. All are meant to share in the God-given goodness of creation.

It is natural for individuals to seek their own good—a good job or home, a good education, good health, and so on. But a strictly individualistic understanding of the good is too narrow. We must also consider the **common good,** or the conditions that benefit all of creation's members. Individuals and groups within society have the responsibility to consider and serve the common good when they make economic choices.

For example, the common good is not served when one student in a classroom dominates a discussion. That student's ideas might be interesting, but the other students' opinions are left out. The learning experience of all suffers, even that of the dominant student. On a larger scale, the common good is violated when a factory dumps waste into a river used for recreation and commercial fishing. The company might cut its costs by dumping (it can be expensive to dispose of waste properly), but the health of the people who use the river, as well as the life of the river itself, is endangered.

At the Second Vatican Council, the Catholic church taught about the common good: "Every group must take into account the needs and legitimate aspirations of every other group, and still more of the human family as a whole" (*The Church in the Modern World,* number 26). The writers of the U.S. Constitution also recognized the need to serve the common good. In the preamble to the Constitution, they wrote that one of the motivations behind the document is to promote the general welfare. In the second half of the twentieth century, it has become increasingly obvious that the common good is more than a matter of looking after *human* welfare alone. It is also a matter of the safety and preservation of the environment and its life-giving resources.

Working for the common good is an ongoing project of justice. Three major obstacles, however, stand in the way: individualism, the assumption that the world's resources are unlimited, and the assumption that human needs are unlimited.

An Obstacle: Individualism

Individualism is a particular way of understanding the role of each person in society and creation. It sees the person as self-contained and separate from others—relating with others, yes, but not really dependent on others or responsible to them. In this view, individuals define and understand themselves in terms of their own wants and needs, not in terms of their place within a community.

In terms of economics, the basic assumption of individualism is this: The world is made up of separate individuals, each seeking his or her own good, indifferent to the success or failure of other individuals seeking *their* own good. Furthermore, society is simply the sum total of individuals seeking their own good. There is no need to look after the common good because a good society will emerge automatically as more and more individuals achieve their own goals.

In this individualistic view of economics, moral concerns are kept to a minimum. Genuine fairness and kindness, for example, are not required in economic dealings because social relationships are limited to the impersonal world of contracts, rules, and laws. "Fairness" equals "whatever you can get away with legally," rather than a genuine sense of justice.

10. Find a news article reporting an event in which the common good is either served or violated. Write a paragraph explaining how the common good was promoted or harmed.

The basic assumption of individualism, however, proves to be faulty. In reality, the self-contained individual does not and cannot exist. As the U.S. bishops put it, "Human life is life in community" (*Economic Justice for All,* number 63). Individuals depend on one another for goods and services. We are **interdependent**, at times receiving and at times giving. Even the things that make us unique—our thoughts, feelings, goals—come about through our relationships with others. The need for responsibility toward others and our community is built into our human nature.

Catholic social teaching follows the lead of Jesus, who called us to community when he said, "'This is my commandment, that you love one another as I have loved you'" (John 15:12). This call applies as much to economic life as to personal life. As the U.S. bishops point out: "Moral responsibilities and duties in the economic sphere are rooted in this call to community" (number 63).

An Obstacle:
Assuming that Resources Are Unlimited

Besides individualism, another deep-seated notion gets in the way of our working for the common good. This is the **assumption of unlimited resources** in the world. This assumption is perhaps most clearly seen in the environmental crisis. For example, forests are cut down so land can be developed for all kinds of uses—shopping malls, agribusiness, highways, and so on. The forest itself has a role to play in maintaining the quality of the atmosphere, and when this resource is removed, the atmosphere suffers. Climate changes for the worse. A forest is a limited resource, and once it is gone it might not be renewed for hundreds of years, if ever.

An Obstacle:
Assuming that Human Needs Are Unlimited

Besides seeing world resources as unlimited, many people make the **assumption of unlimited human needs,** too. Viewing our own needs as limitless can cause us to put ourselves before others, even if the most basic needs of others are not being met. While some members of the human family have more than enough goods and continue to seek more, others go without the basic necessities. If society is to be just, people must recognize that there are limits to what individuals and societies need to survive and thrive, so that the world's limited resources can be justly distributed.

11. Thinking back to a novel, movie, or TV show, write about a character who is interdependent and knows it, who has no illusions of being self-contained.

Once a forest has been cut down, it might not be renewed for hundreds of years, if ever.

12. Write a paragraph answering this question: *What are the limits of my needs?*

A New Look at a Common Product

Her only name is Sadisah, and it's safe to say that she's never heard of Michael Jordan. But she *has* heard of the shoe company he endorses—Nike, whose logo can be seen on the shoes and uniforms of thousands of professional and amateur athletes in the United States. Like Jordan, Sadisah works on behalf of Nike. You won't see her, however, in the flashy TV commercials that smugly command us to JUST DO IT!—just spend upward of $130 for a pair of basketball shoes. Yet Sadisah is, in fact, one of the people who *is* doing it—making the actual shoes, that is, and earning paychecks such as this one in a factory in Indonesia.

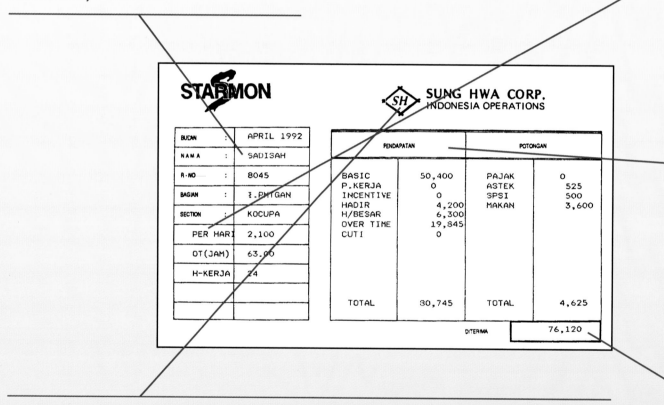

In the 1980s, Nike closed its last U.S. footwear factory and established most of its new factories in South Korea, where Sung Hwa Corporation is based. Sung Hwa is among many independent producers Nike has contracted with. Nike's actions were part of a "globalization" trend that caused the loss of 65,300 footwear jobs in the United States between 1982 and 1989. Workers in the U.S. rubber-shoe industry earn an average of $6.94 an hour. Nonunionized Third World workers in the same jobs earn far less.

But when South Korean workers gained the right to form unions, higher wages ate into Nike's profits.

The company shifted new factories to poorer countries such as Indonesia, where labor rights are generally ignored and wages are but one-seventh of South Korea's. Today, to make eighty million pairs of shoes per year, Nike contracts with several dozen factories in Indonesia, China, Malaysia, Thailand, and Taiwan. By shifting factories to places where labor is cheaper, Nike has posted year after year of growth. In 1991, the company grossed more than $3 billion in sales and reported a net profit of $287 million, its highest ever.

The words on the pay stub are in the language called Bahasa Indonesia. The message, however, is bottom-line capitalism. "Per hari" is Sadisah's daily wage for seven and a half hours of work—twenty-one hundred Indonesian rupiah. At the current rate of exchange this equals $1.03 *per day*—less than 14 cents per hour. That rate is less than the Indonesian government's figure for "minimum physical need." A recent survey found that 88 percent of Indonesian women working at Sadisah's wage rates are malnourished. And most workers in this factory are women in their teens or early twenties. They have come to the city from rural areas to seek work and a better life. Sadisah's pay allows her to rent a shanty with no electricity or running water.

"Pendapatan" is the earnings column, and five lines below the base pay figure for the month (50,400 rupiah) is a column for overtime. Sadisah and other workers in this factory are compelled to work overtime, for which they receive an extra 2 cents per hour. Each production line makes about sixteen hundred pairs of Nikes a day. According to the column at left, next to "OT(JAM)," Sadisah worked sixty-three hours of overtime during this pay period.

At this factory, it takes .84 person-hours to produce each pair of shoes. Working on an assembly line, Sadisah assembled the equivalent of 13.9 pairs every day. The profit margin on each pair is enormous. The labor costs to manufacture a pair of Nikes that sells for $80 in the United States is approximately 12 cents.

Here are Sadisah's net earnings for a month of labor. She put in six days each week, ten and a half hours per day, for a paycheck equivalent to $37.46—about half the retail price of one pair of the mid-priced Nikes she makes. Boosters of the global economy claim that creating such employment around the world promotes free trade. But how many Western products can people in Indonesia buy when they can't earn enough to eat? The answer can't be found in Nike's TV ads showing Michael Jordan sailing above the earth for a $20-million endorsement fee—an amount, incidentally, that would take Sadisah 44,492 years to earn.

(Based on Ballinger, "The New Free-Trade Heel")

Applying Faith-Based Principles to Economic Systems

Faith-based economic principles can help us evaluate the two dominant economic systems of the twentieth-century: **socialism** and **capitalism**. Socialism, also called a "command economy," has taken various forms in different countries, most notably Marxist communism and collectivism. (However, distinctions do exist among the different types of socialism, including a democratic version of it in Sweden.) Capitalism is also termed "liberal capitalism" and a "free-market economy." Let's briefly consider these systems in light of faith-based economic principles and the importance of the common good. The descriptions that follow are necessarily the extremes of socialism and capitalism. Neither system, in fact, exists in pure form in any country today. However, characteristic features of each system are at work in the world.

Socialism Versus Capitalism

In socialism, the government owns the means of production—factories, farms, and so on. The government decides what and how much will be produced, and where it will be produced. It also controls the cost and distribution of goods that are produced.

In capitalism, the means of production are privately owned by corporations and individuals. What and how much is produced, and where it is produced, are decided by the competitive market—by the people buying and selling the goods. The market also determines how goods are distributed and what they will cost, because goods go where the market will pay for them.

The differences between capitalism and socialism result in very different ways of producing and distributing goods and services. The real issue for Christians, however, is this: How do these systems measure up to the faith-based economic principles and the concern for the common good discussed earlier?

As we will see, neither system measures up as it should.

A Poor Justice Record for Both

Failure to care for creation: Both socialism and capitalism rely on large-scale, factory production of goods, which requires large amounts of energy that deplete the earth's scarce resources. Neither system practices good stewardship, and both are responsible for the environmental damage that threatens all of life on earth.

Failure to share the wealth: The use of large-scale production methods also harms workers under both systems. Such production often requires workers to engage in dangerous, repetitive, uncreative work for which they are not well paid. Both systems fail to share the wealth.

Trust in possessions: Both systems base their measurement of success on growth—a constant increase in what has been produced and consumed—rather than on the well-being of society and creation.

Failure to serve the common good: Both economic systems are managed with a hierarchical model—decisions are made from the top down, and only a few people are empowered to make decisions or are even consulted on them. This leads to choices that fail to look out for the common good.

Catholic Thought: The Real "Justice Test"

Certainly we can find exceptions to the above disappointing record: some companies in capitalist societies truly do practice good stewardship, share their wealth with workers, and look out for the common good. And some socialist countries have done well at ensuring that all citizens at least do not go hungry or homeless. But Catholic social teaching has long been critical of both socialism and capitalism in their usual forms. Pope John Paul II says that the two major economic systems are "imperfect and in need of radical correction" (*On Social Concern,* number 21). He judges that capitalism and socialism are not providing for the well-being of all, but only for some.

In 1991, with the collapse of the Soviet Union and the communist governments in several other nations, it appeared that the socialist system had failed. Pope John Paul believes that if the surviving system after the cold war—capitalism—is to provide a just economy, it must meet certain requirements. First, economic management must allow for human creativity; and second, economic freedom must be "at the service of human freedom in its totality," which is ethical and religious at its heart (*On the Hundredth Anniversary,* number 42). In other words, any economy, capitalist or otherwise, must serve humanity and indeed the whole creation community, not the other way around.

So the real "justice test" for any economic system is this: Is the system serving humanity and the whole creation community, or are humanity and creation serving the system?

We have considered the effects and dangers of living crazily. We have also looked at faith-based principles that can guide economics and economic systems. But how does

13. Looking at our society's economic system, how well is the system serving humanity and the whole creation community? Rate the system on a scale from 1 to 10, with 1 being the lowest and 10 being the highest. Explain your rating in a one-page essay.

all of this apply to our daily life and decisions? To consider that question, let's look in more detail at living simply, the opposite of living crazily. Living simply requires us to consider our economic choices in the context of our faith and the common good of the whole creation. It requires that we examine our lifestyle to determine what changes, if any, will make the way we live more just.

For Review

- What is the root meaning of the word *economy?* How does this meaning shed light on global economics?
- Summarize the three faith-based economic principles.
- What is the common good?
- Related to economics, what is the basic assumption of individualism?
- Briefly explain the difference between socialism and capitalism.
- What question is the real "justice test" for any economic system?

Moving Toward Simple Living

Christina is a high school senior living in Philadelphia. Her family has lived a simple lifestyle for as long as she can remember:

> I am the oldest of five children. In our family, we never play with war toys. We rarely watch anything on television. We sing lots of songs and we pray together. We have carnivals in our backyard to raise money for our friend who is a Jesuit missionary in Sudan. We very seldom shop for our clothes in shopping malls or big department stores. We're not poor. However, we choose to live in solidarity with the poor. We're happy people.

Jeremy, a recent college graduate who grew up in the same inner-city Philadelphia parish as Christina, remembers her family and their simple way of finding happiness:

> They chose to live very simply, without most of the material things that families take for granted. They didn't wear designer clothes or have a lot of fancy things in their house. They grew their own vegetables and baked

Living simply is a way of showing our awareness of poverty. This slum in Sao Paulo, Brazil, provides a foreground to the city's commercial center.

their own bread. I remember noticing that they didn't even watch TV. But they didn't seem to mind. I think by choosing not to watch TV, they were choosing to spend more time with each other, and this helped make their relationships to each other closer. They were the happiest family I've ever met.

Jeremy recognized that the simple lifestyle of Christina's family was rooted in their strong Catholic faith and their concern for justice:

They cared a great deal about their community, and they did not want to live a life of excess when there was a lot of poverty around them. They were very active in our church, and they worked with others in the neighborhood to provide an after-school program for kids who needed attention and a good meal.

Christina grew up with a strong understanding of the reasons behind her family's choice to follow a simple lifestyle:

My parents had a banner in our house that read, "Live simply, that others may simply live." That is what they have tried to do. As a senior getting ready for college, I'm very grateful that they've had the courage to live this message in their lives. Through their example, I've come to appreciate simple living. I have also learned to understand how much our actions have an effect on the lives of others.

Their lifestyle choice was challenging. Like any child, Christina was touched by peer pressure and expectations that she should be like everyone else:

> Living simply isn't always easy to do. I remember being in fourth grade and being teased for not having a *real* Cabbage Patch doll. It didn't feel good being so totally "uncool." But as Christians we are called to go against the flow. Thinking about it now, I realize that workers may have been paid unjust wages to produce those dolls. What is "cool" isn't necessarily right.

Jeremy says that knowing Christina's family has made him more conscious of the impact material things can have on relationships. For him, this family is an example of how fulfillment can be found in love instead of possessions.

For her part, Christina values this lifestyle that has been very freeing for her, and she intends to live the same way as an adult:

> Living simply has affected me in many ways. Now I am drawn to simple things. Sunsets in October. White roses. Gardens. Poetry. Music. I know that my lifestyle choices touch many people throughout the world.

Lifestyle Choices: Having Versus Being

A person's lifestyle is an outward expression of the way he or she understands life. Just as an artist's choice of color or shape can be seen in her painting, the choices we make about life can be seen in how we live. Our choices can have both positive and negative effects on the world around us, which is something that Christina in the preceding example understands. In our own personal life and in the groups we belong to, we have the opportunity to make lifestyle choices that support justice and the Kingdom of God.

Pope John Paul II points out that the basic element behind lifestyle choices is whether we focus on "what we have" or "who we are":

> It is not wrong to want to live better; what is wrong is a style of life which is presumed to be better when it is directed towards "having" rather than "being", and which wants to have more, not in order to be more but in order to spend life in enjoyment as an end in itself. It is therefore necessary to create life-styles in which the quest for

14. What simple things appeal to you? Write an essay or poem about a seemingly simple or common thing or experience that means a lot to you.

truth, beauty, goodness and communion with others for the sake of common growth are the factors which determine consumer choices, savings and investments. (*On the Hundredth Anniversary,* number 36)

Economic choices about our lifestyle, the pope says, are moral choices—for or against justice, right, and the goodness of all that God has made. For most of us, making choices that simplify our life will bring about changes that favor justice. But what does it mean to live simply? How is it done?

What Is Simple Living?

Living simply means, first of all, living with the full awareness that all our actions have consequences. But even more, it means making choices that support the well-being of the community.

Deliberately choosing how and where we spend our money is a lifestyle issue. Each time we spend a dollar on a certain product, we support the whole system that produced and delivered that product. So, for example, when the Christmas shopping season comes around, many people who want to live a simple lifestyle decide to buy handmade crafts from persons who support themselves this way, rather than buy the highly advertised, mass-produced items that are in style that season. Or they decide to make their own presents, or give gifts of time or special help to others, instead of buying material presents. Think of Christina and her family. They probably invested nothing in Nintendo games, but lavished much time and care on one another.

Simple living can influence all aspects of our life: the quality and quantity of the goods we buy, the way we earn our money, our attitudes toward learning and recreation, the ways we relate to friends and family. Simple living can ease us of the burdens of too many possessions and dispel false ideas about who we are—things that get in the way of being compassionate and generous toward others. It can enable us to uncover our authentic self and develop toward our full human potential. It can eliminate the distracting stimuli that prevent us from experiencing deep emotion. In short, simplifying our life can make us more effective, authentic human beings.

Simple Living: The Same as Poverty?

When people hear the suggestion that they should live more simply, they often fear they are being asked to live a deprived life. But living simply is not the same as poverty. Those who are in poverty lack sufficient resources to take

15. Write a brief fictional sketch about a chance meeting between two people. One is a person whose lifestyle is directed toward "having," the other a person who is directed toward "being." Include a short dialog between the two.

care of their well-being. Their rights to life, food, clothing, shelter, rest, medical care, education, and employment may be in jeopardy because they are poor. Civil and political rights, including freedom of speech, worship, and political participation, are also often violated by the limitations and frustrations of poverty.

On the other hand, a simple lifestyle enables one to have what is needed to survive and thrive. It is not a state of destitution, but one of knowing what is enough and sufficient. As Christina noted, she and her family thrived even without many of the items that "everyone else" had.

Poverty and simple living are both economic conditions, but while poverty is involuntary, simple living is chosen. And because both of these economic conditions have to do with how resources are distributed in society, the choice for a simple lifestyle rather than an excessive one can indirectly affect those who are in poverty. In fact, the choice to live more simply is an expression of solidarity with poor people, an attempt to help them regain their rights as persons created in God's image.

Why Choose Simple Living?

Every person or group that chooses to live simply will have various motives for doing so. Some of the reasons behind a simpler lifestyle are philosophical and religious; others are based on common sense. The following list offers some of the reasons that people choose to live more simply in the contemporary world:

- to express solidarity with the world's poor and reduce the negative impact of society's overconsumptive lifestyle
- to become more in touch with nature and grow in our appreciation of its processes and creatures
- to give ourselves more opportunities to work with others, sharing our time and possessions with our neighbors

16. Imagine yourself in destitute poverty that has been forced on you by circumstances. Then imagine yourself in a simple lifestyle that you have chosen. Describe in writing how you would feel in each situation.

Lifestyles: Comparing Poverty, Simplicity, and Excess

Poverty	Simplicity	Excess
• is involuntary	• is consciously chosen	• is voluntary, though many are coerced into excessive lifestyles by advertising and peer pressure
• is repressive and debilitating	• is liberating and enabling	• is addictive and enslaving
• fosters a sense of helplessness, passivity, and despair	• fosters a sense of personal empowerment, creativity, and opportunity	• fosters a false sense of self-esteem
• degrades the human spirit	• nurtures the human spirit by highlighting life's beauty and integrity	• cheapens the human spirit

- to reduce our use of scarce resources, decreasing pollution and the harm done to ecological systems
- to live a healthier life, one with less tension and anxiety, and more rest, relaxation, and inner harmony
- to save money
- to reduce the need to work long hours
- to have more time for meditation and prayer

17. Which of these reasons for living simply would be most persuasive for you? Explain why in writing.

Starting to Live More Simply

Just as there are many good reasons for living simply, there are many ways of going about it. Simple living does not require following a strict, universal formula, like "Do *A*, *B*, and *C* and your lifestyle will be simplified." But simplification can begin close to home. If our circle of concern includes decreasing pollution, then we must start with our circle of influence—the amount of waste and pollution we contribute ourselves.

Taking the effort to recycle is a step toward a simpler lifestyle.

18. Brainstorm a list of ways that you could simplify your life (1) today, (2) two years from now, and (3) ten years from now.

In the kitchen: Our first circle of influence is our own household. In fact, the typical kitchen can be a starting point for simpler living in family life:

- Cook simpler, more nutritious meals with less meat and fats. Avoid prepackaged or processed foods and junk food.
- Use fewer electric appliances, such as can openers, when hand-operated appliances are available, effective, and safe.
- Buy more locally grown food and locally made products.
- Plan cooking so that a minimum amount of energy is used for heating and cleaning up.

In the community: Neighborhoods and community members can work together to simplify life on a larger scale:

- Use fewer disposable products.
- Set up neighborhood systems for repair and recycling.
- Plant home and community gardens.
- Place more value on family ties and friendship than on making money.

In social institutions: On an even larger scale, churches, cities, and regions can contribute to simpler lifestyles at the same time as they develop and grow:

- Build simpler, less expensive facilities for church and civic activities.
- Build energy-efficient public transportation systems within cities and between small cities and towns.
- Actively promote carpooling among workers who must commute to their jobs.

Justice is served by each attempt, large or small, to make economic choices that are responsible and concerned with the common good. Such attempts serve justice immediately, and they provide the foundation for economic justice in the long run.

For Review

- What is expressed in a person's lifestyle?
- Summarize what is meant by "living simply."
- What is the difference between poverty and simple living?
- Give three reasons that might motivate a person to live simply.

Economic Justice in the Long Run

Living simply is a good way to begin the process of economic change in society, at a very personal level. Achieving economic justice in the long run, however, is a complex task that will require years and even decades of committed action. Many systems and bureaucracies will need to be reformed. New methods for measuring economic well-being will need to be developed. But as the bishops of the United States remind us:

> We cannot be frightened by the magnitude and complexity of these problems. We must not be discouraged. In the midst of this struggle, it is inevitable that we become aware of greed, laziness, and envy. No utopia is possible on this earth; but as believers in the redemptive love of God and as those who have experienced God's forgiving mercy, we know that God's providence is not and will not be lacking to us today. (*Economic Justice for All*, number 364)

Success may come in small pieces that seem insignificant, but each success must be recognized and celebrated as a sign of the Great Economy—the Kingdom of God in our midst.

Each success, no matter how small, must be recognized as a sign of the Kingdom of God in our midst.

7 Nourishing Wellness

I live and work at a Catholic Worker house, a "house of hospitality" where we offer temporary shelter to the homeless. We are small, serving up to ten guests at a time, so that we can have a more personal relationship with the people who come to us.

Dinner at our house reminds me of the story Jesus told about the rich man who invited his friends to a lavish party, only to be turned down by them. Undaunted, he sent his servants out to the streets and alleys of the town to invite the poor and the crippled, the blind and the lame to the feast.

I imagine that the scene in our dining room every evening must be the modern version of that great party, a combination of chaos, laughter, and good food. Seating is often pretty tight at our long dining room table, but if more people happen to show up at the last moment, they are always welcome. As we say, "There's always enough food and enough space." Guests will pull out another stool or folding chair or, in a pinch, the piano bench.

Everyone bumps elbows as they eat, but it's a cozy sort of crowded. Many of the dozen or more people around our table may be strangers to one another, but not for long—not when there's lasagna, bread, butter, and salad to be passed, and milk and water to be poured for the children too young to pour it themselves.

At a Catholic Worker dinner table, everyone is welcome and there is always enough to go around.

The guests at our table are America's hidden poor. You might see them at K mart or the grocery store and not guess that maybe they don't have enough money to make the next rent payment, or to buy diapers or food. When they come to us, they usually have lost their place to live and much of their possessions. Worse, they sometimes have lost hope and a sense of self-worth.

So when we sit down around that long, wooden table, it's not just the body we hope to nourish; it's the spirit as well. Here, at this table, people joke around, tell stories, share their troubles, become friends with one another. Here, at this table, we recognize that we are one another's brothers and sisters in Christ, feasting at the "great party," where everyone is welcome and there's always enough to go around. (Jerry Daoust)

In God's goodness, God longs for everyone's **wellness,** for all persons to be full of vitality and healthy in body, mind, and spirit. Jesus lived out God's longing in his ministry of healing the sick, in his feeding of hungry crowds, and in his sharing of food and companionship at table with persons who were outcast and marginalized in his society.

Christians today carry on this activity of justice when they are actively concerned about the wellness of their fellow human beings—their nourishment and health.

1. Think of an experience that reminds you, even a little, of dinnertime at this Catholic Worker house. Write about what features of your experience were similar to those in the account here.

Chronic Hunger: Wellness Denied

Wellness begins with the body's proper nourishment. Without an adequate diet, physical wellness and vitality are impossible. So the problem of chronic hunger in the world is especially pressing to Christians who want to see God's Reign of Justice become a reality.

The Problem of World Hunger

Ordinary, everyday hunger can involve growling stomachs, maybe even lightheadedness and irritability. This kind of hunger is a normal part of human life: it is the body's way of telling us it is time to eat.

Chronic hunger, however, is not a part of normal human experience. Those who are chronically hungry never have enough food to give the body the nutrients needed to grow and maintain itself properly. Worldwide, more than one billion people do not have access to the food and water they need. Some are so lacking in daily nourishment that they barely have the energy to do even the most simple activities.

Who Are the Chronically Hungry?

Chronic hunger occurs throughout the world, in rich nations as well as poor. But the chronically hungry people of the world share some common characteristics:
- They are poor.
- They lack access to social services such as education and health care.
- They lack political power.
- They are often victims of injustice, oppression, and poor government planning.
- They often live in remote rural areas or are members of ethnic minority groups.
- They live, and die, for the most part, in the developing countries of the Southern Hemisphere.

Chronic hunger is at its worst in Africa, which has the highest proportion of hungry people (one-third of its population). Of the seven million children who die each year from hunger-related causes, five million are African. The Asia-Pacific region has the highest number of hungry people (528 million).

Though the United States is the world's most economically developed country, it is not immune to chronic hunger. Chronic hunger impacts thirty million Americans, including

Chronic hunger occurs throughout the world. A woman in Moscow weeps after receiving a food package through the Red Cross.

twelve million children. One out of every eight children in the United States suffers from chronic hunger.

Two Forms of Chronic Hunger

Chronic hunger has two basic forms. **Starvation** is the most severe; **malnourishment** is the most widespread.

Starvation: A familiar picture of chronic hunger comes from news coverage of people starving to death: throngs of people with blank stares and bodies that are not much more than skin and bone crowd into feeding centers awaiting bowls of cooked grain. Starvation occurs when the body does not receive enough calories to maintain itself. The metabolism slows down and the body begins to feed on itself. In other words, lacking food, the body's own fats, muscles, and tissues become the body's fuel. The body actually consumes itself and quickly deteriorates. The immune system breaks down, making victims of starvation susceptible to disease. Brain chemistry is also damaged, causing the victim's mental functions to deteriorate. Technically, starvation begins to occur when an individual has lost one-third of his or her normal body weight. When the loss goes beyond 40 percent, death is near.

Malnourishment: Malnourishment is the most common form of chronic hunger. Malnourishment may not be obvious to an observer, but it is a silent killer nonetheless. A victim of malnourishment gets enough calories to prevent his or her body from feeding on itself. But the diet of a malnourished person is extremely limited, often consisting of just three or four foods. As a result, he or she does not receive all of the vitamins and minerals needed for proper physical and mental development and maintenance. Malnourishment saps a person's strength and leaves him or her vulnerable to many life-threatening diseases.

The Myths About Hunger

If food is so basic a human right, a necessity for survival, why are so many people denied that right? The problem of world hunger is not simple; its causes are complex and interconnected. But before we look at its real causes, we need to dispel some common myths about the causes of world hunger.

Myth: Not Enough Food for Too Many People

It is commonly assumed that there is simply not enough food to feed the world's exploding human population. This, however, is false. In fact, enough food is currently grown

2. Do the statistics about hunger in the United States surprise you? Write a brief reaction to them.

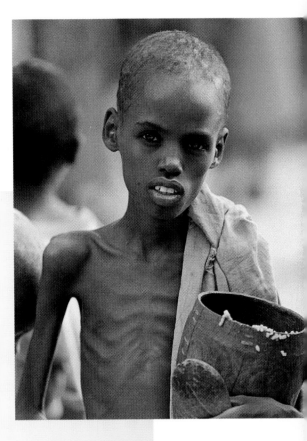

Starvation is the most severe form of chronic hunger. This young boy in Somalia is one of hundreds of thousands of hungry and starving people who have been displaced due to drought and civil war.

3. Reflect on this question in a one-page essay: *How does chronic hunger violate human dignity?*

worldwide to supply every child, woman, and man with thirty-six hundred calories a day, enough to cause weight gain. Almost every hungry country produces enough food for its people. The problem is not the amount of food but the way it is distributed. Redistributing a small amount of each country's food supply would eliminate hunger.

Myth: Droughts and Natural Disasters as Causes

Another common assumption is that most hunger is caused by droughts and other natural disasters. But the people of the world have fed themselves for centuries despite drought, floods, and other effects of weather. Various traditional cultures have developed strategies for coping with food loss due to natural disasters. For example, they have collectively stored food and distributed it among themselves during periods of major crop failure. Today, disruptions such as civil wars interfere with traditional life and the coping strategies that have been developed. In addition, many "natural" disasters are actually caused by human action, such as the droughts in Africa caused in large part by the elimination of forests. When natural disasters occur, poor people are the most vulnerable.

Myth: Lazy Poor People

Perhaps the cruelest myth is the belief that poor people are too lazy to earn the money they need for food. On the contrary, most of the people in the world's hungry countries are hardworking and want to support themselves. They are unable to do so because they are losing access to the resources needed for self-reliance—land, water, tools, animals, credit, and markets for their crops. In the United States, too, poor people generally are willing to work. Most of the hungry poor in this country either work at jobs that pay unjustly low wages, are unable to find jobs, or cannot afford to work because of the high cost of child care.

Dispelling myths about the causes of hunger is the first step toward understanding its real causes. As we will see in looking at those causes, world hunger is not inevitable. It can be solved and prevented if we have the will to do so.

The Connection Between Hunger and Poverty

The most obvious cause of hunger is poverty. People are hungry because they are poor. Finding the true causes of hunger means uncovering the complex causes of poverty.

4. Choose one of the hunger myths presented here. Write a one-page essay explaining your understanding of the material. Before reading the text, would you have agreed or disagreed with the hunger myth? How do you feel about it now?

From Self-sufficiency to Hunger

In the following account, notice what is happening to this Guatemalan family as land is taken over by wealthy people for cash crop exports:

> We are members of the Tzul family. We are peasants, or farmers, in the highlands, the mountainous area in western Guatemala. Our great-grandmother said our family has always lived here, that we come from this earth. We believe we have the right to go on living here because this is where our ancestors are buried.
>
> We are *indigenous people*. We are also called *Indians* descended from the Mayans. We speak Quiché language and practice Quiché customs. Weaving our clothing helps us teach our history to our children; wearing the clothing helps us maintain our culture.
>
> On our tiny plot of land, we raise most of our own food. We grow corn for our tortillas, which the women make every day. For lunch and dinner, we eat *frijoles*, or black beans, with the tortillas. Sometimes we buy rice and milk, and for special occasions we eat eggs or chicken. In season, we have tomatoes, peppers, bananas and *tamarindos*, a fruit that grows on a tree near our home. Although there is not much variety, we are healthy when we have enough food.
>
> Nearby are huge coffee plantations where we work. These lands are owned by rich people who live in Guatemala City or the United States. Recently, the landowners began to grow broccoli on land that used to belong to my family. The landowners export the broccoli to other countries. We don't like broccoli anyway, but we would like the land back to produce food for our family.
>
> Although we are very poor, we are able to live together with our community and carry on our traditional ways. It is here, on our sacred land, that we feel happy. (Adapted from Resource Center of the Americas, *Rigoberta Menchú,* page 9)

Much contemporary poverty originates in losing the opportunity to be self-sufficient. Briefly, these are some of the factors that contribute to the existence of poverty and hunger throughout the world:

1. The demand for exports: Wealthy countries demand products like coffee, sugar, lumber, and grains from poor countries, which are under pressure to export more and more goods to bring in outside money for their weak economies. So a poor country's economy shifts away from providing food and resources for its own people. Land is taken over by people or businesses, often huge conglomerates, that can most efficiently farm it for cash crop exports. Such takeovers displace the families and villagers who previously farmed the land. The corporations offer small compensation and no promise of employment. People thus are forced to leave the land and go to the cities seeking work, which is scarce and extremely low paying.

5. Read the account of the Tzul family above. Imagine that *you* are the rich person who owns the land this family needs to farm in order to survive. How do you respond to their story? Write your answer in a page.

2. Government by the elite: Many of the world's poorest and hungriest nations are controlled by governments consisting of the nations' wealthiest members. Government policies tend to favor the interests of the wealthy rather than the poor.

3. Conditions on aid programs: Aid that is offered by wealthy countries to poor countries often comes with strings attached. For example, a wealthy nation may offer financial aid to a poor country, but then require it to use that aid to build roads, bridges, and airports. Such projects are likely to serve the needs of the wealthy in both the giving and the receiving countries, rather than serve the poor, who need food, health care, and education.

4. Debt payments and conditions: Most poor countries have gone deeply into debt to banks in wealthy nations. Paying interest on loans takes money from programs that could eliminate poverty. In addition, desperate countries that borrow from wealthy ones are required by the International Monetary Fund or the World Bank to institute harsh economic measures to "shape up" their economies. This burdens poor people even more.

5. Discrimination: Ethnic, religious, and gender discrimination within poor countries also causes poverty. Religious and ethnic minorities are likely to be more impoverished than other groups. Indigenous peoples and women often suffer from prejudice, even if they are not in the minority.

6. Arms sales: Military spending by poor countries is encouraged by rich countries that make and sell weapons. As a result, money that could fund programs to end hunger and poverty is spent on weapons. The spiral of violence is fueled by the availability of weapons, which increases repression and adds to poverty and hunger.

7. Abuse of land and other resources: The exploitation of a poor country's resources leads to environmental degradation. Damaged land cannot be effectively farmed for local food production.

The End of Hunger: A Real Possibility

Most hunger in our local communities, nation, and world is caused by human actions. In the context of a Christian approach to justice, many of these actions can be considered sinful, stemming from greed. But because the causes of hunger stem from human actions, then the actions that will eliminate hunger are also within our power.

In the United States, for example, the federal government offers nutrition assistance for low-income pregnant women and their young children. This program helps in the crucial years when a child is developing most. But such programs lack sufficient funding to be fully effective. If ten billion dollars were added to the annual budgets of existing U.S. food programs, hunger could be eliminated in about two years, according to the director of a major organization working to reduce hunger. Ten billion dollars is just 1 percent of the federal budget. By cutting back in areas such as military spending, this 1 percent could be redirected toward ending hunger.

6. On a scale of 1 to 10 (1 means no agreement; 10 means total agreement), how do you feel about this statement? *If we really wanted to, we could end hunger in the world.* Explain your answer in writing.

For Review

- Give three common characteristics of chronically hungry people.
- What are two forms of chronic hunger? Describe them.
- Summarize three myths about hunger.
- What is the most obvious cause of hunger? List three factors that contribute to hunger.

A Eucharistic Response to World Hunger

The Eucharist: A Pledge of Commitment

Jesus called himself the bread of life. And on the night before he was crucified, he gave himself to his followers and to all of us as nourishment. Jesus instructed his disciples to bless bread and wine, recognizing it as his very body and blood, to share it, and to eat and drink it in his memory. This practice became known as the **Eucharist.**

The Catholic church teaches that the Eucharist is the center of Christian life. All Christian ministries, including ministries of justice, find their source in the Eucharist and lead us back to this sacrament. The Eucharist, then, is at the heart of a Catholic response to world hunger.

The Eucharist, or the Mass, is a meal in which Christians share the table of the Lord's Supper. It is also a sacrifice—a way for Christians to enter into the mystery of Christ's death and Resurrection for all humankind. When the Eucharist is celebrated today, it is thus more than a private moment between Jesus and the person receiving the consecrated bread and wine. The Eucharist deepens union with Christ, but at the same time unites Christians with one another and with all for whom Christ died and rose. In the Eucharist, we pledge our commitment to the world's poor and hungry people as we are united with all who yearn for fullness of life.

7. Write a one-page reflection on this theme: *The Eucharist is at the heart of a Catholic response to world hunger.*

Mindful of the community spirit of the Eucharist, Saint Paul scolded the Christians of Corinth because at their celebrations of the Lord's Supper, some members were going hungry. If one is hungry while the others feast, Paul said, then something is wrong. Celebrating the Eucharist is an action that should make a difference in the world, a difference toward justice.

Jesus feeds many people with just a few loaves and fishes in this painting by Pablo Mayorga, of Nicaragua.

Sharing Loaves and Fishes

You may recall the stories of the miraculous **multiplication of the loaves and fishes** in all four Gospels. These accounts have a lot to teach us about responding to hunger.

The Miracle Accounts

A great multitude of people had gathered in an out-of-the-way place to hear Jesus teach. When it grew late in the day, Jesus became concerned about feeding all of these people. His disciples felt that it would be best to send the people to the nearest towns, where they could buy food. But Jesus insisted they could do better than that. He took the few loaves of bread and the few fishes that the disciples had on hand, blessed this food, and told the disciples to distribute it among the crowd. Everyone received plenty to eat, and much was left over. (See Matthew 14:13–21, Mark 6:30–44, Luke 9:10–17, and John 6:1–13.)

The miracle of the loaves and fishes foreshadows the Eucharist, even down to the words that describe the blessing, breaking, and distributing of the bread. The Gospel writers saw that the actual feeding of the hungry and the spiritual nourishment of the Eucharist are closely related.

"Life Is a Banquet"

Dorothy Day, a twentieth-century Catholic convert who died in 1980, cofounded the **Catholic Worker Movement** in 1933. The account at the beginning of this chapter is of a house in that movement today, which, like Day's life, is dedicated to the works of mercy. Catholic Workers feed the hungry and shelter the homeless, while protesting the societal structures that create poverty and injustice.

In her autobiography, Day reflected on how the Catholic Worker Movement got started and grew, weaving in the imagery of the loaves and fishes and the Eucharist:

> We were just sitting there talking when lines of people began to form, saying, "We need bread." We could not say, "Go, be thou filled." If there were six small loaves and a few fishes, we had to divide them. There was always bread. . . .
>
> We cannot love God unless we love each other, and to love we must know each other. We know Him in the breaking of bread, and we know each other in the breaking of bread, and we are not alone any more. Heaven is a banquet and life is a banquet, too, even with a crust, where there is companionship. (*The Long Loneliness*, page 285)

Dorothy Day, cofounder of the Catholic Worker Movement, wrote that "we know each other in the breaking of the bread."

Bringing the World to the Eucharist, Bringing the Eucharist to the World

In many churches, when the bread and wine are brought to the altar as offerings to God, other foods are also brought forward. These foods are distributed to soup kitchens, homeless shelters, and other organizations that serve hungry people. Such offerings have been made throughout the history of the church, which has always recognized that supporting hungry and poor people is an act of the Eucharist.

Archbishop Oscar Romero, of El Salvador, recognized that everything that Christians bring to church on Sunday—joy, sorrow, hope, pain—is offered in the Eucharist. Nourished by that celebration, the people go out to continue the eucharistic action by working and struggling for justice. Romero said this in a 1978 sermon:

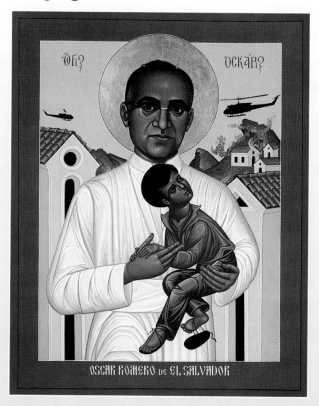

OSCAR ROMERO DE EL SALVADOR

> How beautiful is the Mass,
> especially when celebrated in a cathedral filled
> like ours on Sundays,
> or also when celebrated simply
> in village chapels with people full of faith,
> who know that Christ, the King of Glory,
> Eternal Priest,
> is gathering together all that we bring him
> from the week:
> sorrows, failures, hopes, plans, joys, sadness, pain!
> How many things each one of you,
> brothers and sisters, bring to your Sunday Mass!
> And the Eternal Priest gathers them in his hands
> and by means of the human priest who celebrates
> lifts them up to the Father
> as the product of the people's labor.
> United to my sacrifice present on this altar,
> the people are made godlike
> and now leave the cathedral to keep on working,
> to keep on struggling, to keep on suffering,
> but ever united with the Eternal Priest,
> who remains present in the eucharist
> so that we can meet him the next Sunday also.
> (*Violence of Love,* page 64)

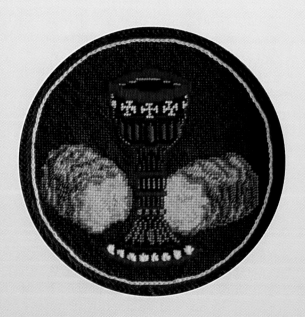

The archbishop was assassinated in 1980 due to his support for the poor and oppressed people of his country.

Imagine what the world would be like if rich countries and rich Christians lived out the eucharistic lesson of the loaves and fishes miracle: *If we share, there will always be enough.*

8. Have you ever witnessed a kind of loaves-and-fishes miracle—that is, a time when scarce things were shared, and then there seemed to be enough for everyone? Reflect on your experience in writing.

Toward Eliminating World Hunger

The elimination of world hunger requires both **immediate responses** and **long-range solutions**. The more than a billion hungry people throughout the world need food today. Those facing starvation especially must be helped immediately. They cannot wait for political situations to calm down or for their country's social services to be re-established. Humanitarian relief efforts are a necessary part of the response to hunger. Many organizations (such as Catholic Relief Services and Oxfam) and governments have developed systems for emergency famine relief and for supplying food on an ongoing basis in areas where long-term food shortages exist.

Such programs are praiseworthy, but they are only the beginning of a permanent solution to world hunger. Efforts that provide immediate relief must be linked with efforts to eliminate the real causes of hunger. All such efforts require hard work, patience, and sacrifice; they are eucharistic responses to hunger. And, of course, breaking the cycle of hunger means breaking the cycle of poverty. Here are some ways to address hunger for the long term.

Promoting Self-sufficiency

An old proverb says, *Give a man a fish, and you feed him for a day; teach a man to fish, and you feed him for a lifetime.* This proverb hints at the kind of actions needed to bring about a lasting solution to world hunger. To secure food on a regular basis and become **self-sufficient**, individuals and communities need access to basic resources like land, jobs, and financial credit. Many of those who are hungry have provided for themselves and their families in the past, but social, political, and economic upheaval have taken away their access to the needed resources. Numerous organizations that work toward justice for poor people are devoted to "helping them help themselves" on a long-term basis. The following are examples of just two such organizations:

Catholic Relief Services: Catholic Relief Services (CRS) was started in 1943 by the U.S. bishops. Besides its emergency relief work in war-torn and famine-stricken countries, CRS assists poor people in their efforts to provide for themselves. CRS encourages the poor people that it works with to participate in the decisions and structures that affect their lives.

The organization's work in Baranquilla, Colombia, is typical of the way it operates. This city's population has grown quickly since 1960. People migrated to the city due, in part, to the deterioration of farming conditions and to the military and drug-related activities in the countryside. Half of the one million people of Baranquilla do without electrical, water, and sewage systems. Many are unemployed or work at low-paying jobs.

Responding to this state of affairs, the Archdiocese of Baranquilla turned to Catholic Relief Services. Together they set up a fund that provides small loans to groups that wish to start businesses. Participants in the program are offered training in management, marketing, and other business skills that will help their new enterprises succeed. Among the newly launched businesses are those engaged in carpentering, craft making, shopkeeping, tailoring, and raising small animals. In its first year, the fund led directly to 500 new jobs, and another 340 jobs were created indirectly.

Heifer Project: Heifer Project International, a Christian-based movement, has been helping people help themselves for more than fifty years. The project's founder, Dan West, wanted to do more than pass out food to hungry people one bowl at a time. Instead, he provided people with heifers—young milk cows—which allowed them to produce some of their own food.

Since 1944, the project has provided millions of animals, fowl, bee hives, and fish to hungry families all over the world. The families are also trained in how to care for their animals.

Sharing is an essential part of Heifer Project's work. Each person who receives a Heifer Project gift is expected to "pass it on" by giving one of the animal's offspring to a neighbor or by sharing her or his new skills in animal care with the community. This people-to-people method provides food and income, and leads to self-reliance. It also removes the stigma often experienced by those who receive charity, and it fosters friendship, dignity, and hope.

Heifer Project International has provided millions of animals to hungry families all over the world.

Changes in Government Policies

Organizations like Catholic Relief Services and Heifer Project International can go only so far to eliminate hunger. The political and economic policies of wealthier nations have helped create poverty in many of the hungry nations. Attempts by poor people to become self-sufficient are ultimately dependent on improvements in the larger political, social, and economic structures under which they live. Changes in **national and international policies** are a critical part of worldwide efforts to provide food for all people.

Organizations like the Christian-based **Bread for the World** promote structural changes that will improve the lives of those who suffer from hunger and poverty. In recent years, Bread for the World has urged the U.S. Congress to support resolutions that would change the focus of U.S. foreign aid. This aid has traditionally been based on U.S. political, military, and economic interests. Bread for the World supports changes that would focus foreign aid on ending poverty and hunger.

Lifestyle Changes

In chapter 6, we saw that those who are well-off can help to reduce world hunger by living simpler lifestyles. We may not see an immediate connection between our lifestyle and hunger in the world, but it is there nonetheless. If many more people consumed less and demanded fewer products from impoverished countries, the wealth that these countries do have could be redirected toward reducing hunger. It is also important to simplify our lifestyle to express our solidarity with those whose basic rights and needs are not being met.

In our efforts to end world hunger, it helps to keep a eucharistic perspective. In the midst of a challenge that seems overwhelming, we need to see our small steps and actions within a larger vision. Whether writing a letter to a representative, raising money for a hunger project, volunteering at a soup kitchen, or trying to eat less junk food, we can see our struggles and longings for justice as part of something greater than ourselves. Our efforts are united, through Jesus' death and Resurrection, to the whole Body of Christ. Thus our efforts have power and strength beyond what we can see or even imagine.

Bread for the World lobbyists promote structural change by supporting legislation that changes the focus of U.S. foreign aid.

9. Of the various types of action you could take to end hunger, which would you choose? Why? Write your answer in a paragraph.

For Review

- How does the Eucharist relate to feeding the world's hungry?
- What is the eucharistic lesson of the miracle of the loaves and fishes?
- Name three kinds of long-term responses that are needed to end hunger.
- Give examples of two organizations working to end hunger.

Health Concerns in the Hungry World

Wellness of body, mind, and spirit comes first and foremost from having good, nourishing food to eat. **Adequate health care** also ranks high as a necessity. Like food, a basic level of health care is a fundamental human right demanded by justice. As the U.S. Catholic bishops state in their 1993 *Resolution on Health Care Reform*, "Every person has a right to adequate health care. This right flows from the sanctity of human life and the dignity that belongs to all human persons, who are made in the image of God."

Lack of Good Food and Good Water

Health issues in impoverished countries are almost completely connected with hunger and poverty. A person who is starving rarely dies of hunger itself; rather, he or she dies of a disease contracted due to the body's weakness and inability to defend itself. Those who are malnourished but not starving are also vulnerable to many diseases and conditions. **Nutritional deficiencies** can cause diabetes, heart ailments, vision problems, obesity, skin diseases, and other problems. In infants and young children, malnutrition can cause permanent damage to physical and mental development.

In some countries, water must be carried several miles from its source to the homes where it will be used. The burden of transport is often the responsibility of women.

The factors behind hunger and poverty are also responsible for the unhealthy drinking water and unsanitary conditions that the world's poor people must contend with. When bodies are already weakened by hunger, exposure to **bad water** and **poor sanitation** further threatens people's health. The effects of these problems are staggering:

- Five million adults every year are afflicted with water-related diseases like cholera, typhoid, and diarrhea.
- Every year five million children younger than five years die from dehydration—the depletion of the body's fluids—caused by diarrhea.
- Each year 200 million people pick up parasites from stagnant water sources; these organisms live off a person's body and the food the person takes in.
- Malaria, one of the most debilitating diseases linked to bad water sources, affects 800 million people annually, killing one million infants in Africa each year.

The quantity of available water is also important. Like the earth, the human body is made up mostly of water. Keeping the body properly hydrated requires six to eight glasses of water per day. Most of the world's poor people, however, must travel far distances to obtain safe water, or *any* water, and then they must carry it the same long distance back home, usually on foot.

10. List as many ways as you can think of that people in our society take our supply of safe water for granted. Write a prayer of gratitude for the water we have.

Promoting Health in Guatemala

Attacking the problems of poverty and hunger will improve the health of millions of people worldwide. But direct attention to providing health care in poor countries is also necessary. Health care in the sophisticated sense that we in the highly industrialized world know it is not needed so much as simple but life-saving preventive measures.

Maryknoll lay missioner Jane Redig spent five years trying to develop good health measures among Indians in the mountain villages of Guatemala:

> The main thrust of our work has been to train local volunteers to be health promoters in their villages. The health promoters' role is to share knowledge about prevention. They teach about better personal hygiene; they try to convince villages to put in latrines so that human waste doesn't run into the streams; they encourage everyone to boil water for drinking, cooking, and washing. The health promoters are also trained to do basic diagnostic and treatment work. If they can't help a sick person, they bring him or her to the regional health center—a long distance away—to see a doctor.

The village health promoters have a tough job, and sometimes they're even met with suspicion. But they believe it's worth it because of the improvements they see, such as less diarrhea among the children in villages that have put in latrines.

I've also seen how the village health promoters themselves gain a sense of self-respect—standing up to the doctors at the health center and saying, "No, doing that isn't enough. I've already done that and it hasn't worked." That's pretty significant. They and their communities need that kind of self-respect in order to fight for the structural changes in Guatemala that will help guarantee that people will be healthy in the long run.

Family Nursing in a Mexican American Community

Sr. Anne Darlene Wojtowicz, a member of the Sisters of Charity of Cincinnati, works as a family nurse-practitioner and nurse-midwife in Hidalgo County, the second poorest county in Texas. Most of the people she serves are Mexican American, and many do not speak English.

As a family nurse-practitioner and midwife, Sr. Anne Darlene Wojtowicz tries to ensure that the poor people of Hidalgo County, Texas, receive adequate health care and education.

We do as much preventive care as possible, especially with pregnant women. Here in the valley we have an extremely high rate of children born without brains, with partial brains, or with spinal cord damage. Defects like these happen within the first twenty-four days after conception, so early prenatal care is critical. Good prenatal care means a healthier baby.

We also provide expectant parents with education. Besides classes on labor, delivery, and breast-feeding, we teach basic parenting skills, toy making, CPR, natural family planning—things that help them be better parents. The children are healthier and happier, there is less child abuse, and more kids stay in school. All of this makes a big difference in their lives.

Sister Anne and her colleagues face many obstacles, such as poverty and environmental damage, in trying to help the people of Hidalgo County become healthier:

The main health problems I see in my family practice are diabetes, high blood pressure, and obesity. Poor diet contributes to a lot of this. You can't have a healthy diet unless you have the money to buy healthier foods like meat, fish, and fresh fruits and vegetables.

Pollution, pesticides, and contaminated water probably cause our very high rate of children born with heart problems and increasing cases of cancer.

Also, we don't have a bus system in the valley, except between cities, so it's hard for people to get to the local clinics. And when people need surgery, they have to go a great distance to Galveston or Houston. These hardships lead people to neglect their health.

11. Suppose you could interview either Jane Redig about her work in Guatemala or Sr. Anne Darlene Wojtowicz about her work in Texas. Choose the woman you would interview and list the questions you would ask her.

For Review

- What are the major health concerns in impoverished countries?
- Give two examples of the devastating effects of bad water and poor sanitation.

Health Concerns in the United States

Access to good food and water is the key health issue in the hungry world. Although most people in the United States do not lack these necessities, the need for health care touches everyone.

A Problem of Access

Some of the world's most sophisticated health care is available in the United States. With only about 5 percent of the world's population, the United States spends about 41 percent of all money spent on health care in the world. U.S. health care is the costliest in the world. Yet, when looking at the country's **infant mortality** (death) **rate** and **average life expectancy**—two key indicators of a population's health—the United States ranks poorly compared with other industrialized nations. (The United States is in twentieth place for its infant mortality rate, and in twenty-second place for average life expectancy.)

When it comes to **access to health care**, poor people in the United States are clearly at a disadvantage in their own country. Medical services are often least available in poor areas, and when they are available they are usually not affordable. If poor people do not have cash, medical insurance,

Medicaid, or Medicare (government assistance programs), they receive inferior care, if any at all.

Nor does having an income above the poverty level guarantee a person access to health care. In the United States, one of every nine *working* families has no health insurance. Thirty-seven million people have no health coverage at all. Millions more do not have enough insurance to cover their needs. U.S. health care reform, undertaken by the federal government, is supposed to address this situation, but it is a long way from arriving at a system that covers everyone.

Consider the impact of lack of access to health care on these three individuals:

- Leon is age twenty-six and diabetic. He lost his job and health insurance and has been unable to find new work. With no money to pay his rent, he moved in with his mother. He has applied for state Medicaid to cover the cost of insulin. But because he lives with his mother, he is not eligible for assistance.

- Tavia works as a substitute teacher. She makes too much money to qualify for Medicaid, but too little to afford private insurance for herself and her two sons. By paying on installments, she keeps up with her sons' medical bills, but she needs a hysterectomy (surgery to remove the uterus) to get rid of a noncancerous but painful tumor. She is uncertain how to deal with the situation.

- Diane, a forty-six-year-old woman whose husband left her, could only find a part-time, minimum-wage job in a department store. She wanted full-time work, but the company hires only part-time people to avoid having to pay

for employees' medical insurance. She is too young for Medicare, cannot receive state Medicaid because she has no young children, and so has no medical coverage at all. As a result, she lives quite fearfully, has trouble sleeping, and suffers with an infected tooth she cannot afford to have treated.

The statistics and the human tragedies associated with health care in the United States show great injustice in the system. Though the United States consumes a huge amount of health care in dollars, a significant portion of its people receive inadequate care, or none at all.

Values That Work Against Justice in Health Care

Why is the U.S. health care system so skewed? This course cannot fully answer that question because the issues are extremely complex. Part of the problem is that health care has become a business, with the financial interests of medical institutions, insurance companies, medical supply and drug companies, and professionals often taking priority over health interests. Beyond that, we can examine some values and attitudes in U.S. society that make health care so costly and cause good, basic care to be out of reach for so many people:

- denial of limits and denial of death
- individualism
- priority on high-tech solutions, or cure over care

Denial of Limits, Denial of Death

The reality of human life is that we are limited creatures, that we cannot "have it all," and that eventually we are going to die. We can accept this reality or deny it. **Denial of limits and death** is common in contemporary society. Advertising reinforces this denial by focusing on youthfulness and trying to convince us that certain products will revitalize us or make us young again. We fight the process of aging, with its inevitable narrowing of choices. Popular culture is filled with images in which pleasure and "having it all" is emphasized. These images ignore the existence of suffering and death, stunting our ability to cope with these realities. Denial of death distorts our understanding of life, and the effects of this distortion can be seen in our lifestyles.

Consider a man who smokes heavily, drinks to excess, and often drives drunk. He does so with an attitude that no harm can come to him—he behaves as if he is immortal. And if that behavior leads to a serious health problem, he

12. Imagine yourself in the place of one of these three persons with no health coverage. Write a first-person inner monolog of thoughts you might be having about your situation and how to cope.

expects modern medicine to solve it. Similarly, other unhealthy lifestyle choices—a high-stress job, a fast-paced lifestyle, a diet high in fat—might speak of a denial of mortality.

In contrast, accepting that we are limited creatures who are going to die is a way of treasuring life and living with real vitality. This acceptance is not a morbid, depressing preoccupation with death's inevitability; it is a way of understanding the fullness of life. When we acknowledge death as part of the essence of being human, we are less likely to take the gift of human life for granted. We recognize that because we are finite and our lifetime is limited, we are responsible for honoring our own dignity and that of others. Our lifestyle choices reflect our sense of responsibility.

Christians have only to look to Jesus to see the ultimate example of accepting death and limitation. Jesus accepted his unjust execution because it was the way his earthly work would be completed. He felt pain and suffered deeply, and he called out despairingly to God as he hung on the cross. But still he did not fight death. His earthly life had come to an end, and he entered into his death with dignity. Christians believe that by his Resurrection, Jesus overcame death, and that those who follow Jesus share in the Resurrection.

Death has a new meaning for Christians. Yet the inability to face death and limits is at the core of much injustice in our society.

Individualism

The intensity of individualism in U.S. society shows up within its health care system. *Individual* needs and desires determine which medical procedures are done for a person, provided, of course, she or he has medical coverage or money for the procedures. So if John Doe needs and wants a heart transplant, John Doe gets a heart transplant—as long as he has the coverage and a donor heart can be found. Much less attention is paid to the "common good" health needs, such as good prenatal care for poor women or proper immunization of children against diseases like measles. Preventing disease through such widespread basic health measures is much less costly than treating it. For instance, for every dollar spent on feeding undernourished pregnant mothers, an average of four dollars is saved on Medicaid costs for babies born prematurely or with severe health problems.

In U.S. society, where individual needs so often take priority over the common good, **preventive health measures** do not receive as much support as medical care that responds to sickness and crisis.

13. Write an essay agreeing or disagreeing with this statement: *Accepting the reality of death and limits is a way of living life fully.* Give detailed reasons for your opinion.

14. In writing, agree or disagree with this statement: *If you can afford to pay for any kind of medical procedure, you should be allowed to have it.*

Priority on High-tech Solutions, Cure Over Care

The denial of death and the priority on individualism feed right into another value in U.S. society—the emphasis on **high-tech solutions** to problems, on **cure over care.** We look to technology to solve just about everything. In health care, this plays out in high-tech rescue efforts that attempt to fix or cure conditions that are actually beyond help. Technology is often used to sustain a person's life after the body has lost its ability to do so. In many cases, though, low-cost preventive care or lifestyle changes could have eliminated the need for extraordinary high-tech measures.

For example, a man who has smoked three packs of cigarettes a day for forty years has so damaged his body that due to oxygen deprivation, his digestive organs have permanently stopped working. Without a digestive system, he can remain alive only if he is attached for sixteen hours a day to machines that feed him and remove his waste. The procedure costs a great deal. If he survives for five years, his medical bills will go into millions of dollars.

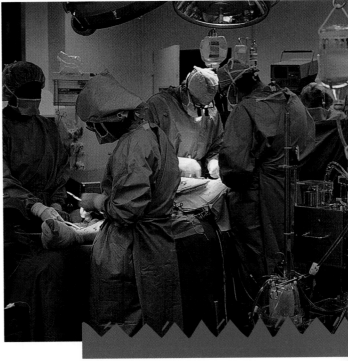

Costly high-tech rescue efforts sometimes attempt to fix or cure conditions that are actually beyond help.

Health care in the United States is often focused in this way. It does all that is technologically possible to help people once they become seriously ill, even if that help provides only short-term survival. Reliance on extraordinary medical solutions leads to the neglect of preventive and maintenance measures that would help people stay healthy in the first place. Medical research also tends to focus on the high-tech cures, taking resources away from the health care that is available to poor people, who primarily need preventive medical care rather than extraordinary procedures.

A family in New Jersey struggled with the dilemma of how far to go with high-tech "solutions" when their mother was dying:

My mother was eighty-two years old when she entered the hospital for the last time. Her breathing was erratic, she could barely walk, she was sometimes disoriented, and she needed help with her essential bodily functions. Up until entering the hospital, she had still lived in her own house. But it was obvious now that she needed full-time attention.

At the hospital, oxygen improved her breathing, but a week later that was not enough. She was put on a respirator, which was very uncomfortable for her. And then it seemed like every day something else went wrong. She got an infection in her lungs, so the doctors gave her

15. If you knew that no high-tech medicine was available to treat heart disease, cancer, serious injury, and so on, would you live your life any differently? Respond in a paragraph.

antibiotics. Every day there was a new tube going into some part of her body. Then her kidneys failed, so they tried dialysis. She improved a bit, but then faded again. She was not even aware of what was going on anymore.

Finally, I went to the doctor and said, "She's an old woman. She's dying. We have to let her go." I just couldn't see sticking more needles in her and hooking her up to more machines. These things weren't helping, they were just dragging out her death. I wanted her to die peacefully.

The doctor agreed that all of these measures would not "cure" her. On my say-so, they stopped all extraordinary procedures except for the respirator. Without it she would suffocate—not a peaceful death. Without dialysis, though, her kidneys shut down completely and she slipped into a coma. It was the most humane way. She died, peacefully, three days later.

Watching medical technology attempt to do the impossible led this daughter to choose care instead of cure for her mother. Her priority was to allow her mother to die in peace and comfort, which was more important than adding a few hours or days to her life.

This decision, incidentally, was not an instance of euthanasia, which is against Catholic teaching. It was based on a sincere weighing of the burdens and benefits of extraordinary treatment for someone who was dying, which is fully consistent with Catholic belief. **Euthanasia,** on the other hand, involves intentionally ending a person's life, not simply allowing the person to die by not using extraordinary means to keep him or her alive.

16. Write your reaction to the choice this daughter made for her mother. What do you think you would have done in her place?

Placing priority on care over cure can enable patients with terminal conditions to die in peace and comfort.

Opting for a Different Way to Go

Denis Wadley was a teacher at De La Salle High School in Minneapolis. He believed that we need to change the way we think about death. His belief originated from a special perspective:

> A year ago June I was diagnosed with terminal cancer. . . . I have been given six months to two years to live.

Doctors offered Wadley various operations and therapies, all with little or no chance of curing the cancer. "A few weeks ago I went off chemotherapy entirely because it was interfering too much with my teaching," he wrote. His decision to accept the inevitability of his death was based on these reflections:

> Most people approach death not as a matter of when, but of whether. To watch most people react to death one could infer that at bottom they think death isn't really necessary, that it's some mistake, that someday someone will find a cure for it. Yet death is the one thing we know will happen to us. Most people aren't ready, and they expect the health-care system to foot the bill for their desperation. But this isn't just a patient's error. Science itself seems to treat death as if it's something we'll eventually be rid of, like tuberculosis or the plague, but until such time we simply have to postpone it as long as possible. . . .

> An additional problem is that with the attitude that death should be conquered, not just coped with, we encourage distraction from that very coping, allowing and even encouraging people to hope well beyond good sense, and then lapse into despair when the last desperate remedy fails. . . .

> Personally, I don't want to be kept alive for the longest possible time; I want the situation to be managed with some dignity and nature to take its course without my clawing after the odd two weeks more that might be possible if I lay there full of tubes at the cost of untold thousands of dollars that could be better spent—a waste of money and, ironically, of time. I see injustice in my good luck in having a total, virtually unconditional coverage program when I consider the comparatively paltry sums spent on preventive medicine and nutrition education—not to mention 37 million people without insurance at all. . . . Fundamentally, our thinking about death must change. . . .

> . . . One should consult one's religious sources—and if you don't have them, get them—and not be afraid to allow one's mind to dwell on it [death] before it becomes an imminent matter. One always behaves better as a result of making up one's mind on principle before facing the instance. Death doesn't have to be a disaster. ("When to Say No to Health Care")

Several months after writing this article, Denis Wadley died as he wished to die, naturally and with dignity.

A Decent Level of Health Care for All

Any health care system needs to pay attention to the basic needs of all. One step in that direction would be to place more emphasis on preventive care and health education, and less emphasis on high-tech rescue care. In their *Resolution on Health Care Reform,* the U.S. Catholic bishops offer general principles to guide any attempt to reform our health care system:

- Its priority must be concern for the poor.
- It must respect human life and dignity.
- It must pursue the common good.
- It must seek to make health care affordable.

Let's briefly look at each of these principles.

Concern for Poor People

"Genuine health care reform must especially focus on the basic health needs of the poor," the bishops insist. This includes anyone who does not have access to health care due to poverty, discrimination, lack of education, or lack of employer or public support for health needs. In the existing health care system, individuals who are better off, at least to the extent of having medical insurance, tend to receive priority treatment. The bishops' principles suggest a different priority: "When there is a question of allocating scarce resources, the vulnerable and the poor have a compelling claim to first consideration." Those who are most in need have a basic right to have their concerns addressed first. A just health care system will ensure that access to care is universal, regardless of the economic status of the person in need.

Respect for Human Life and Dignity

"Real health care reform must protect and enhance human life and human dignity." This principle from the bishops' resolution applies to all members of the human family: "The needs of the frail elderly, the unborn child, the person living with AIDS and the undocumented immigrant must be addressed by health care reform." The bishops see respect for life and dignity as an issue affecting all people, rich or poor, from conception to death. As the resolution states, "A consistent concern for human dignity is strongly demonstrated by providing access to quality care from the prenatal period throughout infancy and childhood, into adult life and at the end of life when care is possible even if cure is not."

Pursuit of the Common Good

The bishops express concern that the making of a just health care system "can be undermined by special interest

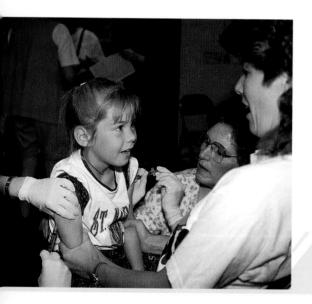

Immunization programs help make health care affordable while serving the common good.

conflict and the resistance of powerful forces who have a major stake in maintaining the status quo." A few politicians or industries cannot be allowed to provide more health care access to some people at the expense of others, especially poor and marginalized people. To ensure that the common good is served, the bishops recommend that both public and private sectors must be involved in developing health care policy.

Affordable Health Care

The final principle the bishops offer has a great impact on the general public: making care affordable. The bishops point out that in the United States "we have the best health care technology in the world, but tens of millions have little or no access to it and the costs of the system are straining our nation, our economy, our families and our church to the breaking point." A just health care system must have built-in mechanisms that help restrain the cost of care.

17. Choose one of the principles for reform offered by the U.S. Catholic bishops. Brainstorm a list of ways in which that principle is *not* being met by our present health care system, and a list of steps that could change this.

For Review

- Briefly describe the problem of access to U.S. health care.
- What three values work against justice in U.S. health care? Give an example of each.
- Summarize the U.S. Catholic bishops' principles for reforming the health care system.

A Child Is Waiting

The work of nourishing the wellness of the world's poor people is of the greatest urgency, but it is especially critical for the children. Nobel Prize–winning poet Gabriela Mistral, of Chile, offers this impassioned plea to us in the more privileged parts of society and the world:

> "We are guilty of many errors . . . but our worst crime is abandoning the children. Many things we need can wait. The child cannot. Right now is the time bones are being formed, blood is being made and senses are being developed. To this child we cannot answer, 'tomorrow.' The child's name is 'today.'" (Quoted in *Bread*)

8 Creating Homes

They sat at a table with their drinks and she explained the shelter's principal rules. Residents had to sign in and out each time they entered or left the building. Curfew was ten o'clock. If anyone tried to come in later, they wouldn't be readmitted. . . . And no drugs or alcohol. Period. If any were discovered, the family would be immediately evicted. "I'll give you a booklet where it's all written down," Lorraine said.

"If we follow those rules, how long can we stay?" Constance said hesitantly.

Lorraine put down her coffee cup. "Right now our limit's two months. It used to be two weeks, if you can imagine that. Two weeks isn't much time to find affordable housing in this city. But in two months it can be done. We'll work with you to make it happen. That's our goal here—to help families find permanent housing. . . . We do as much as we can to get you back on your feet. We'll start tomorrow morning."

"What happens if . . . if we can't find anyplace?" Constance said, staring at her coffee cup.

"There's a long time before we have to worry about that," Lorraine said.

Constance turned her head away.

"Is something wrong?" Lorraine asked.

Constance covered her eyes, trying to fight back her tears. "We've been on the streets, in those hotels"—her voice broke—"nobody should have to live that way. . . ."

Lorraine reached over and took Constance's hand. "You're right," she said sympathetically. "Nobody should." (Harris, Come the Morning, *pages 141–142*)

Homelessness is a stark reality in contemporary society. Homeless people sleep on heating grates outside of city buildings in which daily business transactions may total in the millions of dollars. Because they are considered an eyesore and an embarrassment, homeless people are driven out of parks in which they have found minimal comfort. They are herded into shelters and dangerous, run-down welfare hotels. They are kept out of sight and out of mind, hoping, like the family in the story above, to find the power to get back on their feet.

Just what is a home? It is more than simply a roof over our head, though that is a start and more than many people have. A **true home** is an environment that is physically decent, but that also supports human dignity and human development. A home is a place where we can put down roots, experience stability, and become part of a larger community. It is a place of rest, where body and spirit are nurtured and rejuvenated, so that we can give our best to others.

Society often tries to keep homeless people out of sight and out of mind. A police officer questions a woman camped in a park in San Francisco.

To survive, people *do* need "a roof over their head"—a place to eat, sleep, and bathe, sheltered from the elements. But God desires that human beings should thrive, living *in homes*, not simply *under roofs*. When we see around us so many people suffering without even shelter, we realize how far we are from being a just society where everyone has a home. Homes, in their truest sense, do not just happen. They must be created by human love and effort.

Decent Housing for All

1. What is your idea of a home? Answer in a one-page essay.

Decent housing has long been a major concern of governments, churches, and communities, with many programs aimed at supplying good-quality housing at affordable prices. In spite of these efforts, millions of Americans do not have housing, and millions more have housing that is inadequate.

In 1988, the U.S. Catholic bishops issued a statement entitled *Homelessness and Housing: A Human Tragedy, A Moral Challenge*. It reminds us that for Christians, the reasons to help those who are homeless have their source in the life of Jesus:

> As believers, we find our reason and direction for action in the life of Jesus and the teaching of his Church. We are reminded by the gospel that the first human problem Jesus faced on earth was a lack of shelter. There was

"no room in the inn" for the Holy Family in Bethlehem. Today, we see in the faces of homeless men, women, and children, the face of Christ. We know that in reaching out to them, standing with them in defending their rights, in working with them and their families for decent housing, we serve the Lord. (Number 14)

No Place to Lay Their Head

The National Coalition for the Homeless estimates that at least three million people in the United States are **literally homeless.** Some may live for a time with friends or extended family members. But many more have no choice but to live on the street or in one of the many shelters that have sprung up across the country in response to the housing crisis. Many of these people suffer from mental illness; some are addicted to alcohol or drugs. A growing number are families, with children, who have run into a crisis of some sort, such as loss of a job. Many homeless people have jobs, but a combination of low wages and the high cost of housing has put them out on the street.

Homeless and Jobless

Losing a job is often the reason a person or family becomes homeless. Writer Jonathan Kozol tells of a family in New York City—Peter, Megan, and their five children:

> He was a carpenter. She was a woman many people nowadays would call old-fashioned. She kept house and cared for their five children while he did construction work in New York City housing projects. Their home was an apartment in a row of neat brick buildings. She was very pretty then, and even now, worn down by months of suffering, she has a lovely, wistful look. She wears blue jeans, a yellow jersey, and a bright red ribbon in her hair—"for luck," she says. But luck has not been with this family for some time. (*Rachel and Her Children*, page 1)

While at the beach one Sunday, the family received word that their apartment was on fire. They rushed home, but the fire had already destroyed all of their belongings:

> Peter has not had a real job since. "Not since the fire. I had tools. I can't replace those tools. It took me years of work." He explains he had accumulated tools for different jobs, one tool at a time.

2. In a paragraph, reflect on this statement: *"Today, we see in the faces of homeless men, women, and children, the face of Christ."*

A homeless man in a shelter for men sits beside his Nativity scene. The first human problem Jesus faced was lack of shelter.

3. Imagine you are jobless and have been evicted from your apartment. Make a list of strategies for your immediate and long-term survival.

Each job would enable him to add another tool to his collection. "Everything I had was in that fire." (Page 2)

They were forced by these circumstances to apply for welfare and were placed in a run-down hotel contracted by the city to house homeless families. The conditions at the welfare hotel were quite poor:

The city pays $3,000 monthly for the two connected rooms in which they live. [Megan] shows me the bathroom. Crumbling walls. Broken tiles. The toilet doesn't work. There is a pan to catch something that's dripping from the plaster. The smell is overpowering.

"I don't see any way out," [Peter] says. "I want to go home. Where can I go?" (Page 2)

The accidental and tragic loss of their belongings, including the tools of Peter's trade, led to a cycle of poverty that the family was unable to break. After two years in the welfare hotel, the children were placed in various foster homes. Their family shattered, Peter and Megan had to live on the streets.

Peter and Megan's experience is shocking to us, but it is not uncommon in our society. In 1993, 43 percent of homeless people in the United States were families, including 450,000 children. Millions of Americans live on the edge of homelessness. One missed paycheck, one major illness, or one large repair bill may be all that it takes for individuals or families to see their lives suddenly and drastically change because of the loss of a place to call home. Many do eventually recover from such a loss, but not all.

One missed paycheck, one major illness, or one large repair bill may be all it takes for an individual or family to become homeless.

Homeless and Mentally Ill

The connection between homelessness and **mental illness** originated with the policy of **deinstitutionalization**, begun in the 1960s. Over a period of thirty years, hundreds of thousands of patients were removed from institutions in which they were being treated for mental illness. Theoretically, these patients could expect to find the help they needed in community mental health programs. But many had no home community to return to and were unable to deal with the agencies and bureaucracies that could provide help. Thousands ended up on the streets.

Being homeless, too, left former patients without the stable environment they needed to cope with their illness. Outreach programs have made some progress in treating mentally ill homeless people, for whom treatment must be thorough and ongoing. A stable environment is also needed by those being treated for addiction to alcohol and other

Shelter, with Love and Support

In Washington, D.C., the Christian-based service group **Jubilee Ministries,** helps homeless men and women rebuild their lives. Samaritan Inns, started by Jubilee in 1987, give homeless substance abusers the support that enables them to continue their ongoing recovery from addiction.

At the Inns, formerly homeless men or women live together in a homelike setting. A resident house manager, or Innkeeper, provides support and helps hold residents accountable to their daily Narcotics Anonymous or Alcoholics Anonymous meetings and household chores.

Each resident also meets weekly with the Addictions Counselor and Social Services Coordinator (SSC). The SSC helps each man or woman define a contract of specific goals to address the reasons they became homeless. The SSC also provides financial management assistance, access to job placement and counseling at Jubilee Jobs, outpatient health care through Columbia Road Health Services, G.E.D. tutoring at Academy of Hope. . . . Residents learn to build healthy relationships and hold each other accountable to their own recovery through weekly house meetings and overcomers groups.

Men and women stay at the Inn for an average of six months. The 52% of the participants who successfully complete the program are fully employed and are maintaining the disciplines required to stay clean and sober. They also are ready to move on to more independent living situations.

("Samaritan Inns and Sarah's Circle," *Jubilee Ministries*)

Jubilee's approach demonstrates that ministering to homeless people requires more than just providing shelter. Counseling, education, job opportunities, and a sense of community are also key elements. Another remarkable achievement of Jubilee Ministries is in keeping down costs: Jubilee's comprehensive services to the homeless actually cost less to provide per person per day than the cost of shelter and a meal for one night in one of the city's emergency shelters.

A Samaritan Inn resident sums up the experience: "It's not like I'm here with strangers. I know a lot of people in the building. We look after each other like brothers. And that helps me stay clean."

drugs. In the following case, the treatment of a crack-addicted woman was ineffective for two main reasons: she lacked the will to succeed, and she lacked the stability that a real home would provide for continued treatment.

Tammy had a public housing authority apartment but allowed her drug dealer to use it to manufacture crack. Within a week the apartment was taken over by drug dealers. Tammy lost control of her apartment but was allowed to stay and exchanged sex for drugs. . . . Tammy was forced out one month later. . . .

. . . She was referred into a hospital-based detoxification program. She was discharged to her family five days later. An appointment was made with a . . . substance abuse counselor. No one [of her family] was there to greet Tammy upon discharge. She never kept her appointment with the counselor. Tammy has been seen once by a former friend. She was living in her old apartment, selling herself for drugs. (Brickner et al., editors, *Under the Safety Net,* page 212)

Recovery from drug and alcohol addiction requires complete abstinence. Recovering addicts must take life one day at a time. The stability provided by a home increases an addict's chance of remaining drug free. So for an addict, homelessness makes it more difficult to break the cycle of addiction.

Homeless and Powerless

People who are homeless often experience a sense of hopelessness and powerlessness. Without a home, decent food, and good hygiene, their self-esteem sinks lower and lower. When an opportunity for a place to call home does arise, it must meet the requirements of the welfare system. Mrs. Harrington, a woman sheltered in a welfare hotel in New York, tried to find an apartment. The maximum amount the welfare system would pay for her rent was $270 a month:

Homeless people are often faced with rules and procedures that increase the challenge of finding a home.

"Places I see, they want $350, $400, $500. Out in Jamaica [Queens], recently, I met an older lady. She had seen me crying, so she asked me: 'What's the matter?' I explained to her how long I had been looking for a home. She said: 'Well, I own a couple of apartments.' The rental was $365. She said that she would skip the extra month and the deposit. I had told her what my husband does, my children. I had [my son] Doby with me.

I believe she took a liking to me. So I was excited. Happy! And she handed me the lease and proof of ownership and told me I should take them to my [social] worker, and she gave me her phone number. A nice lady. And you see—you do forget what is your *situation*. You forget that you are poor. It's like a dream: This lady likes me and we're going to have a home! My worker denied me for $365. I was denied. $365. My social worker is a nice man but he said: 'I have to tell you, Mrs. Harrington. Your limit is $270.' Then I thought of this: The difference is only $95. I'll make it up out of my food allowance. We can lighten up on certain things. Not for the children, but ourselves. We'll eat less food at first. Then I can get a job. He'll finish his computer course. The house had a backyard. . . . They told me no. I was denied." (Kozol, *Rachel and Her Children,* page 42)

Mrs. Harrington's efforts gave her a glimpse of a better life for her family. She was willing to make real sacrifices to achieve that life. However, the same system that was willing to pay $3,000 per month for a family to live in a welfare hotel was not willing to allow her $365 per month for an apartment. She remained homeless even though a home was waiting for her.

4. Pretend that you are Mrs. Harrington's social worker. Write a paragraph that explains why you must deny her request to rent an apartment. In a second paragraph, write your personal feelings about her situation.

Unsuitable Housing

A great many of the poor and low-income citizens of the United States live in **unsuitable housing**, that is, housing below a standard that is tolerable. It is all they can afford,

Unsuitable housing, or housing below a tolerable standard, is the best that can be afforded by many poor and low-income U.S. citizens.

and even then it is common for 50 to 70 percent of their income to be spent on housing.

Public Housing

Public housing projects are often the only choice for people with low incomes. These projects are run by the government, and rent is based on the tenant's income. Public housing projects are certainly necessary and have helped millions of families live with dignity. But far too often they fail to provide a safe living environment.

Public housing can become unsuitable housing when the physical structure deteriorates or when living there takes too great a toll on the tenants, emotionally and socially. Such projects are often poorly constructed and insufficiently maintained. When services such as water and elevators break down, the quality of life can quickly deteriorate. Gang members and drug dealers find housing projects to be advantageous places from which to operate. The majority of the tenants live in fear of being victimized by crime. Society also puts a stigma on people living in public housing. This damages the self-esteem of tenants, especially that of the children and the young adults, and often leads to failure in school and work.

Public housing projects that fail to consider the full range of the meaning of home cannot provide real homes for people with low incomes. A home must consist of more than four walls and a roof; the living environment must be decent, safe, and nurturing.

The Inner City

Unsuitable housing also exists in inner-city neighborhoods, which may be overrun by drugs, prostitution, and violence, making life for the majority of residents unbearable. Abandoned houses with broken or boarded-up windows are common. Slum landlords, wishing to extract all they can from their properties with no regard for those who live in them, just collect their rents and let their properties deteriorate. This lowers the quality of life for all inner-city residents, the majority of whom care about their neighborhoods and wish to lead decent lives free of the dangers of crime.

Rural United States

Low-income people living in rural areas also face difficult circumstances when it comes to finding suitable housing. The places they can afford to rent or buy are typically substandard and neglected. "It's appalling," says a woman seeking a place to live in rural Minnesota. "One place we looked at had exposed wiring. In another one, you could see right

5. From a movie, TV show, news article, or your own experience, find an example of people who live in public housing or inner-city neighborhoods who are trying to make their area more livable.

through to the outside around an electrical outlet in the kitchen. You have to watch out for peeling lead paint and crumbling asbestos, too—those are common in the low-rent places."

The housing crisis in our society most visibly affects those who are literally homeless—the people living on the street, in shelters, or in welfare hotels. The "hidden homeless" are those who are making do without a home by doubling up with other families in already crowded apartments or making other, similar arrangements. Low-income people living in unsuitable housing—unsafe, deteriorated, and so on—also feel the effects of the housing crisis. It extends even to the middle class, for whom costs of renting or owning a home are growing faster than incomes.

For Review

- How does the life of Jesus encourage us to take action on behalf of homeless people?
- What are some of the circumstances that cause people to become literally homeless?
- Why does homelessness impede a person's ability to recover from alcohol or drug addiction?
- Describe unsuitable housing.

Responding to the Housing Crisis

Why a Shortage of Housing?

Before we consider how to address the housing crisis, let's take a brief look at some of the reasons for the **shortage of low-cost housing.**

Rising costs of housing: Housing costs, for both renters and buyers, have risen dramatically. Buying a house is way beyond the reach of low-income people and, increasingly, beyond the reach of many families with moderate incomes.

Falling incomes: As housing costs have gone up, real incomes (that is, incomes adjusted for inflation) have gone down. Also, more jobs created in recent years have been low-wage, service jobs. Individuals and families simply cannot afford adequate housing.

Building at the high end: As more people work for less money, the need for low-cost housing has increased. But the supply of low-cost housing has decreased significantly. New rental units being built tend to be at the high end, where developers can make a higher profit. Many high-rent apartments are standing vacant while people with low incomes have no place to live.

Funding cuts: Government neglect has added to the housing crisis. Funding for low-cost public housing was cut from thirty billion dollars in 1980 to less than nine billion dollars in 1990. Often, too, funding has gone to poorly designed programs that serve fewer people than they could.

6. Choose one of the four causes of the housing shortage. In a page, speculate on one step that private groups or government bodies might take to address this cause.

Emergency shelters like this one provide relief for the immediate need of those who have no place to sleep but the streets.

A Compassionate Community Responds

As the housing crisis has worsened, concerned individuals and groups across the country have responded in a wide variety of ways, both to immediate needs and to the need for long-term solutions. Many Christians, fueled by a sense of compassion and a desire to live out their faith, have moved into action. Here are some examples.

Emergency Shelters

The most immediate need generated by the housing crisis has been to provide emergency shelter for the hundreds of thousands of people who have no place to sleep except the streets. Christian churches have been deeply involved in this response, many in cooperation with local governments. The New York Coalition for the Homeless, consisting of around two hundred church and synagogue congregations in New York City, houses over two thousand people a night. The coalition's efforts are part of a citywide program to shelter New York's estimated sixty thousand homeless people. A church organization in Chicago, the Interfaith Coalition for the Homeless, works with its city government to house more than twenty-five hundred people per night.

Houses of Hospitality

Offering **hospitality**, a welcoming spirit and generous attention to comfort, to a stranger in need has a long history in the Judeo-Christian tradition. For the ancient Israelites, closing one's home to the homeless violated the laws of the Covenant. Jesus teaches us that offering hospitality to the stranger is the same as offering it to Jesus himself: "'"For I was a stranger and you welcomed me. . . . Truly I tell you, just as you did it to one of the least of these who are members of my family, you did it to me"'" (Matthew 25:35–40).

Movements such as the Catholic Worker, described in chapter 7, carry on the tradition of giving shelter to the homeless, one of the **works of mercy.** Today, more than one hundred Catholic Worker houses of hospitality are open in the United States, all run by volunteers.

Habitat for Humanity volunteers work alongside the families who will eventually live in the houses they build.

Building Homes with Poor Families

Habitat for Humanity was founded in 1976 in response to the haunting question in the Christian Testament, "How does God's love abide in anyone who has the world's goods and sees a brother or sister in need and yet refuses help?" (1 John 3:17). Habitat offers people of faith a chance to put their faith into practice, to love their neighbors not just with words, but with actions. Here is how it works:

Volunteers with Habitat work alongside poor people to build or renovate homes that the poor people will move into. No government funding is used. It is basically a hand up, not a handout, because the prospective homeowners are required to work not only on their own house but on other Habitat houses as well—at least five hundred hours of work. The homeowners then pay for the materials with a twenty-year, no-interest loan. Their payments go to a fund to help build more Habitat houses. One family's experience goes like this:

On Monday, Patrick and Lydia Bushie's first home, Lot 18, Habitat Place in Winnipeg [Canada] is just a basement. By Saturday the house is ready for them to move in with their children Lisa and Desmond.

Patrick explains how he and his family feel about their new home: "It's a house built with love, so many people's love that I have lost count. The people who are building care that the work is done right or they do it over. It's really something to own this house. We've always been renters." (Adapted from Mitchell, "Homes That Love Builds")

Effective Action on the System

Working with Habitat for Humanity or volunteering at a homeless shelter is often the first and most common way that those who want to help homeless people become involved. The need for and the value of such efforts should not be underestimated, but we also must recognize the need to take actions that go even further, to address the whole system.

7. Find out if the Catholic Worker, Habitat for Humanity, or a similar movement is active in your community. Interview someone who participates in the movement and write a report on that person's experience.

Having a good home is a basic human right. High-quality public housing can help realize that right for all.

In their 1988 statement on homelessness, the U.S. Catholic bishops offered several major goals that they believe should be included in a national housing policy:

From Building Homes to Building a Community

In the summer of 1967, the Central Ward of Newark, New Jersey, experienced five days of race-related violence. Twenty-three people were killed, more than a thousand were wounded, and property damage exceeded $15 million.

The Central Ward was written off by many of Newark's leaders. They chose to focus instead on commercial development downtown, in an attempt to import economic stimulation. For some of the ward's residents, though, that was not enough. In the months following the violence, a group began to meet informally at Queen of Angels Catholic Church. This group was convinced that with determination and commitment they could make a difference in the future of their neighborhood.

The people from Queen of Angels became the **New Community Corporation** (NCC) in January 1968. They were led by Fr. William J. Linder, a Catholic priest deeply committed to the people of his Central Ward parish. In the decades since, NCC has developed a great variety of projects that serve the people of the Central Ward; its annual budget has grown to more than $100 million. NCC has shown that the work of creating real homes goes far beyond simply providing shelter, and that real homes exist only within real communities, where people are concerned about one another and basic needs are taken care of.

> Starting with a complex of 120 apartments built in response to the Central Ward's staggering need for decent, affordable housing, New Community has grown to become New Jersey's largest non-profit housing developer. Many people consider it America's most successful, comprehensive community development corporation. It now owns 10 developments with more than 2,500 apartments in 62 clean, well-maintained, graffiti-free buildings that are home to more than 6,000 people. With few exceptions, residents would previously have only had the grim choice of the Central Ward's towering public housing projects, with their debilitating squalor, or the ward's grossly deteriorated private housing.

> New Community's activities have now spread far beyond housing (which it is now even building and operating in New Jersey towns outside of Newark). The group does job training through a center that serves thousands every year and places nearly 1,000 clients in jobs annually. It offers an array of medical care and day-care services. Its economic development ventures provide jobs and a solid economic base for a Central Ward otherwise bereft of significant economic activity.

> New Community runs its own businesses. . . . It employs a sizable work force, including social workers, maintenance staff and its own sizable security forces. Its six for-profit businesses and affiliated non-profit service operations have created almost 1,200 permanent jobs, filled mostly by previously jobless Central Ward residents. Today, New Community is one of Newark's biggest employers. (Guskind and Peirce, *Against the Tide*, page 4)

Some of NCC's other achievements include these:
- Babyland Nursery provides day care for 630 infants and toddlers.
- Extended Health Care Facility provides care for elderly members of the community.
- The *NCC Clarion*, the corporation's newspaper, has a circulation of forty-two thousand.
- NCC runs a shelter for victims of domestic violence.
- The NCC Pathmark Supermarket, owned jointly by NCC and Pathmark, opened in 1990 and is the first such food market to open in Newark since 1967. It provides Central Ward residents with the kind of market that many Americans take for granted.

Despite NCC's successes, the city of Newark still has serious problems. Drugs, violence, crime, AIDS, and a continuing shortage of decent housing persist in making life difficult for many Newark residents. But the NCC is an enduring sign of hope in a still-hurting city.

- *Preservation:* Effective policies to help preserve, maintain, and improve what low-cost, decent housing we already have.
- *Production:* Creative, cost-effective, and flexible programs that will increase the supply of quality housing for low-income families, the elderly, and others in great need.
- *Participation:* Encouraging the active and sustained involvement and empowerment of homeless people, tenants, neighborhood residents, and housing consumers. We need to build on the American traditions of home ownership, self-help, and neighborhood participation.
- *Partnership:* Ongoing support for effective and creative partnerships among nonprofit community groups, churches, private developers, government at all levels, and financial institutions to build and preserve affordable housing.
- *Affordability:* Efforts to help families obtain decent housing at costs that do not require neglect of other basic necessities.
- *Opportunity:* Stronger efforts to combat discrimination in housing against racial and ethnic minorities, women, those with handicapping conditions, and families with children.

(Number 12)

8. Choose one of the six goals that the U.S. Catholic bishops say are necessary for a national housing policy. In a paragraph, speculate on why this goal cannot be met without working on issues like poverty, discrimination, and economic justice.

To fulfill goals like these, proponents of better housing must think in terms that go beyond charity, shelters, and public housing projects. The hard work of creating homes cannot be accomplished in isolation from related issues like poverty, discrimination, and justice in the economy. Nor will efforts to create real homes be successful if they are made with the attitude that the desire for good homes for all is just a dream, a wish, or a high ideal. Having a good home is a basic human right. Each person has a right to expect a decent home and a good living environment, not just dream of it.

For Review

- Summarize two causes of the housing shortage.
- Give two examples of how Christians have responded to homelessness with compassion.
- Explain three of the goals that should be included in a national housing policy, according to the U.S. Catholic bishops.

When a House Is Not a Home

What Makes a Home?

As we have seen in this chapter, a home, in the truest sense of the word, is much more than four walls and a roof. Home is a place where human dignity is respected and each person is free to develop his or her potential. A real home, one that helps us thrive, is all of these things:

A safe place: In a real home, each person feels physically, emotionally, and psychologically safe and secure.

A nurturing place: In a true home, persons are nurtured and cared for out of love and respect. In this way, home serves as a solid foundation upon which we can build our character.

A stable grounding point: A true home is a grounding point for those who live there. From this stable place, they can move beyond home to participate fully in their communities.

A source of identity: A true home gives people a sense of who they are. It is an important part of how they define themselves.

Domestic Violence

For many people, the kind of home described above is not a reality. For them, "home" is oppressive and dangerous, a place of violence. **Domestic violence** takes the form of battering, emotional and psychological abuse, or sexual assault—all strategies that attempt to control a person through fear and intimidation. Although men are sometimes its victims, women and children are the likeliest victims of domestic violence. Three million to four million women are battered each year by their husbands or partners. These victims are homeless in the sense that they lack a real home, and many become literally homeless when they try to escape the violence by moving out.

No safety: Violent homes are places of physical, emotional, and psychological danger, not safety. Volunteers working with battered women report that most of these women are hurt more by the mental and emotional anguish connected to the violence than by the physical attack itself. In fact, physical violence is not necessary to make a home unsafe. Verbal violence can also do tremendous harm, as does sheer neglect of a person's basic needs.

9. Reread your response to activity 1, if you did that one earlier. Did your idea of a home contain the characteristics described in this chapter? Add a paragraph to your first essay, reflecting on these aspects of home.

No nurturing: Homes that are violent do not nurture. Those who live in them are deprived of the love, respect, and support they need to develop as fully as possible. They do not receive the solid foundation upon which to build their character.

No stability: Homes wracked by violence do not provide people with stability and grounding so they can contribute to the community as whole persons. Instead, people raised in violent households often become abusers themselves, or they become lifelong victims of abuse.

A poor source of identity: Victims of domestic violence commonly lack a good source of identity. The self-esteem of battered women is often so beaten down that they do not believe they are even capable of caring for themselves or their children. Many of them stay in abusive relationships precisely because they think so little of themselves.

10. Are you aware of anyone who lives in a situation of domestic violence? If so, write a description of how she or he is affected by it.

Safe, Temporary Homes for Victims of Domestic Violence

The ultimate solution to domestic violence is to stop the violent behavior of abusers. Women in these situations should never be given the message that the church or the Bible condones the violence or requires their submissiveness. In fact, church counselors and pastors must give a clear message to women and men that violence has no place in the home and that no one has to tolerate it. **Sexist attitudes** underlying domestic violence—that women are to be controlled, are inferior, are basically there to do what men want—can never be acceptable to Christians.

Until abusive partners have a turnaround in their violent attitudes and behavior, the women and children who are in danger need immediate help—safe, temporary housing.

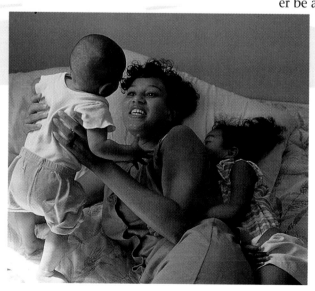

Shelters and Safe Houses: Paths to Home
Whether a woman chooses to take the first step and leave an abusive situation depends on a number of factors—her fear of further violence if she tries to leave, her economic dependence on her partner, her self-esteem and whether she blames herself for the violence aimed at her and her children.

Outreach programs that offer help and safety to abused women and children exist in many communities. Battered women's shelters provide immediate help, giving women a place to live temporarily away from violence. Safe houses, private homes with locations that are kept secret, offer further protection to women, keeping them and their children out of the reach of an abusive partner.

Services like these, staffed by professionals and volunteers, also help abused women discover a true sense of home by helping them regain a sense of worth. This can be a long process, because many women have been in situations of abuse for extended periods. The behaviors and attitudes that come from living under the threat of violence can take years to unlearn.

Covenant House: Homes for Kids in Crisis

Sr. Mary Rose McGeady runs the **Covenant House** crisis shelter for homeless teenagers in New York City. With its six crisis shelters across the United States, Covenant House reaches more than thirty-five thousand of the one million young people who find themselves homeless every year. Many homeless youth are victims of domestic abuse. Sister Mary Rose tells of sixteen-year-old Ricky:

> When Ricky walked in here yesterday, we didn't ask him a lot of questions about his past. We wanted to make sure he felt welcome. He told us he was 16 and that he had been on the street for six months . . . ever since his mother threw him out of the house.
>
> He was so exhausted when he walked in that he could barely keep his eyes open. He said he had a hard time sleeping on the streets because he was scared all the time. He said there were very scary people on the streets.
>
> He just woke up from his safe bed at Covenant House a little while ago, after sleeping for almost 24 hours. ("God Isn't Done with Me Yet . . . ," page 92)

Ricky was very interested, in a desperate way, to learn how much the state paid Covenant House to take care of him. If the state pays Covenant House for each young person sheltered, Ricky figured, the house would need to keep him in order to receive the money. Sister Mary Rose assured him:

> "Ricky, money has nothing to do with it. I would want you here if I didn't have a penny in the world. We love you. Now, why did you ask that question?"
>
> "Well . . . that's what my mother said when she threw me out. She said she got money from the state for

A Covenant House outreach worker listens as a homeless teenager tells his story. Covenant House offers such teens some of the fundamental aspects of a real home.

the foster children she took in and if I was gone she could take in one more foster child.

"So she told me to get out. She said she wasn't making any money on me. I'm her son! She said those other kids were worth more than me. She told *me* to get out, Sister!"

Ricky looked up at me, lost in his words. Tears rolled down his face. "Can you believe that Sister," he kept saying. "Can you believe that?"

I reached out for him, and hugged him for a minute. I could believe it. . . . Tragically, I hear stories like this all too often. But it doesn't make Ricky's story any easier to accept. (Page 93)

Homeless teenagers like Ricky come from every racial and economic background. The biggest challenge they face is staying alive. Two-thirds either attempt or consider suicide; three-quarters become involved in prostitution, pornography, drugs, or other crimes in order to make money to live on; some are killed in the process.

Covenant House provides these young people with food, clothing, shelter, medical attention, counseling, and educational and vocational training. In the process, they are able to experience some of the fundamental aspects of a real home: safety, a nurturing environment, a stable grounding point, and a source of identity.

Violence—physical, emotional, or psychological—has no place in a real home. In the name of justice and love, the entire Christian community has an obligation to help victims of domestic violence in whatever way it can. Abusers also need help in stopping their violent behavior. Outreach programs do indispensable good, but Christians must also work to create a community where violence in the home does not happen in the first place.

11. Imagine that Ricky has come to you with his story. What will you say to him? Write your response in a paragraph.

For Review

- Summarize what a real home is.
- Briefly describe how a house where domestic violence occurs fails to live up to being a real home.
- What types of emergency help are available for victims of abuse?

When Country Is No Longer Home

War, hunger, and political persecution throughout the world have driven more than forty million persons from their homes and shattered their lives. In 1993, over sixteen million of these were international **refugees**, whose only hope of survival was to leave the country that had always been home to them. They had no choice but to search for a new land that would welcome them, or at least let them survive.

A look at the contemporary refugee crisis reads like an encyclopedia of nations and ethnic groups. Among those displaced by wars and internal persecution are Afghans in Pakistan and Iraq; Burmese in Bangladesh; Eritreans in Sudan; Guatemalans in Mexico; the Khmer along the Thai-Cambodian border; Laotians in Thailand; Mozambicans in Malawi; Palestinians in Gaza, the West Bank, Lebanon, and Jordan; Tamils in India; Tibetans in Nepal and India; and Vietnamese in Hong Kong. Huge numbers of refugees have fled Haiti, Bosnia, Rwanda, Cuba, Burundi, Liberia, and Somalia, all countries torn by terrible violence in the 1990s. Typically, refugees are placed in camps with minimal health and hygiene standards. Others stay on the move, their lives endangered as they remain in flight, hoping for a better life.

Top: Vietnamese refugees in Hong Kong are taken to a detention camp in a locked police truck.
Bottom: A stream of Rwandan refugees crosses the border into Tanzania.

Welcoming the Stranger: Entertaining Angels

Making room for refugees in our hearts, our communities, and our nation is a large task. It involves helping people to rebuild their lives after great trauma, often in strange surroundings with unfamiliar languages and customs. Unfortunately, refugees who immigrate to new lands are often met with suspicion and hatred, blamed for the economic and social problems experienced by their new country. But the Christian tradition strongly supports the rights of refugees and immigrants, encouraging us to treat them as if they were angels, messengers from God: "Let mutual love continue. Do not neglect to show hospitality to strangers, for by doing that some have entertained angels without knowing it" (Hebrews 13:1–2).

Cardinal Roger Mahony is the archbishop of Los Angeles, an area that has attracted perhaps more immigrants than any other area in the United States. As a church leader, he is deeply concerned about the tendency to show bias against immigrants and refugees. He comments:

> Our biblical tradition encourages us to encounter the "strangers in our midst"—not with fear and negativity, but with compassion and hopeful expectation. Our social teaching challenges us to embody this sentiment in our personal actions, in our response as a community and in public policy. ("You Have Entertained Angels Without Knowing It")

To better understand the background of many of the refugees who come to our shores, let's look at the experience of a boy who was driven from his homeland because of war. We will see lives lost and disrupted by circumstances far beyond the control of the victims themselves.

12. Have you always welcomed the stranger? Write a page-long essay outlining your attitude toward refugees and immigrants.

The Experience of Refugees: "Disposable People"

Vang Yang was born in 1966 in Laos, a country in southeast Asia. Ethnically, he is of a group known as the *Hmong,* which means "free people." During the Vietnam war, the Hmong fought for the United States; as a result, after the war, they were persecuted by the communists, who were the victors. Many Hmong fled to Thailand, hoping eventually to reach the United States. Vang Yang, the youngest of eight children, was fortunate. After terrible experiences, he escaped and finally reached the United States. His story has much in common with that of many refugees:

> Life in Laos was good for a small boy who was the darling of his older sisters, and Vang had fun. He came and went and did as he pleased. In the nearby town of Muong Ja there were little shops with all kinds of things to see and buy, and Vang spent many happy hours exploring them. But life didn't turn out to be so easy. There was a war, and its backwash grew in volume and intensity until even a small boy became aware of it. The Yangs were finally overwhelmed by it. (*Dark Sky, Dark Land,* page 58)

All of the villagers packed what they could and left. They went on foot, walking all day and stopping at night to rest.

The Yangs lived in the forest for a year and a half, during which time they were relatively safe. But the war came steadily closer. Through binoculars, they could see trucks and tanks on roads far below their hideout. Distant planes dropped bombs. One day a missile crashed into a house in their forest village. It was time to move again.

This time, the forty to fifty families headed north through the forest, making a wide semi-circle and eventually turning back south. They stayed away from roads, struggled across small rivers, through thick forest growth and up and down steep slopes. For thirty days they traveled. Vang's brother Youa was the leader. He was young, but he was also vigorous and intelligent, and people trusted him. (Page 58)

When they finally reached the Mekong River, which they would cross into Thailand, two hundred people were gathered with just a small canoe to ferry them across. All through the night the canoe went back and forth, but when daylight came, the Yangs were among those who had not yet crossed.

Vietnamese refugees, already in exile from their homeland, attempt to escape further persecution in Cambodia.

With light coming on fast, Vang, his mother and sisters and the others—about thirty or so people—hid in the bushes away from the river. Vang's sister's little baby was hungry, so Vang's mother gathered some wood and began building a fire to cook rice. Just then, a communist patrol came walking along the path by the river. They saw Vang's mother and began shooting without hesitation. Vang's mother fell over dead, covered with her own blood. Vang and his sisters ran, choking, sobbing, and terrified, trying to get away. They ran deep into the forest. When they finally threw themselves down to catch their breath, one of Vang's sisters was missing. They didn't know what to do. Vang couldn't imagine going on living without his mother. He was just a little boy and needed someone to take care of him. He wouldn't be able to survive alone with his two sisters in the forest, so they turned back and gave themselves up.

Vang got a last look at his mother, lying still in her own blood. (Page 59)

With thirty others, Vang was taken prisoner. They were forced to walk for a day and a half, but Vang and some others managed to escape. A week later they again reached the Mekong River and were able to cross. They lived for some time in a refugee camp in Thailand. Eventually, Vang and his brother were accepted for residence in the United States.

The Yangs held a celebration. Friends came to wish them bon voyage. But when the day came to leave, there was great sadness. Buses pulled onto the Ban Vinai soccer field to take them to Bangkok. Vang said a tearful good-bye to his sisters as they crowded around to wish him well.

"If we don't ever see you again, goodbye," they cried out as the buses moved slowly away. "Maybe some day we'll get our country back." (Page 60)

Vang Yang did find some measure of peace. He survived his ordeal, and in the United States he had the support of other Hmong refugees and much of the community. He attended school, made friends, joined the Boy Scouts, and participated in many of the typical activities of American teens. He is now married and has two children. Still, he is haunted by his refugee experience, especially the loss of his mother.

The situation of most refugees around the world is like that of Vang and the Hmong. They are hostages, in a sense, of some nation's or faction's political, military, or economic interests. In the eyes of leaders who are using them to fulfill political objectives, refugees are stripped of their humanity and personhood. Once these political goals are met, refugees become "disposable"—the throwaway by-products of conflict and war.

13. Put yourself in Vang's place and imagine how you would feel arriving in the United States after such a terrible ordeal. Write your thoughts.

Responding to the Plight of Refugees

Responding to the needs of millions of refugees worldwide is a vast undertaking. Several levels of action are needed:
1. providing for refugees' basic needs, for instance, through contributions to aid programs like Catholic Relief Services
2. looking into and improving conditions at refugee camps in other countries and in our own
3. assisting refugees in returning home safely
4. welcoming refugees into our own country
5. holding our government accountable to use our resources to help resolve violent conflicts justly, so people won't need to become refugees

The World Community Pulls Back

At every level of need faced by refugees, the response of the world community has been grossly inadequate. The number of refugees doubled between 1982 and 1992, but the budget of the United Nations High Commission for Refugees, which helps refugees, has been significantly reduced. Aid from industrialized countries has dwindled sharply as they face economic problems of their own. For instance, the United States spent twenty-five dollars per refugee in 1980; that figure dropped to twelve dollars in

1992. More and more countries, either unable or unwilling to take on the burden, are also closing their borders and refusing to accept fleeing refugees.

A Christian Response

The Christian community has the opportunity to lead in reaching out to the world's refugees and immigrants. The Scriptures and Catholic Tradition support and even require hospitality and outreach.

Building skills for returning home: Catholic Relief Services sponsors programs around the world that support refugees, teaching them trades and skills to help them produce food, clothing, and shelter. With such skills, refugees who finally return home can help rebuild their communities. This happened in El Salvador in 1990, when nearly twelve thousand refugees returned home despite the continuing civil war in their country. "They returned with new tools, new skills, and with a new sense of community and confidence. Despite the war, they will continue the development process begun in the [refugee] camps—resettled communities of hope for their country" (*The Big Picture,* page 31).

Warmly welcoming newcomers: When refugees and immigrants come to our own borders, how should Christians respond? Cardinal Mahony of Los Angeles says:

> The stranger in our midst reminds us that the social purpose of economic wealth is not what it achieves for the individual, but how it promotes the common good of society. While each and every human being has a right to private property, to a decent standard of living, we have a responsibility to share, as Pope John Paul II has reminded us, not only "from our abundance, but also from our very substance."

> The hearts of Christians whose lives are centered on God cannot help but see Jesus in today's immigrants. . . . The proof of our hospitality is measured not by its

14. Find out what church or community programs exist in your area to welcome refugees and immigrants. Talk to someone involved with one of these programs and write a report on it.

Former Salvadoran refugees re-enter their home village in a religious procession.

exercise when the arrival of strangers is convenient, but precisely when it is inconvenient. In our parishes we must strive to enflesh this effective love by truly serving all. . . .

I encourage you to remember the words from the Third Letter of John: "My friends, you have done faithful work in looking after these brothers, even though they were complete strangers to you" (v. 5). Let these sentiments be our guide as we strive to build up our community. ("You Have Entertained Angels Without Knowing It")

For Review

- What factors cause people to become refugees?
- According to Cardinal Mahony, how does our biblical tradition encourage us to respond to "strangers"—refugees and immigrants?
- List five levels of action that respond to the needs of refugees.

A Prayer for the Homeless

For these things we pray:
A decent home in a good living environment,
A place of safety,
A place of nurture,
A grounding point from which to give and receive,
A source of identity.

This is our prayer for all our sisters and brothers
        who are homeless.
Fill our hearts, God of life and hope, with compassion to
        befriend the homeless,
            the victims of domestic violence,
            and the refugee.
Stir up within us a spirit of hospitality
        and a spirit of justice.
And grant us the wisdom and the courage
        to do all that we can
            to help our homeless sisters and brothers create
            the homes to which they have a right,
            for they are creatures made in your image.

15. Find a newspaper or magazine photo of refugees. Study it closely and prayerfully. Is Jesus present in the picture? Write a story or poem based on the photo.

A young Guatemalan refugee displays her picture of *home.*

9 Providing Good Work

Listen to me, college boy, you can
keep your museums and poetry and string quartets
'cause there's nothing more beautiful than
line work. Clamp your jaws together and listen:
  It's a windy night, you're freezing the teeth out
of your zipper in the ten below, working stiff
jointed and dreaming of Acapulco, the truck cab.
Can't keep your footing for the ice, and
even the geese who died to fill your vest
are sorry you answered the call-out tonight.
You drop a connector and curses
take to the air like sparrows who freeze
and fall back dead at your feet.
Finally you slam the SMD fuse home.
Bang! The whole valley lights up below you
where before was unbreathing darkness.
In one of those houses a little girl
stops shivering. Now that's beautiful,
and it's all because of you.
                ("Bill Hastings," by Todd Jailer)

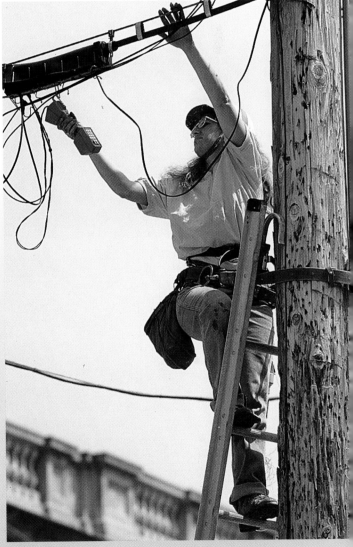

Each day, millions of people go to work, performing an amazing variety of tasks. They are teachers and technicians, carpenters and cooks, dancers and dentists. The laborer who strains muscles and the scientist who stretches the intellect are both engaged in work, as are the mother or father caring for children and the high school student participating in class and reading a textbook after dark.

Paid work helps us provide for the necessities of life by giving us income. This type of work, whether for oneself or for an employer, is what is typically understood as work. But work is larger than that.

Although pay is important, what is perhaps more significant for human dignity is whether we sense that our work makes a positive difference in the world. Bill Hastings, the subject of the poem that begins this chapter, found his difficult, even grueling work *did* make a difference. That was enough for him to proclaim, "there's nothing more beautiful than line work."

Work is sustained effort expended for a purpose, effort that makes a difference in the world. It is a fundamental dimension of human life; we all need to work. So work is more than a job, and the effort of parenting and of studying is work just as surely as is a line worker's job.

1. Make a list of all the activities you do that can be considered work. Next to each one, write what the purpose of the work is or the difference it makes in the world.

Participants in God's Work

Christians believe that God calls human beings to work. As creatures made in the image of God, our work is a reflection of the work of God. In the Genesis Creation story, God tells humankind, "'Be fruitful and multiply, and fill the earth and subdue it'" (1:28). God commands the first humans to use the resources of creation to meet their needs and those of their descendants. Humankind can fulfill this command only through work. In this way, human work participates in God's creative work.

The value of our work is based on more than what we produce or earn. Evaluation of work must also consider the worker's experience.

What Is the Value of Work?

When we consider the value of our work, we are likely to think immediately of the amount of money we are paid for it. Or we might think of the product that is the result of our work—the car at the end of the assembly line, or the hamburger served to a hungry diner. If we are the owner of a business, the value of work might be thought of in relation to the company's year-end profit. Catholic social teaching, however, emphasizes that understanding the value of work solely in terms of end results is inadequate because it fails to consider the worker.

Objective and Subjective Aspects

Pope John Paul II, in his encyclical *On Human Work,* explained that work has two aspects: an **objective** aspect and a **subjective** one. The objective aspect of work refers to the product of the work—the item made or the service performed—and the tools, machinery, and technology involved. The subjective aspect of work is the worker and his or her experience.

Consider, as an analogy, a team sporting event. The *object* of the game is to win. But the *subjects* of the game, the individual players, are most likely to perform well when they are motivated simply by the desire to do their best. Steve Hamilton, a former major league pitcher, recognized this:

> With some guys, winning is everything. It's the whole ball of wax. If you don't win, it's a waste. I do my best, but if you judge your life on winning, you're hurtin'. I know we play for money. These guys say, "If I don't win, I don't make any money." But if I go out and play, there's a certain satisfaction in knowing I've done as good as I can. No matter how hard I try, I could never be a Sandy Koufax. But if I can be as good as Steve Hamilton, I feel I've been successful. (Terkel, *Working,* page 488)

Similarly, the value of work is based on how it affects the worker, not simply on its result, product, or profit. Work, as a creative event, is meant to transform the worker. At its best, in other words, work should help a person fulfill her or his calling or mission as a person. The worker, participating with God, must be given prime consideration in any evaluation of work.

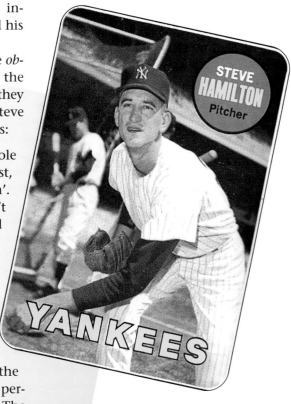

"If I go out and play," said pitcher Steve Hamilton, "there's a certain satisfaction in knowing I've done as good as I can."

Supporting Human Dignity

The value of work is based on whether it supports the dignity of the human person. Whether work is physically hard or intellectually challenging, it must meet the test of human dignity, enabling the worker to achieve a measure of fulfillment as a human being.

So work exists for the sake of human beings, not the other way around. When work exploits our humanity, or when we seem to exist for the sake of work, our dignity is violated. Such work is not the kind of activity God has called us to do.

A steelworker described his working life to journalist Studs Terkel. He referred to himself simply as a laborer. "Strictly muscle work . . . pick it up, put it down, pick it up, put it down" (*Working,* page 1). He feels more like an object than a subject of work, as if he is just another tool or machine used in the process of building. "A mule, an old mule, that's the way I feel" (page 3). The hard labor itself is not the problem. For this worker, it is the lack of recognition and sense of accomplishment, which are matters of human dignity:

2. Think of three people you know who work, and list the objective and subjective aspects of their work.

It's not just the work. Somebody built the pyramids. Somebody's going to build something. Pyramids, Empire State Building—these things just don't happen. There's hard work behind it. I would like to see a building, say, the Empire State, I would like to see on one side of it a foot-wide strip from top to bottom with the name of every bricklayer, the name of every electrician, with all the names. So when a guy walked by, he could take his son and say, "See, that's me over there on the forty-fifth floor. I put the steel beam in." Picasso can point to a painting. What can I point to? A writer can point to a book. Everybody should have something to point to. (Page 2)

Meeting Family Needs

Work that supports human dignity is a foundation for family life. Paid work provides the heads of families with the financial means to support those who depend on them. Families must be fed, clothed, and sheltered. Their medical and educational needs must be met. In a community that aims to be just, work must provide enough income to meet these needs. And if a family remains in need even though one or both adults are working, justice is not being done.

In addition to providing for a family's needs, work is part of the education of the family. Children need to see their parents putting forth effort and being industrious for a purpose. This is one way that children grow into full humanness—by having models who show them how to be creative with their life through work. When children see a parent oppressed by work—treated as a mere tool of production or of the organization—then work fails to be educational for family members. Likewise, when a parent is not able to get work or loses a job, it is a demoralizing experience not only for the worker but for the whole family.

Enhancing the Common Good

Every worker is a member of the larger society, so work that supports human dignity will enhance the common good. Just the opposite happens when work violates human dignity: the common good itself is violated, and the quality of life in the larger society deteriorates. Pope John Paul II says that "work serves to add to the heritage of the whole human family, of all the people living in the world" (*On Human Work,* number 10).

In quiet, unspectacular ways, persons who work honestly and carefully do build up the "heritage of the whole human family." A woman recalls her father, who as a young man started with nothing but eventually developed his own home-remodeling business:

> If I were to choose one main way of remembering Dad, it would be as a working man, an honest laborer. He had a wonderful personality for the business world. He made more friends and acquaintances on his rounds than we could count. He did lots of favors for his customers and always preached that they were right, no matter what. He built up his home-remodeling business, spent hours on the road, and, during the hard, early years of his marriage, worked around the clock to provide for our family. His customers still comment today on his gentlemanly presence and on the excellent, enduring quality of his work.
>
> . . . He did not have a big vocabulary, nor did he need it. He knew how to care for people and make them happy. What God hid from the wise and clever, He revealed many times through Dad. He was a great witness, without knowing it, to the beauty of labor lived for the higher purpose of love for God and family. (Muto, *Meditation in Motion,* pages 130–131)

This man's devotion to his family, work, and customers made him an example of someone whose work contributed to the common good, building up the heritage of society.

3. What lessons about work have you learned in your family? Write a brief essay describing them.

4. Write a character sketch of someone you know who has served the common good, quietly and unspectacularly, through her or his work.

Caring for Creation

In the Creation story, when God tells the first human beings to "'fill the earth and subdue it'" (Genesis 1:28), God is inviting humankind to do work that reflects God's work. The work of humankind is to be stewards, or caretakers, of the earth. All the resources of the earth must be managed and maintained so that today's needs are met without depleting the resources that are available for future generations. Good stewards attempt to decrease the use of nonrenewable resources, such as oil, because these will eventually run out. They try to use renewable resources—the power of the sun, wind, and water, for example—whenever possible and minimize human damage to the water, air, and soil.

Laura Wharton, an energy engineer for a nonprofit organization, tries to be a good steward in her work:

> As an engineer, I try not to do anything that will be harmful to the environment; that's not so much making a positive impact but lessening negative ones because much of what's being engineered today will end up polluting the earth. I try to reduce that. (O'Connell, "Work of Human Hands")

The stewardship practices of each generation affect the generations that follow. Poor stewardship leaves a legacy of depleted resources and pollution, while good stewardship assures abundance and purity to future generations.

We have seen that God calls humankind to work, and each person has an obligation to work, in the sense of putting forth effort to make a difference in the world. And

Amish farmers have long been recognized as good stewards of the earth.

from the perspective of justice, the value of work is determined by how it affects the worker as much as by the products or profits of the work. The human person must be the primary focus in any consideration of work.

The Rights of Workers

With the obligation to work come a number of rights. Although workers have a just claim to these rights, historically they have had to struggle to attain their rights. Because of the crucial connection between paid work and meeting a person's or family's basic needs, this discussion focuses on the rights of persons in paid work. Workers are paid either for being employees of a person or company or for working on their own as farmers, small-business owners, freelance artists, and so on.

5. Before reading further, make a list of what you think are the basic rights of workers.

The Right to Employment

Catholic social teaching holds a strong position on the right to **employment.** Pope John Paul II states that **unemployment**, the lack of work available for those who can work, is always an evil (*On Human Work,* number 18). Work is our source of material support and, as the U.S. bishops point out, it is a key factor in building economic justice in the nation:

Full employment is the foundation of a just economy. The most urgent priority for domestic economic policy

is the creation of new jobs with adequate pay and decent working conditions. We must make it possible as a nation for every one who is seeking a job to find employment within a reasonable amount of time. Our emphasis on this goal is based on the conviction that human work has a special dignity and is a key to achieving justice in society. (*Economic Justice for All,* number 136)

Besides supporting us materially, work is also a major source of human fulfillment. Without it we experience a deep sense of loss:

> Thomas S. has been laid off from his job at a steel company for over a year. He has been looking for work every day since then. "I believe in God," he says, "but I don't go to church very much. I hope God has something to do with my situation and my finding work. I feel depressed more than anything—working all these years and not getting anywhere. I got more done when I worked; now I don't feel like doing as much. I get lazy." (Gossé, *The Spirituality of Work: Unemployed Workers,* page 11)

We *need* to work, as much for our dignity as for food and shelter. We therefore have a right to work.

The Right to Just Pay

Justice demands that workers receive fair **remuneration**—that is, compensation for their work—enough to meet their needs and offer some security. Employers who maximize their own gain by paying unfair wages to employees violate a fundamental demand of justice.

Some countries have established **minimum-wage** laws, which set the lowest wage that can be legally paid to an employee. In the United States, such laws have been in place since the early part of the twentieth century, and their effectiveness has long been debated. The amount of the minimum wage, although it rises occasionally, does not ensure that a worker and his or her family will live above the poverty level (a level of income below which one is classified as poor by government standards). In 1994, a full-time minimum-wage job paid $8,840 per year, but the poverty level was $7,369 for a single person and $14,800 for a family of four.

In response to this problem, Catholic social teaching calls for a "**family wage**," so that a single salary will provide sufficient pay "for establishing and properly maintaining a family and for providing security for its future" (*On Human Work,* number 19).

6. Has someone you know experienced forced unemployment? Write a reflection on the effect it had on him or her.

Compensation for work can also be given in the form of benefits. Medical coverage falls into this category. Health insurance for workers and their families is provided by many employers. Even so, millions of employed people do not have adequate health insurance. As we saw in chapter 7, this is a grave injustice that needs to be turned around.

Other benefits include regular periods of rest. Catholic social teaching holds that such periods should consist of a day of rest each week, preferably Sunday, and longer vacation periods during the year. Overwork can cause fatigue, illness, and poor job performance. It can also have a negative influence on the family and social relationships of workers. A just community seeks a balance between work and rest, for everyone's welfare.

The Right to a Safe Workplace

Workers are entitled to workplaces and manufacturing processes that are safe. Much work is, by its nature, dangerous. Construction workers balancing on steel beams several floors above the ground or hospital staff who care for patients with infectious diseases cannot escape a certain measure of danger. Still, employers have a responsibility to minimize work hazards by creating proper procedures and providing the equipment and training necessary for safety.

The consequences of neglecting worker safety are seen in a fire that occurred at the Imperial Food Products chicken processing plant in Hamlet, North Carolina, in 1991. Twenty-five workers were killed and fifty-six injured. An official report issued by the state said most of those killed or injured had attempted to escape but were confronted by locked or blocked exits. The report also said the plant failed to meet national safety standards for fire doors and had no sprinkler system or escape plan. Researchers say that such neglect is a widespread problem; they claim that many plants have most doors locked on the inside to prevent theft by employees. The state of North Carolina was also at fault by ignoring workplace safety, failing to inspect plants for such violations.

Strong evidence of neglect in this case led to charges of involuntary manslaughter against the plant's owner, who received a twenty-year jail sentence. In this case of neglect, the workers were treated as objects of work—as nothing more than tools with which to complete a task. The dignity of these workers was not respected by their employer, and the result was tragic human suffering and terrible damage to families and communities.

Workers on an oil rig in the North Sea are often faced with hazardous conditions, but their employer has a responsibility to minimize danger by providing proper equipment and training.

Cesar Chavez: Justice in the Fields

Cesar Chavez was born in 1927 to a family of migrant farmworkers near Yuma, Arizona. As a boy and then a young man, he worked in the fields, served in the U.S. Navy, and became active in community organizing and voter registration efforts.

In 1962, Chavez began the organization that came to be known as the United Farm Workers (UFW), a labor union with the goal of protecting the rights and safety of migrant farmworkers. When Chavez started organizing, migrant farmworkers' rights were severely neglected and violated.

Since then, the situation of migrant workers has improved somewhat, largely due to Chavez and the UFW's efforts. But they are still one of the most oppressed groups of workers in the United States.

Chavez died in 1993. The following excerpts are from a homily entitled "What Cesar Chavez Believed" by Bishop Ricardo Ramirez at a memorial service for Chavez. They tell us a great deal about what Chavez believed and stood for:

> Welcome to this celebration in honor of Cesar Chavez. The march we have just finished along the streets of Las Cruces is our simple way of recalling and reliving the many marches Cesar led in his struggle to bring about justice for those who work in the fields and who harvest the food that ultimately comes to our tables. . . .
>
> Cesar Chavez knew that God so loved the world and that the world was worthy of being saved. He focused his life on a segment of society, the poor who work in the fields. He certainly did not aim to save the world; that only the Son of God could take on, but Cesar was enlightened and guided by the light of the Gospels and the person of Jesus Christ. His life was authentic, and from that authentic and virtuous life came the authority he had to lead to the promised land of justice for all.
>
> Throughout his lifelong march for justice, Cesar was guided by the Judeo-Christian traditions of respect for the dignity of the human person, of the nobility of work, of the responsibility of all to contribute to the common good and that we are stewards of the Earth. He reminded us of the connection between the economic life of society and morality: There is a good way and a bad way of going about providing for ourselves materially. His work reminds us that there is a

Above: Speaking at a Philadelphia rally in 1987, Cesar Chavez demanded that a super-market chain stop selling pesticide-contaminated grapes.

The Right of Association

Many workers take their rights for granted. If they do, it is because they have not had to sacrifice for them. Workers of previous generations have struggled and sometimes even died to see their rights respected. Workers' rights, however, are not universally recognized, and workers must often join together to secure them. For this reason, workers have the right to form **associations**, called **labor** or **trade unions**, in order to promote and defend their vital interests.

moral imperative that protects workers and those who employ them. Part of that imperative is that all who are able to work should work and that work needs to be compensated justly.

In his later efforts against the use of harmful pesticides, he clearly associated himself with those who dream and work for a cleaner world. This too is a biblical mandate, for we human creatures of God have been given the responsibility of caring for the Earth—we are its chief stewards. Cesar wanted to make sure that the place of work for farm laborers would be safe and the food we eat be free of any contamination. . . .

I believe that one of the unique contributions of Cesar Chavez was his constant message that there is no work that is less noble than another. All work, whether it is done in pristine, air-conditioned surroundings or whether it is done in the inclemency of heat or cold, whether one goes home from work dirty and soaked with perspiration or goes home clean, work is work. All work is good in the sight of God, and it is always ennobling.

. . .

I am deeply impressed by Cesar Chavez's simple yet profound theology. In February 1969, he rose from his sickbed after fasting for many days and said, "It is for God, not us, to know what is going to be the eventual outcome of what we're doing. All we can be sure of is what we are doing right now, today. There is no such thing as means and ends. Everything we do is an end, in itself, that we can never erase. That is why we must make all our actions the kind we would like to be judged on, as though they might be our last. . . . That is why we will not let ourselves be provoked by our adversaries into behaving hatefully." . . .

May the memory of Cesar Chavez long live in our hearts, and may his efforts inspire us to continue in all noble and just causes in spite of adversity and setback. *Si se puede! Viva Cesar Chavez!*

Catholic social teaching has long considered union membership a right of workers. In 1891, **Pope Leo XIII** issued a momentous encyclical entitled ***On the Condition of Workers*** (also widely known by its Latin title, *Rerum Novarum*). It was written during a period when impoverished masses of workers in Europe and North America were being exploited by the owners of industry. The encyclical expressed a point of view that was not popular with the profiteers. Pope Leo came down firmly on the side of poor people, advocating for

7. From what you know of unions today, how well do you think they help workers not only *have* more but *be* more? Summarize your thoughts in a paragraph.

Garment workers who sought to form a union in 1913 helped pave the way for many rights that workers now take for granted.

their right to work, to earn just wages, and to form associations, or unions. *On the Condition of Workers* marked the beginning of modern Catholic social teaching on issues of justice. Its messages have been reaffirmed and developed by popes and bishops in the century since it was written.

Because unions seek to protect and expand the rights of so many people, they are a significant part of the struggle for justice around the world. Work builds community. Workers and owners, employees and employers, need to be part of this community. The struggle for workers' rights ought not be a struggle of one faction against the other. Rather, it is a struggle for justice, which requires the participation of the full community.

A **strike**, or work stoppage, by employees is one of the methods used by unions in the struggle for justice. Catholic social teaching sees the strike as a legitimate tool, but one that should be used only as an extraordinary measure. Workers who legitimately strike should not be punished by employers for participating in the work stoppage. And workers must ensure that their strike will not prevent the community's essential services from being carried out.

Above all, labor unions exist to help workers achieve and maintain their rights as human beings created with dignity. Pope John Paul II sums up the overall goal of unions in this way: "It is always to be hoped that, thanks to the work of their unions, workers will not only *have* more, but above all *be* more: in other words, that they will realize their humanity more fully in every respect" (*On Human Work,* number 20).

For Review

- What is the connection between human work and God's work?
- What are the two aspects of work? Explain them briefly. On what should the value of work be based?
- Summarize how work can support human dignity, meet family needs, enhance the common good, and care for creation.
- Briefly describe three rights of all workers.

Work and Faith: A Mission in Life

Christians are entrusted with a **common mission**: to meet God in Jesus and to follow Jesus in his saving mission of healing, feeding, and serving—doing justice. We all have our own particular ways of doing justice, through our relationships with family, friends, and strangers, and through our work. This is our own **unique mission** in life, our **calling**. With this in mind, it is important to seek work that uses our special talents, gifts, and abilities to fulfill our mission to bring about God's Kingdom of justice. The work we do can be much more than just a job that pays our bills. It can and should be a vital part of the mission we are called to by God.

Our Calling

God desires that there be a good fit between who we are, as unique persons created in God's image, and what we do with our life. Such is the unique mission we are called to by God. But God's call to a certain mission is not often as clear to us as the sound of a friend calling to see if we want to go out on Friday night. Writer Frederick Buechner offers this advice:

> There are all different kinds of voices calling you to all different kinds of work, and the problem is to find out which is the voice of God rather than of Society, say, or the Superego, or Self-Interest.
>
> By and large a good rule for finding out is this. The kind of work God usually calls you to is the kind of work (*a*) that you need most to do and (*b*) that the world most needs to have done. If you really get a kick out of your work, you've presumably met requirement (*a*), but if your work is writing TV deodorant commercials, the chances are you've missed requirement (*b*). On the other hand, if your work is being a doctor in a leper colony, you have probably met requirement (*b*), but if most of the time you're bored and depressed by it, the chances are you have not only bypassed (*a*) but probably aren't helping your patients much either.
>
> Neither the hair shirt nor the soft berth will do. The place God calls you to is the place where your deep gladness and the world's deep hunger meet. (*Wishful Thinking,* page 95)

Of course, our unique mission can change from one phase of our life to the next, because we ourselves change and the needs of the world change. Discerning the work God calls us to during any phase of life is a major challenge, and finding that kind of work in a real-world situation can be equally challenging. A woman summed up these two challenges concisely: "'I think most of us are looking for a calling, not a job. Most of us . . . have jobs that are too small for our spirit. Jobs are not big enough for people'" (Terkel, *Working,* page xxix).

Often, the way work is organized in society prevents workers from finding a sense of mission. Systems of work that are governed purely by profit or efficiency, rather than by the quality of work, turn workers into mere tools of production. Being expected to perform one's job passively and mindlessly, without any input from the worker, certainly cuts off any sense of mission about the work. Workers in these situations are likely to feel frustrated and unfulfilled, having no personal identification with the work that fills so much of each day.

Justice requires that the human spirit not be miniaturized to fit into jobs. Work must be organized so that the person can be influential, even in the "smallest" of jobs. The intersection of our deep gladness and the world's deep hunger should lead to a place where we can use our skills, satisfy our heart, and make a positive difference in the world.

It may seem like a luxury to expect one's work to be a calling with a sense of purpose or mission, not just a job. These days, most people are happy to find any job at all after high school, technical school, or college—let alone work that feels like a calling. Times are difficult, and the economy tends to simply absorb people into limited job slots, rather than allowing them to find their own calling while supporting themselves in the process. The situation is not hopeless, however. An individual can turn what would seem to be a job slot into a calling by the approach he or she takes to the work.

Turning a Job Slot into a Calling

Any person, doing just about any type of work, can hear God's call to mission. We expect priests and ministers to perform their work with a sense of mission. Caregivers for sick people and elderly people often seem connected with a call to mission, as do artists. But what about the millions of people who work in jobs that we might think of as too small to contain a sense of mission? Consider the experience of Maxine, a supermarket cashier:

> Cashiering in a supermarket may not seem like a very rewarding position to most. But to me it is.

8. Write brief descriptions of five kinds of work or occupations that could possibly be a meeting place between your own "deep gladness" and the world's "deep hunger."

You see, I feel that my job consists of a lot more than ringing up orders, taking people's money, and bagging their groceries. The most important part of my job is not the obvious. Rather it's the manner in which I present myself to others that will determine whether my customers will leave the store feeling better or worse because of their brief encounter with me. For by doing my job well I know I have a chance to do God's work too.

Because of this, I try to make each of my customers feel special. While I'm serving them, they become the most important people in my life. (Pierce, editor, *Of Human Hands,* page 49)

The call to mission that Maxine hears enables her to focus on the people she is serving. She finds her deep gladness in the interaction with the people she meets, and in these people she often finds aspects of the world's deep hunger. She must complete her cashier tasks promptly and accurately, but that is just one part of the job:

Compassion, however, is the most vital tool of my trade. There are many sad stories to be heard while ringing up

Any worker, in nearly any job, can hear a call to mission.

Worker-Ownership: Cause for Hope

Seeking work that provides a sense of mission can be a challenge. For many people, owning a small business seems to be one of the best ways to attain a sense of mission. But people of low income who have this dream are typically frustrated in pursuit of it.

In the past decade, however, the Campaign for Human Development (CHD), an arm of the U.S. Catholic bishops that funds many projects aimed at self-help and justice, has given more than three million dollars in low-interest loans and grants to poor workers trying to start businesses. CHD's efforts have played a part in establishing seventy-five worker-owned cooperative businesses.

Many of these companies are inspired by similar cooperatives in Mondragon, Spain. The Mondragon cooperatives were developed in the 1940s under the direction of a Spanish Catholic priest. Fifty years later, twenty thousand people are participating as worker-owners of Mondragon's two hundred cooperatives, doing about $200 million worth of business a year.

Annie Donavan, an adviser to the U.S. Catholic bishops, explains the need for worker-owned cooperative businesses today:

> "The economic systems that are now in place are such that the human dimension is not always accounted for in the workplace. . . . Poor people, especially, are left out of economic decisions that affect their lives.

When people own their own businesses, the mere process of having a stake in the business enterprise and decisionmaking is empowering. This helps poor people, particularly, feel less alienated, like they have a place in the community and they're doing something that benefits themselves and other people."

Worker-ownership has given thousands of workers reason for hope. Their rising level of satisfaction and fulfillment surely points to the value of alternative ways of organizing work and the economy, ways that can build a just society. (Based on Scott, "Minding Their Own Business")

---

9. Do you know anyone whose attitude toward her or his work transforms a job slot into a calling? Write a short essay or poem about the person.

grocery orders. Many times I find I'm called upon to help nurture the emotional state of shoppers—just as the food they're buying will provide nourishment to their bodies. Hearing of death, terminal illness, fatal accidents, and broken homes is all part of my job. During such times I try my utmost to listen with my heart, not just my ears. Often a single word of understanding or a mere look of genuine concern is just the right dose of medicine to help heal a bruised heart. When I succeed in easing some of the pain of another human being, it is then that I realize just how important my job as a simple cashier is. (Page 51)

Creating New Work Structures

An individual can make a calling out of what seems to be a fairly mundane job. But companies, too, need to structure jobs so that people can be more creative and feel more respect for the work they do.

Fortunately, some companies are being organized in new ways today, thus turning boring job slots into work that feels more creative, responsible, and purposeful. Forward-looking companies have been moving toward increased **employee participation** in decision making. When work is done in a fragmented way, on orders from the top down, workers do not see how their work fits into the whole. Now, by being in **cooperative work groups**, workers can have more say in how the work is done.

Some companies are even moving toward **employee ownership**, along with putting decisions about new products, equipment, raises, benefits, and so on, in the hands of the workers. These changes are happening in a minority of companies, but more are moving in this direction. Such changes are signs that a more just way of organizing work may be emerging. In fact, the U.S. Catholic bishops have been supporting the growth of **worker-owned cooperatives** through their **Campaign for Human Development**, which funds projects aimed at self-help and justice for poor people.

If our work is filled with a sense of mission, we become more aware that we are participants in God's work. In her interactions with her customers as a cashier, Maxine works with God by offering care and concern to everyone who comes her way. Similarly, in cooperative work settings or worker-owned businesses, where workers are given a sense of responsibility and ownership for what they produce, the connection between human work and God's creative activity in the world is more readily experienced.

Jesus: A Man of Work

In his mission, teachings, and actions, Jesus never lost sight of the fact that he and his listeners were workers.

"He Is a Carpenter"

When Jesus first taught in his hometown, "many who heard him were astounded. They said, 'Where did this man get all this? What is this wisdom that has been given to him? What deeds of power are being done by his hands! Is not this the carpenter?'" (Mark 6:2–3). The people of Jesus' own town immediately identified him as a worker. When he chose his disciples, he selected workers. His parables on the Kingdom of God often used human work and workers to demonstrate truths about the Kingdom. The way Jesus lived and taught showed deep respect for all who work and toil to participate in God's Kingdom of justice, from shepherds to doctors, farmers to scholars.

Work and the Cross

Jesus' mission—the work of his ministry—was to proclaim good news to the poor and marginalized, to usher in the Reign of God's love. He healed and fed outcasts, and challenged the leadership that neglected those in need. Jesus' work led inevitably to his death and Resurrection. Shortly before he was condemned to die, Jesus prayed, "'I glorified you on earth by finishing the work that you gave me to do'" (John 17:4). The work of Jesus' followers is linked to his **cross.** Pope John Paul II explains the connection:

> Sweat and toil . . . present the Christian and everyone who is called to follow Christ with the possibility of sharing lovingly in the work that Christ came to do. This work of salvation came about through suffering and death on a Cross. By enduring the toil of work in union with Christ crucified for us, man in a way collaborates with the Son of God for the redemption of humanity. He shows himself a true disciple of Christ by carrying the cross in his turn every day in the activity that he is called upon to perform. (*On Human Work,* number 27)

Jesus willingly accepted his death as part of the work of salvation. In a similar way, we must accept the challenges and hardships connected with our daily work, because it continues God's work.

"Carrying our cross," however, does not imply that we should meekly accept working conditions that are unsafe or wages that leave us in poverty or jobs that degrade our humanity. Accepting such conditions would prevent us from fulfilling our mission. Rather, to carry our cross in our daily work is to accept willingly its inevitable frustrations and challenges as part of the "sweat and toil" needed to accomplish God's work. Cecilia, a nurse, recognizes these burdens in the conflicts she encounters in her hospital work:

> In a hospital situation, it is necessary to know how to deal with conflict in many forms. Patients frequently are in conflict with themselves, their feelings, their reactions to pain, to disease, to illness. They may be irritated with the service and action of the medical staff and with other patients. Illness and hospitalization put stresses on family relationships, and at times there may be painful conflicts with those they love. Working with these realities gives a nurse insight into causes and effects of conflicts that apply also outside a hospital. (Pierce, editor, *Of Human Hands,* pages 97–98)

Working through these conflicts and obstacles amounts to carrying a cross. For Jesus, the cross led to Resurrection. In

10. Identify aspects of work that you do—whether in a job or as a student or a family member—that meet the description here of "carrying your cross." Reflect in writing on how you can approach these aspects of work as ways to grow or accomplish good things, rather than as situations to avoid.

Cecilia's case, the cross of conflict brings her to an enriched understanding of her work, a kind of resurrected life:

> Through the years many of the lessons my patients taught me have been a resource to draw upon; their testing of my abilities has strengthened my purpose; their life-sharing relationships have been a ministry to me. (Page 97)

The awareness that our work participates in God's work comes with a responsibility: to harmonize our activities with God's desire that human beings should survive and flourish. Our work must become action that promotes justice.

For Review

- What is the mission that all Christians have in common?
- What is one good "rule" for finding out what our unique calling or mission is?
- Explain how a job slot can be turned into a calling. How can work be restructured to give people a sense of mission?
- What does it mean to carry our cross in our daily work?

Education: A Matter of Justice

Most of us have our first work experience in school. Being a student and getting an education is work. **Education**, however, is an ongoing process of learning that takes a lifetime. Education does not begin with kindergarten and end with a high school or college diploma. It does not consist of merely learning certain facts and passing certain tests. At its best, education provides us with opportunities to discover and understand our mission in life. Education should prepare us to contribute to building a just community.

Because the worker is the most important aspect of work, the educational formation of the worker is vital. An educated worker is better equipped to ensure that his or her rights are respected, that the work being done contributes to, rather than damages, the well-being of people and the environment—in short, that the work promotes justice.

The relationship between education and justice is two-fold: justice demands the right to education for all; at the same time, education must provide the means for pursuing a just world. Education informs us of the need for justice in the world, and work enables us to play a part in bringing justice about. Together, education and work are the means by which we can find our unique mission—the intersection of our own deep gladness and the world's deep hunger.

The Right to Education

At the Second Vatican Council, the bishops of the Catholic church recognized the twofold relationship between education and justice. They strongly supported the right all people have to education and indicated that education could promote justice in the world:

> All men of whatever race, condition or age, in virtue of their dignity as human persons, have an inalienable right to education. This education should be suitable to the particular destiny of the individuals, adapted to their ability, sex and national cultural traditions, and should be conducive to fraternal relations with other nations in order to promote true unity and peace in the world. (*Declaration on Christian Education,* number 1)

This "inalienable right" to education is not universally respected, however. Even when it is, educational techniques do not always respect the particular learners and their situations. When these rights are not fully respected, education fails to "promote true unity and peace"—justice—in the world.

"Savage Inequalities"

Each of us has a limited perspective on education. We are aware, for the most part, of our own schooling and what kind of opportunities it opens up to us. Writer and social critic Jonathan Kozol can broaden our perspective. Between 1988 and 1990 he visited more than thirty public schools throughout the United States. In spite of civil rights legislation and Supreme Court decisions that attempt to ensure an equal quality of education to all children in public schools, Kozol found that equality across schools and school districts was not the rule:

> Public schools remain still separate, still unequal. . . . Almost everywhere I went, in inner-city schools, I saw good teachers overburdened with large classes, working with too few supplies, in physically repellent buildings,

struggling against the odds of poverty in the streets and parsimony in school budgets, sometimes prevailing, sometimes drowning, sometimes simply holding on for sheer survival. ("Let's 'Throw' Money at the Pentagon and Allocate It to Education")

A high school that Kozol visited in impoverished East Saint Louis, Illinois, illustrates the "savage inequality" that exists:

- "The football field . . . is missing almost everything—including goalposts. There are a couple of metal pipes—no crossbar, just the pipes. Bob Shannon, the football coach, who has to use his personal funds to purchase footballs and has had to cut and rake the football field himself, has dreams of having goalposts someday." (Kozol, *Savage Inequalities,* page 25)

- "Advanced Home Economics" is a class that provides "preparation for employment." Asked what types of jobs the students are trained for, the teacher responds, "'Fast food places—Burger King, McDonald's.'" (Page 27)

- "The science labs at East St. Louis High are 30 to 50 years outdated. John McMillan, a soft-spoken man, teaches physics at the school. The six lab stations in the room have empty holes where pipes were once attached. 'It would be great if we had water,' says McMillan." (Page 27)

- "The chemistry lab is the only one that's properly equipped. There are eight lab tables with gas jets and water. But the chemistry teacher says he rarely brings his students to the lab. 'I have 30 children in a class and cannot supervise them safely. Chemical lab work is unsafe with more than 20 children to a teacher.'" (Page 28)

- A history teacher says, "I have no materials with the exception of a single textbook given to each child. If I bring in anything else—books or tapes or magazines—I pay for it myself. The high school has no VCRs. They are such a crucial tool." (Page 29)

- The same teacher also has this to say: "I have four girls right now in my senior home room who are pregnant or have just had babies. When I ask them why this happens, I am told, 'Well, there's no reason not to have a baby. There's not much for me in public school.' The truth is, that's a pretty honest answer." (Page 29)

- "'I don't go to physics class, because my lab has no equipment,' says one student. 'The typewriters in my typing class don't work. The women's toilets . . .' She makes a sour face. 'I'll be honest,' she says. 'I just don't use the toilets. If I do, I come back into class and I feel dirty.'" (Page 30)

An overcrowded school in New Hampshire demonstrates the "savage inequalities" that exist among schools in the United States.

11. Imagine that you are a student in the school described here. Write a journal entry about how you feel about yourself and your future.

This school system, with all its inadequacies, violates the students' right to education. The system is overcrowded; it lacks essential equipment and educational tools; its physical facilities are broken down. As a result, students are deprived of the education they have a right to. Spending years in an educational system that cannot provide them with a vision for the future leaves many students with low self-esteem. This education system does not enable students to find their unique missions in life.

Why So Unequal?

The causes of this particular failure of education in East Saint Louis are complex. They are economic and racial—economic, because the school system is in a low-income area and therefore has a low tax base from which to draw funding, and racial because the city is populated primarily by African Americans. This failure cannot in any way be blamed on the students—they are victims of a violation of the right to education. One girl, Samantha, spoke about trying to transfer from East Saint Louis to a school in a nearby white community:

> "My mother wanted me to go to school there and she tried to have me transferred. It didn't work. The reason, she was told, is that we're in a different 'jurisdiction.' If you don't live up there in the hills, or further back, you can't attend their schools. That, at least, is what they told my mother."
>
> "Is that a matter of race?" I ask. "Or money?"
>
> "Well," she says, choosing her words with care, "the two things, race and money, go so close together—what's the difference? I live here, they live there, and they don't want me in their school." (Kozol, *Savage Inequalities,* page 31)

Students like Samantha are aware of the educational opportunities that are available in other communities. But they are unable to take advantage of them, and the resources within their own communities are not sufficient to raise the level of education in their system.

Injustice in education penetrates the lives and hearts of children. Aside from the fact that the quality of their education is lower than that of students in higher-income areas, Kozol points out the sense of rejection they experience:

An education system should support each student's God-given dignity.

The worst thing [these students] suffer is the terrible sense that government is no longer on their side, that they are despised by their nation, and are seen, if they are seen at all, as human deficits, as societal expendables, in short, that they are written off as valued human beings. ("Let's 'Throw' Money")

An education system that leaves students feeling the way Kozol describes is clearly inadequate and unjust. It violates the God-given dignity of each person, and it fails to support the cause of justice in the world.

U.S. citizens are accustomed to hearing about the crisis in education, and many proposals to solve the problem have been debated. The most pressing concern from a justice perspective is to reduce the inequality across schools and school districts, such as that found by Kozol in his travels to U.S. schools. The disparity is caused by vastly different resources going into schools in poor and minority areas versus those in wealthy and white areas. It is plainly sinful to make poor and minority children endure the consequences.

12. Imagine again that you are the student in the school Kozol describes. Write another journal entry, this time reflecting on where you can turn for help and what steps you can take to improve your situation.

Education for Justice

Whether an education system is public or private, religious or secular, traditional or progressive, it must promote justice. In the 1971 document *Justice in the World,* the world's Catholic bishops offer insights into how education can further the cause of justice.

Respecting Human Dignity

Education must *always* respect a person's dignity (*Justice in the World,* number 55). This means treating him or her as a child of God, with unique potential, capable of growing into full humanness and contributing to the human community.

This principle is violated when students who are perceived as having lower ability are shunted into inferior schools or classes. They are treated as if they possess less human dignity than those with higher ability.

John Duffy, a teacher in Maywood, Illinois, works in a school where there is tracking of students according to ability. He teaches a group of lower-ability students. But that does not keep him from respecting them and expecting good things from them:

"I don't treat them as low-ability kids." For example, they are working on an interpretive art project—a poster contest that displays some school-based application of

the Bill of Rights. It's an enrichment activity, Duffy points out, "you know, like all the high-ability classes get to do." And he has organized his U.S. history course around current events being used to illuminate and explore historical issues. No lectures, no drill, no mere memorization activities. Duffy refuses to fall into the trap of spoon-feeding the material to passive students, which only increases their passivity. (Wood, *Schools That Work*, page 67)

As a result of Duffy's respectful attitude, students in his classes who are considered low achievers do much better than expected, and their classrooms are lively and creative. Unfortunately, this is not typically the case when students are expected to be of lower ability. In this school, an extremely caring, energetic teacher who insists on honoring the potential of his students makes the difference.

Emphasizing Community
Education must discourage the narrow form of individualism in which the rights and needs of the individual take precedence over those of the community (*Justice in the*

World, number 50). Education takes place in the community and is for the benefit of the community. If it encourages students to put their narrow self-interest before the community's interest, education fails to promote justice.

Marcia Burchby teaches first grade, and she emphasizes community in her classroom with the help of Dr. Seuss's *The Butter Battle Book:*

> In it, Seuss builds a world whose very existence is threatened by an escalating conflict between the Zooks and the Yooks over which side of the bread the butter should be spread. The debate of butter-side-up versus butter-side-down becomes a metaphor for many of the conflicts in the classroom. [Marcia says,] "When they stop and think, they realize that what they are arguing over is nowhere near as important as their friendship. . . . I want to give them the tools and the space to solve their own problems, without violence, without anger. It takes some time, but so does trying to straighten out every little dispute or argument that comes up during the day." (Wood, *Schools That Work,* page 87)

These first-grade students are fortunate to be receiving an education that supports community instead of pure self-interest. Learning this value early will help them to promote justice in the larger community in the years ahead.

Educating for Life

Education does not stop with graduation from high school or college. Education for justice continues throughout life (*Justice in the World,* number 53). The just community recognizes this fact and organizes its educational programs with this in mind, giving all members of the community opportunities to discover and refine their own potential.

The Uptown Center, which is connected with Northeastern University in Chicago, offers ongoing education that reaches out to marginalized people, who are not often served by educational institutions. In the process, the center finds itself involved in the concerns of its students' lives. The center's director, Sam Lopez, explains:

> The students we recruit at Uptown are ex-cons, former drug addicts, dropouts, unemployed. I feel we can't take them on unless we take on the social ills they bring with them. A person can't go to school if he's having a

Top: Schools can emphasize community from the earliest stages of education.
Bottom: Education continues throughout life, giving all people the chance to develop their potential.

housing problem. He can't study if he's having a health problem. If we're gonna be in the community, we've got to deal with what affects these people outside the walls of the center. (Terkel, *American Dreams: Lost and Found,* page 458)

Renewing the Heart

Education for justice seeks not only development of the mind but **renewal of the heart** (*Justice in the World,* number 51). This means it must help us recognize wrongdoing, or sin, at both the personal and the social levels. Becoming sensitive to sin empowers us to be critical of the way things are, not simply to accept the existing injustice of society's structures, values, and practices. Education must enable us to avoid being manipulated by the media, the marketplace, and political rhetoric. Only then can we begin working to reverse injustice (*Justice in the World,* number 52).

The Catholic school system is in a unique position to promote justice in the world. Because Catholic schools are motivated by the Gospel and rooted in a clear set of values, they can speak out forcefully against wrongdoing and injustice in society, naming it sin. They can foster students' critical reflection on the media and other social institutions. Most Catholic high schools offer their students not only religion courses but also opportunities for worship, retreats, sharing of faith, and service to the wider community, especially poor people. Ideally, the Catholic high school is a faith community of students, teachers, administrators, and staff, a community whose purpose, among others, is to renew the heart of all its members. Such a renewal in young people is what makes it possible to dream of a more just society in the future.

13. Besides offering the religion course in Christian justice that you are now taking, in what other ways does your high school promote justice in the world? List as many as you can.

For Review

- What is the twofold relationship between education and justice?
- Briefly describe how children in inadequate schools are deprived of their right to education and experience a violation of their dignity.
- Summarize the insights offered by Catholic social teaching into how education can promote justice in the world.

A Teacher's Testimony: Education as Vocation

The relationship between work and education is summed up quite well by Kathleen O'Donnell, a worker who is a teacher. Her work satisfies her deep gladness and society's deep hunger. In her life, teaching is a mission as well as a job, and so she is a servant of justice:

> "Teaching is a job, . . . but it is also a profession and also a calling. It's a job. It gives me the money to eat and pay my bills. . . . Teaching is also a service needed by the community. My teaching fulfills a need in the community. It is also a vocation for me. At a certain moment the lesson plan has been written and my materials are in place. I close the door of the room and begin interacting with my students. That's my vocation." (Quoted in Droel, *The Spirituality of Work: Teachers,* pages 22–23)

10 Sustaining the Earth

Jasmine tried to calm herself by gazing up at the star-lit sky. She hoped the poem she had selected for their last evening at the Nature Learning Center was appropriate—and that the campfire would give off enough light so she could read it!

Each of the other nine students, who came from different cities and towns all across the state, had also picked a poem expressing something they'd learned during their weeklong experience at the center. Jasmine had been asked to start things off.

A hush fell over the usually boisterous group of teenagers as Cheryl, who lived at and ran the center with her husband, clanged the cast iron dinner triangle.

"All right everyone, let's get started. Jasmine, are you ready?"

Standing with her paper turned toward the light of the fire, Jasmine took a deep breath and read:

"We live by the sun
We feel by the moon
We move by the stars

"We live in all things
All things live in us

"We eat from the earth
We drink from rain
We breathe of the air

"We live in all things
All things live in us

"We call to each other
We listen to each other
Our hearts deepen with love and compassion

"We live in all things
All things live in us

"We depend on the trees and animals
We depend on the earth
Our minds open with wisdom and insight

"We live in all things
All things live in us"
            [Stephanie Kaza, from Roberts and
    Amidon, editors, Earth Prayers, pages 16–17]

"I used to think living in the city made it impossible for me to feel connected to nature," Jasmine continued. "That's why I wanted to come to the Nature Learning Center. But what I learned here, and what this poem says, is that no matter where I am, I am connected to nature and to the earth."

1. How connected to nature do you feel? Are you aware of nature every day, or just sometimes? Write a page-long essay on this theme.

At every moment of our existence, each of us—in the city, the suburb, or the country—is connected to and sustained by the earth. As with any relationship, our connection to the earth is not a one-way street. People and the earth are interconnected: the earth also depends on us for its continued existence.

How we relate to the earth and use its gifts determines whether the earth itself is sustained, whether it survives and thrives as God intends. **Sustaining** the earth, keeping it well—for its own sake, for our sake, and for the sake of future generations—is a requirement of justice.

Respect for the Earth

Like justice for people, justice for the earth begins with respect. Respect is owed to all that God has made because all of creation is good in God's eyes and is valued by God. Its goodness and worth are given by God and are not dependent on human opinions about what is good, valuable, and worthy of respect. When we see one another and the earth as God does, we are being truly respectful.

Throughout this course, references to respect for persons focus specifically on respect for the *dignity* of the human person: made in God's image and likeness, every person has inherent dignity. Dignity is central to who we are; it is what makes us human. Although it can be violated by injustice, our dignity can never be taken away from us. When we address issues of respect for the earth, we have a parallel to human dignity called the "**integrity of creation.**" Like inherent human dignity, the inherent integrity of creation must be respected.

The Integrity of Creation

To better understand what is meant by the integrity of creation, consider one of these analogies:

- Call to mind one of your all-time favorite songs. Let the melody and the lyrics fill your head. Hear the blend of sounds made by the instruments and the voice. Take special notice of how the melody and lyrics fit and flow together. Stay with the memory for a few moments.
- Or recall one of your school's most successful sports teams. Pick a particular game that stands out as the best of the season. In your mind's eye, see the players working together, almost as if they are reading one another's minds. Notice their skill and attention to the rules. Stay with these images for a minute or so.

Most likely, what makes your favorite song so appealing is its integrity. That is, all the elements—performers, instruments, melody, lyrics—complement and support one another and become something whole and beautiful. Likewise, it is the team's integrity that enables it to be so successful and that makes it such a thrill to watch. Here, too, the players work together to enhance one another's talents. As a result, the team creates something greater than any one member could do on his or her own.

A Whole Community of Life

The integrity of creation is like the integrity of a good song or a successful team. All of the elements of creation are woven together as one united, whole, interdependent **community of life.** Each element is fascinating and valuable in and of itself, but when all are brought together, they become something much greater and more magnificent than any single element. Humans, plants, and animals; rivers, aquifers, ponds, and oceans; deserts, grasslands, and forests; mountains and valleys; soils, rocks, and minerals; wind, rain, snow, and so forth, are like the members of a team or the parts of a song. Each has value, but taken together they have integrity, a good completeness that should not be violated.

2. Write your reflections on how the different elements of the song you chose, or of the team you recalled, worked together to make something whole and beautiful.

The community of life has integrity that should not be violated.

Let All Creation Praise God

In Psalm 148, all of creation is invited to praise God the Creator. The psalm recognizes the kinship that exists among all that God has made:

Praise God from the heavens;
praise God in the heights;
praise God, all you angels;
praise God, all you heavenly hosts.
Praise God, sun and moon;
praise God, all you shining stars.
Praise God, you highest heavens,
and you waters above the heavens.
Let them praise the name of God,
who commanded and they were created.
God established them forever and ever
and gave a decree which shall not pass away.
Praise God all the earth,
you sea monsters and all depths,
fire and hail, snow and mist,
storm winds that fulfill God's word.
You mountains and all you hills,
you fruit trees and all you cedars,
you wild beasts and all tame animals,
you creeping things and flying birds.
Let the rulers of the earth and all peoples
and all the judges of the earth—
young men too, and maidens,
old women and men—
praise the name of God
whose name alone is exalted;
whose majesty is above earth and heaven,
and who has raised the fortunes of the people.
Be this God praised by all the faithful ones,
by the children of Israel, the people close to
    God.
Alleluia.

(Schreck and Leach, compilers, *Psalms Anew*)

3. Find a poem, prayer, song, or essay that praises the oneness and integrity of creation. Does the expression of praise encourage you to treat the world differently? Why or why not? Answer in a paragraph.

A Universal Truth

The native peoples of North America traditionally recognize the integrity of creation by referring to the wind, the sun, the animals and plants, the rivers and mountains, as their relatives or kin. **Saint Francis of Assisi**, too, referred to the elements as his kin: Brother Sun, Sister Moon, Brother Wind, Sister Water, Brother Fire, Sister Mother Earth. Traditional African understandings of the world speak of the interconnectedness of all creation. In many passages from the Hebrew Scriptures, all creation is invited to give praise to the Creator, demonstrating the oneness and integrity of creation.

The world's religious traditions echo one another on this truth: creation has God-given integrity, just as persons have God-given dignity. Just as human dignity must be respected, creation's integrity must be respected if justice is to be done on earth.

Sustaining the Integrity

Beautiful songs and successful sports teams do not just materialize out of thin air. Numerous principles and processes are at work, contributing to a song's or a team's integrity. For songs, rules of harmony and instrumentation are involved, as well as principles of language and poetry. Any sport involves rules and regulations that govern how the game is played and that spell out what kind of conduct is acceptable.

These guiding principles and processes bring the diverse elements of a song or a team together. When they are followed, the elements come together successfully; when they are disregarded, the result is grating noise or fumbling, ineffective teams.

One Process of Millions

Likewise, a myriad of principles and processes are at work to sustain, or keep well, the integrity of creation. They keep the whole community of life going and prevent it from disintegrating into chaos. **Photosynthesis** is an example of a process that is vital to sustaining creation's integrity. In this process, plants and certain other organisms use light energy from the sun to convert carbon dioxide, water, and minerals into breathable oxygen and organic compounds such as sugars, carbohydrates, proteins, and fats. These compounds provide food for almost all living organisms on the planet. Photosynthesis is the fundamental process responsible for maintaining all life on earth. Without it, there would be no

Photosynthesis, which is the fundamental process responsible for maintaining life, is one of millions of processes that sustain creation's integrity.

food produced to sustain the vital functions of living—growth, repair, reproduction, and so forth. In fact, without photosynthesis the earth would eventually run out of oxygen. Life as we know it would end.

From the Viewpoint of Faith

The Christian tradition holds that God established the principles and processes of the natural world to govern and maintain the community of created life as an integrated whole. Human action that inhibits or prevents these processes, like photosynthesis, from taking place violates the integrity of creation.

These God-given principles and processes have a role in establishing justice and peace. As Pope John Paul II put it, "No peaceful society can afford to neglect either respect for life or the fact that there is an integrity to creation." He continued:

Theology, philosophy and science all speak of a harmonious universe, of a "cosmos" endowed with its own integrity, its own internal, dynamic balance. This order must be respected. The human race is called to explore

On Earth Day, elementary school students share what they have learned about stewardship: the earth's soil must be treated with respect.

this order, to examine it with due care and to make use of it while safeguarding its integrity. (*The Ecological Crisis,* numbers 7 and 8)

From the viewpoint of faith, the principles and processes that sustain creation's integrity must be respected.

Stewards of the Earth

The integrity of creation and the built-in principles and processes that sustain it attest to God's wisdom as Creator. Think how marvelous it is! Each element within the order of creation—air, soil, water, plant species, animal species, including the human species—has specific functions to fulfill for the greater good of the whole community. Humans, though, have a unique role. Like all parts of creation we have functions to perform, but we must also perform them consciously and responsibly.

As the Genesis Creation story illustrates, the unique role God assigned to humans is that of **stewards** of the earth. By assigning us this role, God places the continued well-being and flourishing of creation in our hands. Stewardship is an awe-inspiring responsibility whose importance cannot be underestimated. Because humans are created with free will, we have the ability to make disrespectful as well as respectful choices about the integrity of creation. Fortunately, the Christian tradition guides us on how to be good stewards.

Love Your Neighbor, Love the Earth

Good stewardship, like all works of justice, is grounded in the Great Commandment: Love your neighbor as yourself. It may seem strange to think of nonhuman creation as our neighbors, but the Great Commandment calls us to love as God loves. And God's love encompasses all of creation.

So Christian faith broadens the command of love to include all of our companions in the creation community. But this does not weaken our responsibility toward our fellow human beings. We do not choose either the earth or human beings over the other. Just the opposite is true: stewardship strengthens our commitment to human beings, especially to the poor among us and to future generations. The U.S. Catholic bishops state this clearly:

Christian love forbids choosing between people and the planet. It urges us to work for an equitable and sustainable future in which all peoples can share in the bounty of the earth and in which the earth itself is protected

4. Besides photosynthesis, what is a natural principle or process that sustains the natural order? Describe it briefly in writing, and then point out how this principle or process has been violated by humans.

5. Give a written example of an environmental issue that *appears* to pit people against the planet. For instance, "Saving forests from destruction will put the loggers out of work." Show how the issue need not be approached as a "people versus the environment" conflict.

from predatory use. The common good invites regions of the country to share burdens equitably in such areas as toxic and nuclear waste disposal and water distribution and to work together to reduce and eliminate waste which threatens health and environmental quality. It also invites us to explore alternatives in which our poor brothers and sisters will share with the rest of us in the banquet of life, at the same time that we preserve and restore the earth, which sustains us. (*Renewing the Earth*, page 11)

A Call to Serve

With love of the earth as its foundation, stewardship is seen as a service, and good stewards are called to serve. Like someone who provides the service of a caretaker—maintaining an estate or caring for sick people, for example—a steward of the earth provides the earth with loving service.

Jesus and the early Christians placed a great deal of emphasis on the service aspects of loving one's neighbor. As stewards, our duty is to serve all of God's creatures. Minnesota farmer Mike Rupprecht sees great honor in the call to serve through stewardship of the earth:

Stewards are called to serve the part of creation that has been entrusted to them.

I want to do everything I can to take good care of this one little part of God's creation that has been entrusted

to me. I believe I'm supposed to be here doing what I am to farm more sustainably and take care of the land. I strive to do the best that I can. And I hope that I set an example that others can see.

If Mike were caring for an ailing relative, we might expect him to describe that task in similar language—the language of service.

Stewardship as Caring, Creative Cooperation

Mike has realized that in order to serve as a caretaker of the creation community, he must enter into a creative and cooperative **partnership with the earth.** Over the past several years, Mike and his wife, Jennifer, have been learning about the natural processes that create and sustain healthy soils and a diverse plant and animal community on their farm. To them, farming sustainably means making sure that what they do on the land enhances and supports these natural processes. For Mike and Jennifer, healthy land is one of the most important gifts they can pass on to their daughter, Johanna.

In the process of gearing their farming activities to cooperate with nature, two significant transformations have happened for the Rupprechts. First, farming has become more fun: they get to be more creative. Second, farming has become more profitable: they are better able to support themselves financially. What's more, the Rupprechts' partnership with the earth has led to greater cooperation with other farmers and concerned people in their community. They see themselves as part of a larger effort to weave together concern for people and concern for the earth.

Good stewardship grows out of respect for the integrity of creation. An attitude of respect is important, but the attitude needs to be made visible in actions. The work of good stewardship is evidence of that respect.

6. Brainstorm a list of things you could do in your daily life to demonstrate good stewardship.

For Review

- What is the starting point of justice for the earth?
- Describe what is meant by "the integrity of creation."
- What viewpoint does Christian tradition hold about human responsibility for the integrity of creation?
- What is the unique role of human beings within the order of creation?

We Have Forgotten Who We Are

Unfortunately, the creation community is presently in a very damaged, wounded state. It has not been cared for, and we are seeing the results in pollution, the extinction of plant and animal species, the eradication of whole ecosystems, the disappearance of pieces of the protective ozone layer around the earth, global warming ("the greenhouse effect"), and dire predictions of environmental disaster by scientists. It is clear that humankind has not lived up to God's expectations for us as stewards.

This prayer of sorrow from the United Nations' Environmental Sabbath Program laments that we have often failed to hear the call to be loving stewards of our planet, and loving neighbors to all of its inhabitants:

> We have forgotten who we are.
>
> We have forgotten who we are
> We have alienated ourselves from the unfolding
>   of the cosmos
> We have become estranged from the movements
>   of the earth
> We have turned our backs on the cycles of life.
>
> We have forgotten who we are.
>
> We have sought only our own security
> We have exploited simply for our own ends
> We have distorted our knowledge
> We have abused our power.
>
> We have forgotten who we are.
>
> Now the land is barren
> And the waters are poisoned
> And the air is polluted.
>
> We have forgotten who we are.
>
> Now the forests are dying
> And the creatures are disappearing
> And humans are despairing.
>
> We have forgotten who we are.
>
> We ask forgiveness
> We ask for the gift of remembering
> We ask for the strength to change.
>
> We have forgotten who we are.
>
> (Roberts and Amidon, editors, *Earth Prayers*,
> pages 70–71)

Toxic waste dumps are an indication that humans have forgotten their connection with nature.

When we forget who we are, as stewards, the whole community of life suffers. Instead of supporting the integrity of creation, we cause its "dis-integration."

If "we have forgotten who we are," we must ask, Why? *Why* have we forgotten who we are? The prayer points to some answers. Let's look at some of them.

Separating Ourselves from Nature

The experience of a young woman named Anita during her first year of college is a kind of parable about the **separation from nature** that goes on at an earthwide level:

> I was so excited to be in a premed program in New York City. It was tough, but I was determined to become a doctor. I didn't want to miss out on any part of the experience. I took as many classes as my adviser would let me; I joined a sorority; I went to every possible event, on- or off-campus. Most days I was up at 6 a.m. and not in bed before 1 a.m.
>
> I kept this schedule for nearly the whole first year—until the last month of the second semester, in the spring. That's when I came down with mononucleosis. All of a sudden, I was so weak and tired I couldn't make it to half my classes. There was no way I was going to be up for final exams.
>
> To recuperate, I moved off-campus to my aunt and uncle's house. My aunt is a horticulturist and landscape designer, but she is also very interested in what she calls the rhythms of the human body. When she learned I'd been pushing so hard with so little sleep, she knew right away why I'd gotten sick. She said it was because I had ignored my body's natural rhythms and needs. This threw my system off balance and weakened it and left me wide open for getting sick.
>
> At first I didn't buy it. But she made some specific recommendations—like eating the right kinds of foods for my body type and following a daily routine that fits the body's natural ups and downs—and after a week I definitely felt better. Usually it takes months to recuperate fully from mono, but I recovered much more quickly.

A Cultural Attitude

Anita failed to consider the natural needs and rhythms of her body, so she became ill. Being forgetful about who we are—that is, becoming alienated from our condition as a part of nature—is common in much of Western culture today. The U.S. Catholic bishops point out that although our

7. Have you ever apologized by saying, "Sorry, I'm just not myself today"? If so, you know what it means to "forget" who you are. What can you, as an individual, do to regain your sense of self? And what do you think a forgetful society needs to do? Write a page-long reflection.

Being forgetful of nature's cycles is similar to ignoring our body's needs and subjecting it to stress and fatigue.

8. Have you ever gotten out of touch with your own natural needs and rhythms and pushed yourself too hard? Reflect in writing on what happened to you.

Tradition teaches respect for the integrity of creation, we modern people have only a dim sense of the natural order and rhythm at work in creation: "As heirs and victims of the industrial revolution, students of science and the beneficiaries of technology, urban-dwellers and jet-commuters, twentieth-century Americans have also grown estranged from the natural scale and rhythms of life on earth" (*Renewing the Earth,* page 6).

Alienation, or separation, from nature leads us to assume that human-made solutions to problems are always superior: Whatever the problem—social, political, or ecological—the best solution must be human-made and **technological.** As a society we have succeeded in manufacturing much of what we need. So it seems logical to us that all of life should operate like a machine or factory, controlled by technology. This mind-set is society's forgetfulness that people are a part of the natural order. Like Anita's forgetfulness, it leads to illness.

Earth Out of Balance

Human separation from the needs and cycles of nature has serious consequences for creation. Anita's experience demonstrates what happens when we ignore the body's natural ways of maintaining balance: the system gets overloaded and breaks down. The following examples show that when we push the earth like we push ourselves, the result is the same—breakdown.

Farming without nature: Much of the pork, beef, poultry, and dairy products on the market are produced in farms that are more like factories. **Factory farming** is a classic example of ignoring nature. To get as much production as possible out of each animal, the animals are treated like machines rather than as living creatures. Artificial growth hormones, for example, are often used to obtain maximum production.

Living conditions for the animals are extremely stressful, even brutal, and lead to serious health problems among the livestock. Large quantities of antibiotics are needed just to keep the animals alive, and traces of these drugs remain in the food when it reaches the market. Even with lots of antibiotics, high death rates are common among factory-farmed animals. Dairy cows can give milk for eight to ten years on traditional farms, but live half as long in typical factory-style dairies. The breakdown that results from factory farming is evident in the poorer quality of food it produces and the inhumane treatment of the animals.

When farms are operated as if nature does not matter, animals are treated like machines rather than living creatures.

9. What are other examples of "farming without nature," besides the inhumane treatment of livestock? Describe one of them in a paragraph.

The wrong activity in the wrong place: The tropical **rain forests** of South American countries like Brazil provide another example of pushing nature beyond what it can handle. Every year thousands of acres of forest are cut down or burned to clear the land for farming. Although rain forests support an incredible variety of plant and animal life, and are vital to the earth's oxygen supply (rain forests are sometimes called "the lungs of the earth"), their soils are not good for farming. Their thin, nutrient-poor soils can support farming activity for only a few years before they are depleted. These areas are then abandoned and more forest is cleared. A tremendous value—that of the rain forest—has been eliminated for short-term gains by farming. Great harm comes from ignoring the particular characteristics of a local ecosystem and trying to force it to support activity that it cannot, by its nature, sustain.

System overload: Global warming and other climatic changes predicted by scientists are also symptoms of human separation from nature. Climate changes like these are signs that the planet's built-in "air purifying system" is overloaded and breaking down.

Two main culprits are behind this breakdown. First, human-made **pollutants**, like by-products from burning fossil fuels, are being discarded into the earth's atmosphere at a greater rate than the system can naturally handle. Second, every year is marked by great **losses of biological activity and diversity.** Forests, wetlands, and other natural habitats

Top: Rain forests like this one, in Brazil, have been cut down or burned to clear land for farming—an activity that the soil is not suited for.
Bottom: By-products from burning fossil fuels are being discarded into the earth's atmosphere faster than the natural system can handle.

are replaced by shopping malls, highways, and housing developments. The natural processes, such as photosynthesis, that take place in these environments play a key role in the earth's system of air purification. When such environments are lost, nature cannot readily purify the atmosphere. Life on earth is threatened by the breakdown that occurs due to the combination of increased pollution and decreased natural activity and diversity in the environment.

Abusing Our Knowledge and Power

Human separation from nature has led to an attitude that we are "**rulers over nature.**" According to this attitude, nature must always conform to human needs, desires, and schedules. It can be controlled and manipulated in any way that we see fit. Such an attitude violates our role as stewards of creation and is detrimental to creation's integrity.

More Power-Over

The attitude that we are rulers over nature is similar to an attitude found in abusive human relationships, where one person or group imposes power over another. Ruling over nature reflects the same abuse of our God-given capacity for power as when we attempt to control and manipulate other people.

A power-over approach to nature assumes that if we have the knowledge and technology to control nature, we have the right to do so. Besides, the impact of human actions on the integrity of creation is secondary: If a forest is in the way of an airport, it can be obliterated. If a river's course impedes a highway, it can be changed. Using power over nature is not the practice of good stewards of creation.

A Not-So-Natural Disaster

The great flood of 1993 on the Mississippi and Missouri rivers points to the negative consequences of abusing our knowledge and power in our relations with the earth. The potential for the flood existed long before the exceptionally heavy rainfall. Ironically, the flood had its origins in flood control projects designed to contain big rivers like the Mississippi and the Missouri.

A variety of engineering marvels is used to harness and confine the rivers: levees and other types of containment walls, locks, dams, channels, and reservoirs. These human-made devices keep the river flowing along a specifically designated path instead of in a naturally meandering pattern. Containing the river makes it more convenient for hauling grain, coal, and other raw materials. When a river is used for

10. Find a newspaper or magazine article about a recent event in which humans have separated themselves from nature. Brainstorm some actions that could repair the environmental damage described.

transporting such commodities, cities, towns, and farms tend to be built along the river's banks. These towns lie on what is called the river's "floodplain," an intricate network of **wetlands** that acts as a sponge during naturally occurring flood cycles. When wetlands are removed in favor of development, the river loses its capacity to safely overflow its banks. Damage to human-made developments along the banks, like towns and farms, is inevitable.

The High Cost of "Ruling Nature"

When human beings try to control large rivers like the Mississippi and the Missouri, living, dynamic ecosystems are severely damaged. Wetlands are frequently destroyed, and much of the river's biological life is severely diminished. According to the assumptions behind flood control projects, however, rivers are not living entities; they are just unruly bits of nature that need to be brought in line, because "the best river is a straight river." And in the past, ecosystems were seen as static and unchanging. It was thought that individual parts could be singled out and controlled without affecting the other parts. Today we know that this is not true, although we have not completely changed our behavior accordingly.

The great flood of 1993 was a consequence of trying to rule over nature. The attempt to rule over nature backfired, devastating human communities. Although the Mississippi was contained to some degree by human engineering, the river was unable to handle the high amounts of rain that fell across its watershed region. The excess water had nowhere to go but into the towns and farms on the floodplains. Sooner or later, the negative effects of abusing our knowledge and power over nature outweigh the short-term advantages, such as temporary control of a river's path.

11. Can you give another example of the human attempt to "rule over nature" backfiring? Describe what happened in a paragraph.

A Missouri farm is completely submerged during the flood of 1993—a flood caused, in part, by human actions.

A Poor Record of Stewardship

Human influence on the North American environment has been a concern throughout the history of the United States. The following passages cover a span of more than a hundred years, and leave some doubt as to whether we have learned from history.

George Perkins Marsh in 1864

Man is everywhere a disturbing agent. Wherever he plants his foot, the harmonies of nature are turned to discords. The proportions and accommodations which insured the stability of existing arrangements are overthrown. Indigenous vegetable and animal species are extirpated, and supplanted by others of foreign origin, spontaneous production is forbidden or restricted, and the face of the earth is either laid bare or covered with a new and reluctant growth of vegetable forms, and with alien tribes of animal life. (*Man and Nature,* page 36)

Aldo Leopold in 1949

Conservation is a state of harmony between men and land. Despite nearly a century of propaganda, conservation still proceeds at a snail's pace; progress still consists largely of letterhead pieties and convention oratory. On the back forty we still slip two steps backward for each forward stride. (Page 243)

Perhaps the most serious obstacle impeding the evolution of a land ethic is the fact that our educational and economic system is headed away from, rather than toward, an intense consciousness of land. Your true modern is separated from the land by many middlemen, and by innumerable gadgets. He has no vital relation to it; to him it is the space between cities on which crops grow. Turn him loose for a day on the land, and if the spot does not happen to be a golf links or a "scenic" area, he is bored stiff. (*A Sand County Almanac,* page 261)

Rachel Carson in 1962

This is an era of specialists, each of whom sees his own problem and is unaware of or intolerant of the larger frame into which it fits. It is also an era dominated by industry, in which the right to make a dollar at whatever cost is seldom challenged. When the public protests, confronted with some obvious evidence of damaging results of pesticide applications, it is fed little tranquilizing pills of half truth. We urgently need an end to these false assurances, to the sugar coating of unpalatable facts. (*Silent Spring,* page 13)

Al Gore in 1992

Human civilization is now so complex and diverse, so sprawling and massive, that it is difficult to see how we can respond in a coordinated, collective way to the global environmental crisis. But circumstances are forcing just such a response; if we cannot embrace the preservation of the earth as our new organizing principle, the very survival of our civilization will be in doubt. (*Earth in the Balance,* page 295)

Old Man River Takes Back His Flood Plain

Serving Only Ourselves

> We have sought only our own security
> We have exploited simply for our own ends

These lines from the Environmental Sabbath prayer of sorrow remind us that the lifestyle we choose can either threaten or enhance the well-being of the whole global community. Our economic decisions have an impact on the environment, for better or for worse. The U.S. Catholic bishops point out that negative impacts on the environment come primarily from the developed, industrialized, consuming countries:

> Consumption in developed nations remains the single greatest source of global environmental destruction. A child born in the United States, for example, puts a far heavier burden on the world's resources than one born in a poor developing country. By one estimate, each American uses twenty-eight times the energy of a person living in a developing country. Advanced societies, and our own in particular, have barely begun to make efforts at reducing their consumption of resources and the enormous waste and pollution that result from it. We in the developed world, therefore, are obligated to address our own wasteful and destructive use of resources as a matter of top priority. (*Renewing the Earth*, page 9)

12. Write a page explaining why you agree or disagree with this statement: *People in the developed world must make a top priority of changing our wasteful and destructive uses of resources.*

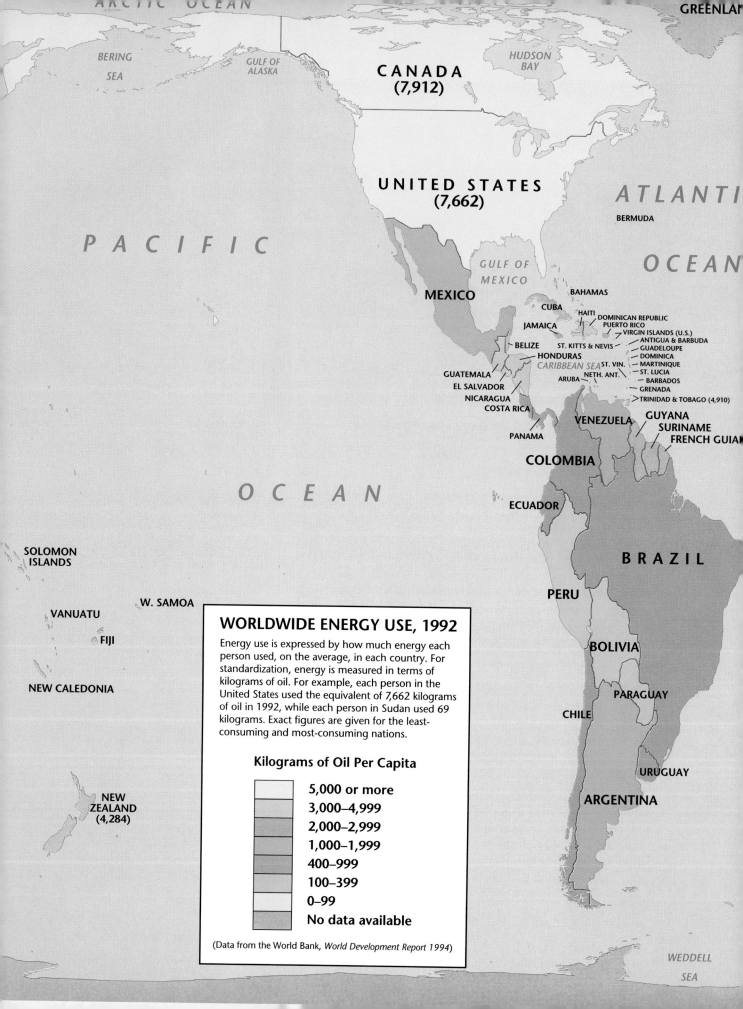

ARCTIC OCEAN

GREENLAN

BERING
SEA

GULF OF
ALASKA

HUDSON
BAY

CANADA
(7,912)

UNITED STATES
(7,662)

ATLANTI

BERMUDA

OCEAN

PACIFIC

GULF OF
MEXICO

MEXICO

BAHAMAS

CUBA
HAITI
DOMINICAN REPUBLIC
PUERTO RICO
VIRGIN ISLANDS (U.S.)
ANTIGUA & BARBUDA
GUADELOUPE
DOMINICA
MARTINIQUE
ST. LUCIA
BARBADOS
GRENADA
TRINIDAD & TOBAGO (4,910)

JAMAICA

BELIZE   ST. KITTS & NEVIS
HONDURAS
CARIBBEAN SEA   ST. VIN.
NETH. ANT.
ARUBA

GUATEMALA
EL SALVADOR
NICARAGUA
COSTA RICA

VENEZUELA   GUYANA
SURINAME
FRENCH GUIAN

PANAMA

COLOMBIA

OCEAN

ECUADOR

SOLOMON
ISLANDS

BRAZIL

PERU

W. SAMOA

VANUATU

FIJI

BOLIVIA

NEW CALEDONIA

PARAGUAY

CHILE

URUGUAY

NEW
ZEALAND
(4,284)

ARGENTINA

WORLDWIDE ENERGY USE, 1992

Energy use is expressed by how much energy each
person used, on the average, in each country. For
standardization, energy is measured in terms of
kilograms of oil. For example, each person in the
United States used the equivalent of 7,662 kilograms
of oil in 1992, while each person in Sudan used 69
kilograms. Exact figures are given for the least-
consuming and most-consuming nations.

Kilograms of Oil Per Capita

5,000 or more
3,000–4,999
2,000–2,999
1,000–1,999
400–999
100–399
0–99
No data available

(Data from the World Bank, *World Development Report 1994*)

WEDDELL
SEA

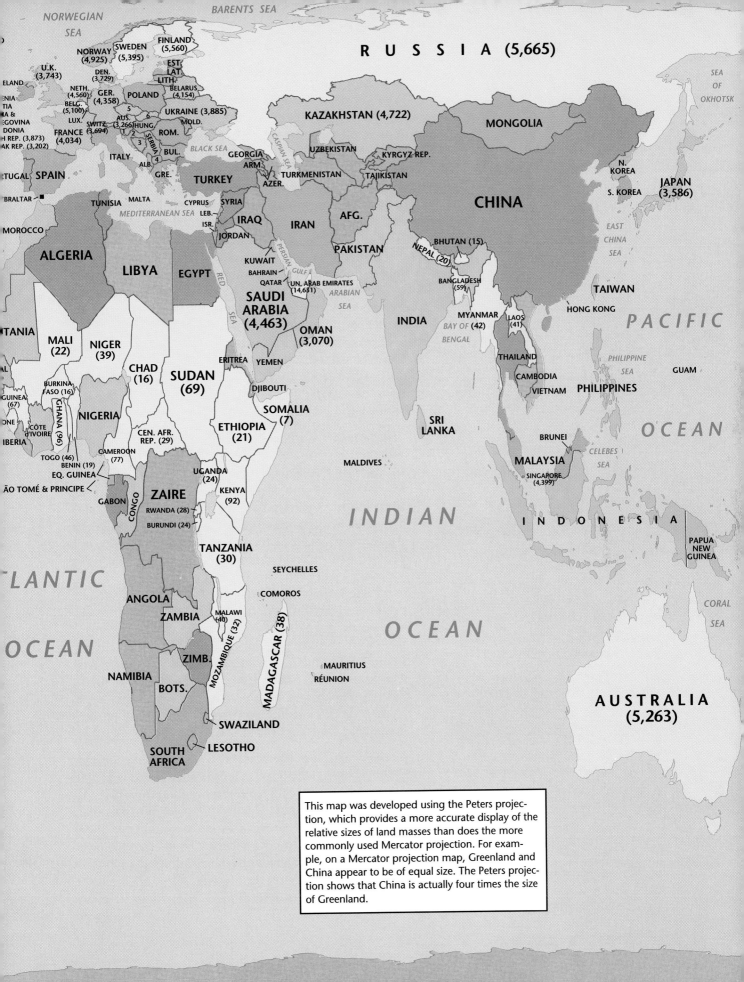

NORWEGIAN SEA

BARENTS SEA

RUSSIA (5,665)

SEA OF OKHOTSK

NORWAY (4,925)
SWEDEN (5,395)
FINLAND (5,560)
EST.
LAT.
LITH.
DEN. (3,729)
U.K. (3,743)
ELAND
NETH. (4,560)
GER. (4,358)
POLAND
BELARUS (4,154)
BELG. (5,100)
LUX.
SWITZ. (3,694)
AUS. (3,266)
HUNG.
FRANCE (4,034)
5
6
1
2
MOLD.
ROM.
UKRAINE (3,885)
KAZAKHSTAN (4,722)
MONGOLIA
ENIA
TIA
MA &
EGOVINA
DONIA
H REP. (3,873)
AK REP. (3,202)
SERBIA
3
BUL.
ALB.
4
ITALY
GRE.
BLACK SEA
GEORGIA
ARM.
AZER.
UZBEKISTAN
TURKMENISTAN
KYRGYZ REP.
TAJIKISTAN
N. KOREA
S. KOREA
JAPAN (3,586)
PORTUGAL
SPAIN
TURKEY
CASPIAN SEA
CHINA
BRALTAR
TUNISIA
MALTA
CYPRUS
LEB.
SYRIA
ISR.
IRAQ
JORDAN
IRAN
AFG.
EAST CHINA SEA
MOROCCO
ALGERIA
LIBYA
EGYPT
RED SEA
KUWAIT
BAHRAIN
QATAR
GULF
PERSIAN
SAUDI ARABIA (4,463)
UN. ARAB EMIRATES (14,631)
PAKISTAN
NEPAL (20)
BHUTAN (15)
BANGLADESH (59)
TAIWAN
HONG KONG
PACIFIC
ARABIAN SEA
INDIA
MYANMAR (42)
LAOS (41)
ANTIA
MALI (22)
NIGER (39)
CHAD (16)
SUDAN (69)
ERITREA
YEMEN
OMAN (3,070)
BAY OF BENGAL
THAILAND
PHILIPPINE SEA
GUAM
BURKINA FASO (16)
GUINEA (67)
ONE
CÔTE d'IVOIRE
IBERIA
GHANA (96)
NIGERIA
DJIBOUTI
SOMALIA (7)
CAMBODIA
VIETNAM
PHILIPPINES
OCEAN
TOGO (46)
BENIN (19)
EQ. GUINEA
ÃO TOMÉ & PRINCIPE
CEN. AFR. REP. (29)
CAMEROON (77)
ETHIOPIA (21)
SRI LANKA
BRUNEI
CELEBES SEA
MALAYSIA
GABON
CONGO
ZAIRE
UGANDA (24)
KENYA (92)
MALDIVES
SINGAPORE (4,399)
INDONESIA
RWANDA (28)
BURUNDI (24)
PAPUA NEW GUINEA
TANZANIA (30)
SEYCHELLES
INDIAN
LANTIC
COMOROS
OCEAN
OCEAN
ANGOLA
ZAMBIA
MALAWI (40)
MOZAMBIQUE (32)
MADAGASCAR (38)
MAURITIUS
RÉUNION
OCEAN
CORAL SEA
ZIMB.
NAMIBIA
BOTS.
SWAZILAND
AUSTRALIA (5,263)
SOUTH AFRICA
LESOTHO

This map was developed using the Peters projection, which provides a more accurate display of the relative sizes of land masses than does the more commonly used Mercator projection. For example, on a Mercator projection map, Greenland and China appear to be of equal size. The Peters projection shows that China is actually four times the size of Greenland.

Consumption Here, Hunger There

The use of nature's resources on one side of the globe can have a direct influence on the quality of life and the environment on the other side. An example is found on the island of Mindanao, in the Philippines. The island is known for its lush, thick forests and at one time provided its inhabitants with plenty of fish, corn, and rice. But since the 1970s, more and more residents of Mindanao have become hungry. And most of the children now suffer from malnutrition.

This change was caused by the exploitation of the island's natural resources. The exploitation was carried out by outsiders—miners, logging companies, and large agricultural companies like Dole and Del Monte. The food companies took down forests to open plantations for producing tropical fruits such as pineapples. Most of the resources exploited by these outside agents would eventually be sold in rich countries like the United States and Japan.

Although such activity was supposed to stimulate the economy, the island's peasants were hit hard when the loss of forests began to affect their daily life:

> The peasants watched the rivers change shape, turn muddier, less deep, yet more violent during the big rains. In formerly flood-free areas, the river would now overflow its banks, inundating adjacent fields with mud from the increasingly barren hills around them. . . . The river would sometimes even swallow the edges of the fertile fields along its side. In the last five years, one peasant who cultivated land on the banks of the Tigua lost nearly half of the land he farmed.
>
> There were other changes, too. Creeks nourished by once-forested watersheds disappeared during the dry season; landslides became common during the rainy season. And the rat population, which had previously found food in the forests and had been kept in check by forest predators, now ravaged farmers' fields at night. "People are hungry because the rats are eating everything," [says a] young woman solemnly. (Broad and Cavanagh, "Halting the Plunder")

As the situation of the peasants worsened, they took action. They began with civil disobedience, picketing and blocking the logging trucks from reaching the work sites. Although the loggers responded with some violence, this strategy of protest brought a degree of success. But even more needed to be done to stop the plunder. Thirteen of the peasants were chosen to go to Manila, the Philippine capital, to ask the government to stop the logging. They fasted outside the office of the Department of Environment and Natural

Resources, and after ten days were invited to meet with President Corazon Aquino. After speaking with the protesters, she decided to support their position.

The life of the peasants of Mindanao was hurt by economic practices based on greed and plundering of natural resources. Those who use the products made from the resources of Mindanao may never hear this story. Or they may not ever see its connection to their own economic choices and lifestyle, which probably do rely to some degree on products obtained through wiping out forests in the Philippines. But justice requires that we try to be aware of the effects of our actions, both social and environmental, no matter how distant.

13. Do some research to find out about one item you use, buy, or benefit from that comes from the developing world—for instance, sugar, coffee, or chocolate. Write a report on what effects its production has on the environment.

A Sin Against God and Creation

The Catholic bishops of the Philippines recognize the importance of the integrity of creation. They have condemned the destruction of tropical forests in the Philippines and have declared, "The environment is the ultimate pro-life issue."

Environmental injustice must be seen plainly for what it is—sin. We are called to renew our hearts and find the strength to change.

In the Environmental Sabbath prayer of sorrow, "we ask forgiveness" for our actions that violate the integrity of creation. Environmental injustice must be seen plainly for what it is—sin. The Filipino bishops do not hesitate to call it by its name:

> "The poor are as disadvantaged as ever and the natural world has been grievously wounded. We Philippine people have stripped it bare, silenced its sounds and banished other creatures from the community of the living. Through our thoughtlessness and greed we have sinned against God and his creation." (Quoted in Malone, "Environmental Degradation and Social Injustice")

When we separate ourselves from nature's ways, abuse our knowledge and power, and serve only ourselves, we are really turning our backs on God. Our actions say to God, "We don't like the way you made things. We can do it better. We will follow our rules, not yours."

In pursuing our own ways, not God's, we have been blind to all the havoc and destruction that human actions have caused in the environment. Now, when circumstances have reached a point at which our own future is threatened, we have begun to see that we have forgotten who we truly are. In religious terms, now is the time to repent and to ask for forgiveness.

Faith assures us that upon repentance and forgiveness, new life comes. With renewed hearts, the gift of remembering will be ours, as will the strength to change, to take whatever action is needed for the sake of the whole planet.

14. What is one thing you need to ask forgiveness for in how you have treated creation? Reflect on it in writing.

For Review

- In general, what is the result of separating ourselves from and ignoring nature's ways?
- Give three examples of pushing creation to the point of breakdown.
- What are the assumptions of a power-over approach to nature? Give an example of how the attempt to rule nature can backfire.
- Summarize, from this chapter, an example of how economic choices on one side of the world affect the environment and people on the other side of the world.

Restoring the Integrity of Creation

The following prayer of healing describes a hopeful view of reality. From it, we get an idea of what the world can be like if we remember that we are the stewards of all that God has created:

> We join with the earth and with each other.
>
> To bring new life to the land
> To restore the waters
> to refresh the air.
>
> We join with the earth and with each other.
>
> To renew the forests
> To care for the plants
> To protect the creatures.
>
> We join with the earth and with each other.
>
> To celebrate the seas
> To rejoice in the sunlight
> To sing the song of the stars
>
> We join with the earth and with each other.
>
> To recreate the human community
> To promote justice and peace
> To remember our children.
>
> We join with the earth and with each other.
>
> We join together as many and diverse expressions
>   of one loving mystery: for the healing of the
>   earth and the renewal of all life.
>   (Roberts and Amidon, editors, *Earth Prayers*, page 94)

The response to "we have forgotten who we are" is to "join with the earth and with each other." In a state of forgetfulness, we exploit resources and abuse power. But in a state of remembering who we are as fellow creatures of the earth, we care for, protect, restore, and celebrate creation.

The starting point for stewardship today is a planet on which the integrity of creation has already been badly violated. Now respecting the integrity of creation must begin with restoring, or healing, those areas that have been violated. This restoration will require fresh, imaginative, varied responses to creation by people everywhere:

15. Have you ever participated in a restoration project, such as restoring an old car, house, bicycle, toy? How does restoration differ from creating something entirely new? Write a page relating this type of experience to restoring the integrity of creation.

- courageously standing up for and protecting the earth
- listening to the earth with humility
- cooperating creatively with the earth and one another
- conscientiously attending to the impact of human actions upon the earth

This section does not provide a comprehensive blueprint for action. Instead, it is meant to simply offer examples of action taken by others who have responded to the ecological crisis with enthusiasm, hope, and imagination.

Standing Up for the Earth

Protecting the integrity of creation often requires people and groups to take **courageous action** in their local communities. It requires commitment and hard work. Months and even years may pass before an environmental issue in a community is resolved. More people need to develop the kind of persistence demonstrated by Andrew Holleman of Chelmsford, Massachusetts.

When he was twelve years old, Andrew took action to prevent a land developer's plan to build 180 condominiums on the wetlands near his home. Andrew's courageous work exemplifies the type of response needed if creation's integrity is to be restored:

Andrew had practically grown up in the wetlands. He could identify most of its plants and animals, some of which were on the endangered list. The wetlands held a special place in Andrew's childhood memories as well: the quiet times he went there just to think, the fun times playing with his brother and sister, and the adventures—like an underwater rescue of a skunk from a steel trap.

Andrew's parents had always encouraged him to respect the environment. So when he heard the news about the developer's plans, he knew he had to do *something* to save the wetlands.

First, Andrew went to the local library. He found a master plan of the town and looked up the state laws that applied to the situation. He also found information showing that development of the wetlands could contaminate the town's drinking water. Then Andrew drafted a petition for local residents to sign to try to stop the developer from building on the wetlands.

Copies of the signed petition went to the Chelmsford Board of Selectmen, the Conservation Commission, the Zoning Board of Appeals, the Board of Health, and the land developer. Andrew also wrote letters to elected officials and a TV anchorwoman. In return, he received letters of support, but no real help.

Development of wetland areas can have a drastic impact on local drinking water as well as the many species of plants and animals living in the wetlands.

Andrew called the local Audubon Society (a nature advocacy group), complaining that no one would give him any real help, but the woman there just told him, "That's no excuse for *you*." She went right on giving him more information to keep him persisting. "I learned that when you really believe in something, you have to stand up for it no matter how old you are," Andrew said.

Eventually, Andrew and his neighbors organized the Concord Neighborhood Association and raised money to hire a lawyer and an environmental consultant. The effort to save the wetlands lasted over ten months. Andrew attended at least two meetings a week and spoke at most of them. Finally, an important test was conducted by the state environmental officials to see if the land was suitable for building. The test results were negative and Andrew beamed with happiness.

When the developer tried to withdraw his application to build on the wetlands, the zoning board wouldn't let him. Instead, by totally denying the application, they made it impossible for anyone to ever build on the wetlands. Andrew's, and the wetland's, victory was complete. (Based on Lewis, *Kids with Courage,* pages 143–150)

16. Would it take courage for you to stick up for creation? Give an example in writing of an incident where you would need courage.

Restoring the integrity of creation will not happen overnight. But it can happen eventually if millions more people do what Andrew Holleman did: stick his neck out courageously to protect the earth from those who would continue to destroy it out of greed or thoughtlessness.

Listening to the Land

We sometimes hear a person referred to as a "good listener." What makes a good listener is not so much the verbal response, but the care with which he or she listens. When we communicate with a good listener, we feel that we have really been heard. And good listeners themselves are enriched by what they learn through listening.

To truly respect the integrity of creation, good stewards must be good listeners: they must **"listen to the land"** to hear what it says about what it needs to survive and thrive. Good listeners hear with an attitude of humility. They do not presume that they know more than the speaker. Similarly, listening to the land requires us to be humble, open to what the land can teach us about what is best for it. And when we have listened closely to the land, what we have heard should guide our actions.

The Consequences of Not Listening

Wendell Berry is a farmer and writer who makes a point of listening to his land, observing it carefully, and letting it show him the best course of action. He listens humbly, readily admitting that he can never know all there is to know about his land. Even with all that care, though, he has made mistakes. He tells of a time when he built a small pond on a level portion of a slope. The project went well, but extremely wet weather caused sudden erosion, and "a large slice of the woods floor on the upper side slipped down into the pond." Says Berry, "The trouble was the familiar one: too much power, too little knowledge. The fault was mine" (*What Are People For?* page 5).

Berry looks at his mistake and sees it as a small example of the troubled relationship between humankind and creation: "I have carried out, before my own eyes and against my intention, a part of the modern tragedy: I have made a lasting flaw in the face of the earth, for no lasting good" (page 6).

The damage to Berry's farm was small, but his experience shows that listening to the land and understanding what it can handle is an important and difficult task. On a larger scale, a similar mistake—such as building condominiums on wetlands—can be tragic for the common good of society and the environment. Good stewardship requires that we listen to the land before taking actions that will affect the environment. A good steward puts the needs of the land ahead of the dictates of the market and of profit making.

17. Think of a time when you were trying to say something important to someone but the person would not listen. In a written reflection, relate that to how the earth must feel when it is not listened to.

Biological Literacy

With typical lack of humility, human beings tend to assume that human-generated ideas are always the best course to follow. Human thinking and ingenuity are, in fact, vital components in the process of renewing the earth. But to be good stewards, we must recognize that the earth has a great deal to teach us about what we must and must not do if the earth is to continue sustaining life.

Good stewards need to be "**biologically literate.**" In the same way that we are computer literate or technologically literate, we need to understand the biological processes—like photosynthesis—that support life. Modern technology can and should support our efforts to become biologically literate. Computers have enabled us to learn a great deal about the natural world. A combination of modern technologies and simple listening to the land has a great deal to offer to the quality of stewardship.

Creative Cooperation

The task of restoring the earth's integrity calls for partnerships of all kinds: we must join with the earth and with one another in a spirit of **creative cooperation.**

Joining with the Earth

The human mind is a powerful tool. When it is used wisely and in tune with the integrity of creation, exciting and mutually beneficial ways of relating with the earth can emerge.

We saw earlier that Mike and Jennifer Rupprecht view their Minnesota farm as a partnership with the earth. Farming seems a logical arena for partnership with the earth, but creative cooperation can apply to all aspects of human life and the environment. Here are other examples of creative cooperation between people and the earth:

From waste to wetlands: Southwest Wetlands Group of Santa Fe, New Mexico, is learning how to develop wetlands in places where none were before. Placed adjacent to buildings such as nursing homes, the new wetlands receive waste water from the facility. Natural bacteria feed on contaminants, plants are nourished, and clean water results. In addition, the wetlands support birds and other wildlife that migrate to the new habitat.

Xeriscaping: Fourth- and fifth-grade students in Ashland, Oregon, learned about cooperating creatively with nature in their xeriscape project. *Xero* is the Greek word for "dry." A xeriscape is a landscape consisting of native plants that do not require artificial watering.

The students worked on the design, construction, and maintenance plans for the project. Part of the fun came from learning which trees, shrubs, and ground covers would thrive in their region, which does not see rain for months at a time. The students also learned which plants would provide habitats for wildlife. This school project is a fine example of creative cooperation. Similar projects, on a large scale, are greatly needed in the many areas of the western United States where water is scarce.

Green architecture: Green architecture presents opportunities to use technological knowledge and skills to do good things for the earth and for us human inhabitants. Green architecture means designing homes and other structures that cooperate with nature in every step of the process:
- Buildings are set so that they harmonize with the land around them.

The task of restoring creation's integrity calls for creative cooperation with the earth and one another.

18. Imagine a house that follows green architecture—one that you would live in. What might be some of its features? Draw a sketch and write a description of the house.

- Buildings are designed in ways that help residents feel intimately connected to their natural surroundings.
- Native and nontoxic building materials are used.
- Environmentally friendly building techniques are used.
- Technologies that use fossil fuels (a nonrenewable resource) for heating or cooling are avoided.

Green architecture creates buildings that reconcile humans' needs and nature's needs. Currently, most buildings developed through green architecture are fairly expensive. To fully serve justice and the whole human community, these buildings must become more available to persons of low income.

Joining with One Another

Restoring the integrity of creation requires partnership and creative cooperation among all the peoples of the earth. The project of restoration will require collaboration and negotiation from the local to the international level.

Local and regional conflicts: Environmental disputes require people to join together sincerely for problem solving. Analysis of such conflicts, however, often finds two or more parties at odds with each other even though all claim to have the same goal—to protect the environment.

Of course, conflicts can almost always be resolved in more than one way. So all parties must cooperate by listening to each other, listening to the land, and even letting go of preconceived ideas about the proper solution. Those who attempt to help restore the earth must also put "earth before ego." The needs of the earth are more important than the needs of an individual or organization to insist they have the "right" response to a problem.

Global cooperation: At the Earth Summit in June 1992, leaders of almost every nation on earth gathered in Rio de Janeiro, Brazil, to discuss the global nature of the environmental crisis. This meeting represented a significant step toward the global cooperation needed to solve the crisis. The process, however, must be ongoing and progressive. Constant diligence is needed to ensure that the goodwill and eloquent words of such high-profile summits will materialize into actions that make a real difference.

A Sustainable City

Renewable energy would be gathered by way of wind farms and wave generators. This energy could supplement, and eventually replace, fossil fuel energy.

Recycling of waste materials such as glass, metal, and paper would take place in specially designed processing plants.

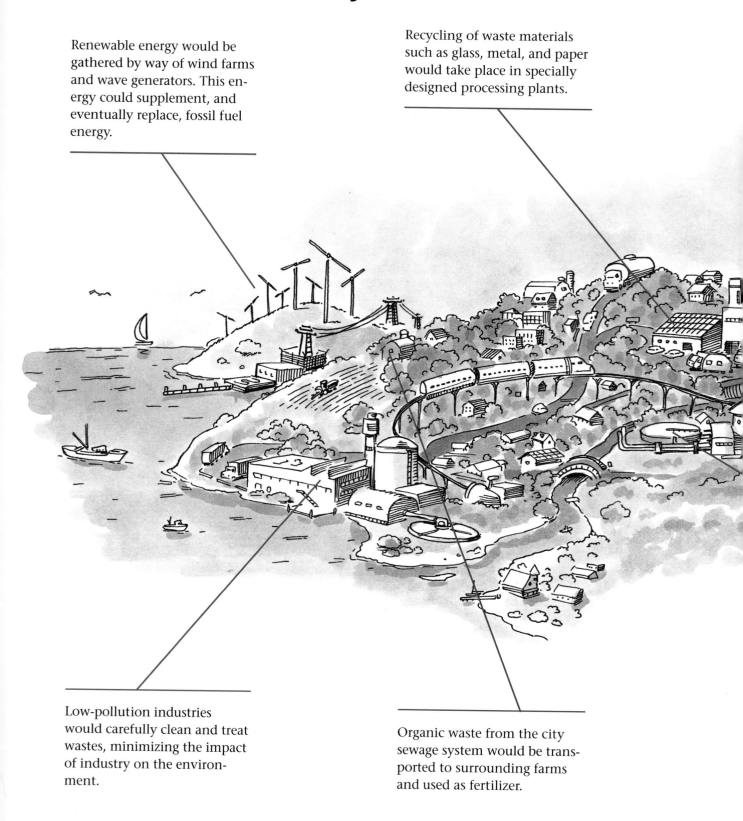

Low-pollution industries would carefully clean and treat wastes, minimizing the impact of industry on the environment.

Organic waste from the city sewage system would be transported to surrounding farms and used as fertilizer.

Greenery in the city, planted in parks and other open spaces, would help clean urban air and provide wildlife habitats.

Public transportation, powered by renewable energy sources, would be the dominant form of transit.

The water supply would take advantage of nonpolluted river water, which would need no chlorination and little other treatment. This water would be used in homes and industry for purposes other than drinking.

Solar energy would be collected by solar panels placed on homes and other buildings throughout the city.

Earthwise Living

As noted earlier, the consumption of goods and resources by the world's wealthiest nations is the greatest source of global environmental destruction, as well as a major contributor to world poverty. **"Earthwise living"** must include examining and changing patterns of consumption in society and the methods by which goods are produced.

A Matter of Impact

Consumption, in and of itself, is not a bad thing. We all need goods and services to live. Rather, the issue revolves around questions like these:

- How much consumption is necessary, and when do we reach the point of excess?
- What goods and services are we consuming? Are they of good or bad quality? Are they reusable? Do they really enhance our life, or do they actually detract from our quality of life?
- Where were the products made, and by whom? How were they made, and out of what kind of materials? What wastes were generated, and how much?
- What did it take to get the products from their point of origin to their point of consumption? How much fossil fuel was used in the process?
- Who can afford to buy or use the goods or services? What were all the real costs involved in their making and delivery? Does the purchase price reflect the total cost?

Many ways of making, transporting, buying, selling, and using goods and services are harmful to people and the earth. We need to learn how to be "earthwise," to sustain

Earthwise living takes advantage of renewable power sources such as the sun and the wind.

ourselves with methods that diminish the harm done to the whole community of life by our activities. Furthermore, we must conscientiously work to make the impact of our activities as positive as possible: "Live lightly on the earth," as a Native American saying goes.

Earthwise Businesses

Living simply is part of the earthwise response to creation. In simple living, the user or consumer of goods makes choices that do the least amount of harm. Those who produce the goods and services we buy also need to cultivate earthwise practices for production and distribution. Society's business community must become more aware of the effects of its practices on the integrity of creation, striving to enhance it wherever possible.

Because consumer goods and services are a major part of a modern economy, businesses can be extremely significant in restoring the integrity of creation. We need business leaders and companies that are motivated to produce quality goods without damaging the environment. The earth is relying on corporations to examine and improve current practices, keeping in mind that every business transaction today has the potential to influence the condition of creation, for better or worse, for generations to come.

Clearly, acting courageously to protect the earth, listening to the land, cooperating with the earth and one another, and living in an earthwise manner play vital roles in restoring creation's integrity. Justice demands that such responses permeate every aspect of human living. Not a single human activity takes place outside of the community of creation. Respectful stewardship involves making sure our actions contribute to the well-being and flourishing of all that God has made. Sustaining the earth from generation to generation depends on it.

19. Consider one consumer item that you use regularly (examples: toothpaste, shoes, candy bar). Using the questions here as a guide, research whether the item is earthwise. Sum up your findings in a report.

For Review

- Summarize the four types of responses needed to restore the integrity of creation.
- What does it mean to be "biologically literate"?
- Explain the notion of earthwise living, both for individuals or families and for businesses or companies.

A Sacramental World

Why is sustaining the earth so important? There are several reasons: it is necessary for survival, it enables us to be true to our calling as stewards of creation, and it plays a part in the establishment of God's Reign of justice and peace. Another important reason is this: The Christian tradition sees the world as **sacramental**, in the sense that it reveals God's presence through millions of visible and tangible signs. Respecting the integrity of creation enables us to discover God's love and greatness in nature.

Human beings, as part of creation, cannot live without using nature's resources. But the way in which we do so indicates whether we recognize creation as a sacrament. Wendell Berry puts it this way: "To live, we must daily break the body and shed the blood of Creation. When we do this knowingly, lovingly, skillfully, reverently, it is a sacrament. When we do it ignorantly, greedily, clumsily, destructively, it is a desecration" (*The Gift of Good Land,* page 281).

Justice calls for us to treat the world as sacramental, in our thoughts, words, and actions. To do so, we must be con-

stantly attuned to God's presence in creation; and when we use creation, we must use it with the awareness that it is a gift from God.

The following prayer from the Jewish tradition affirms the presence of the Creator in all that God has made. Let us join with the earth and with one another in thanksgiving for this sacramental world entrusted to our care:

How wonderful, O Lord, are the works of your hands!
The heavens declare Your glory,
the arch of sky displays Your handiwork.
In Your love You have given us the power
to behold the beauty of Your world
robed in all its splendor.
The sun and the stars, the valleys and hills,
the rivers and lakes all disclose Your presence.
The roaring breakers of the sea tell of Your
    awesome might;
the beasts of the field and the birds of the air
bespeak Your wondrous will.
In Your goodness You have made us able to hear
the music of the world. The voices of loved ones
reveal to us that You are in our midst.
A divine voice sings through all creation.
    (Roberts and Amidon, editors, *Earth Prayers,* page 57)

Epilogue:
Celebrating Life

When [Jesus] came to Nazareth, where he had been brought up, he went to the synagogue on the sabbath day, as was his custom. He stood up to read, and the scroll of the prophet Isaiah was given to him. He unrolled the scroll and found the place where it was written:
"The Spirit of the Lord is upon me,
      because he has anointed me
            to bring good news to the poor.
He has sent me to proclaim release to the captives
      and recovery of sight to the blind,
            to let the oppressed go free,
      to proclaim the year of the Lord's favor."
And he rolled up the scroll, gave it back to the attendant, and sat down. The eyes of all in the synagogue were fixed on him. Then he began to say to them, "Today this scripture has been fulfilled in your hearing." (Luke 4:16–21)

Celebrating Justice and Abundant Life

Throughout this course, by way of stories and examples, we have examined the concerns and activities of a just community. We have focused on how people around the world are working to make the Christian vision of justice, of sharing God's goodness, a reality.

The scriptural passage from Luke shows Jesus beginning his ministry with that vision of justice in his heart and soul. In the passage, Jesus attends a Sabbath service in his hometown. When he stands up to read the Scriptures (Isaiah 61:1–2), he uses the opportunity to launch his public ministry. He applies the words of Isaiah to himself, stating plainly that his mission is to bring about justice. Those who make a commitment to follow Jesus learn from this passage what they, too, should be concerned with.

Life in Abundance

By quoting Isaiah, Jesus makes clear *what* his ministry is about. We might wonder, though, *why* Jesus was so concerned with matters of justice. He was surely motivated by his distress at the situation around him. He witnessed injustice every day and, as a Jew, was a member of a people who were oppressed by the Roman government. Jesus certainly wanted to see that oppression reversed. But his motivation went deeper than that. He knew that God desires **abundant life**, not just the absence of oppression, for all. All creation is intended to thrive and flourish. In the Gospel of John, Jesus states that this abundance is for everyone, that God's goodness is to be shared with all creation. This is what Jesus longs for in his ministry: "'I came that they may have life, and have it abundantly'" (10:10).

Jesus stated that his mission was to bring justice to the captives, the blind, and the oppressed. In modern terms, the **captives** are those who suffer from poverty and those who are addicted to consumerism. The **blind** are those who are kept in darkness by illiteracy and lack of education, as well as those blinded by prejudice. The **oppressed** are the victims of violence, hunger, and homelessness, as well as those burdened by their complex, stressed-out lives. These factors diminish life. They are not what God intends for people and creation. Jesus desired to do the work of God; he wanted to counteract anything that kept God's abundant goodness from being shared with all creation.

In Jesus' vision, working for justice is not only about rejecting and undoing injustice. Ultimately, working for justice is about celebrating the gift of abundant life. Jesus criticized oppressors and called them to repentance, but he also called his followers to celebrate life in the Eucharist. Today, as in Jesus' day, people who act for justice are missing something crucial if they fail to celebrate life. So in the midst of our work for justice—respecting human dignity, making neighbors out of strangers, waging peace, creating homes, sustaining the earth, and so on—Jesus calls us to celebrate.

1. Write a reflection on how you may be captive, blind, or oppressed.

The followers of Jesus celebrate life in the Eucharist. Jesus shares the Last Supper with his disciples in this painting by Milagros Chavarría.

What Celebration Says

We can celebrate life as our wholehearted *Yes!* to God's desire that we have abundant life. We can affirm the belief that life, not death, is the essential character of existence. This yes to life is expressed in every act of justice. It is also expressed in the many and varied celebrations that mark our lives.

Religious rituals like the Catholic Mass and the Jewish Passover celebrate life. Honoring birthdays or wedding anniversaries with parties is also a way of saying yes to life. So too are the other formal celebrations and rituals we engage in, from national holidays to homecoming parades.

Sometimes, it may seem impossible to say yes to life. If we are feeling depressed or uncertain or unloved, affirming life may not come easily. When we hear about suffering and death caused by injustice, we may be tempted to throw up our hands in despair. But every moment of every day offers us opportunities to affirm the gift of life. Placing a fresh flower on the dinner table is a life-celebrating act. Words of praise and gestures of gratitude and affection are small but important ways to celebrate life. The Yes! to life that Jesus calls us to embrace can be heard even in the midst of injustice: in situations where, on the surface, it looks as if death has the upper hand.

Celebrating Life in the Midst of Struggle

In the Slums of Mexico

Let's look at an example of people who can celebrate in the midst of injustice—the slum dwellers of Cuernavaca, Mexico, a city located just south of Mexico City.

While traveling in Latin America to study poverty and other social-justice issues with a group from his church in the United States, Richard Ness visited with a priest who worked with several Christian communities around Cuernavaca. The communities' members were some of Mexico's poorest people, but they came together for Bible study and dialog. They sought to better understand their situation in light of the Gospel and to figure out what they could do to improve their lives.

The priest spoke about the impact of the communities' activities on members' lives. Ness was surprised to learn that one of the first actions inspired by their study and dialog was to clean up and beautify their neighborhoods. By bringing beauty into their lives, the people were affirming their self-worth: "We are not dirt. We should not be treated that way by others. Nor should we treat ourselves that way." The communities' actions were celebrations of life, even in the midst of their poverty and their struggle for justice.

In *La Fiesta,* by Manuel Garcia Moig, villagers say Yes! to God's desire that we have abundant life.

In Black South Africa

The black South African choral group Ladysmith Black Mambazo also celebrates life in the midst of the struggle for justice—through singing and dancing.

Apartheid, South Africa's former political system based on strict racial segregation and rule by the white minority, has officially ended. And in 1994, Nelson Mandela, a black leader who had been a political prisoner for over twenty-five years, was elected president. Black South Africans struggled for decades to remove the yoke of apartheid, and the long transition from oppression to freedom has been difficult. Much was lost in the struggle. Many lives were sacrificed and innocent people imprisoned. But the losses have been accompanied by something we might not expect to find in such a desperate situation—great hope. Ladysmith Black Mambazo gives voice and body to both loss and hope in songs like this one:

Joseph Shabalala, *center,* and the choral group Ladysmith Black Mambazo give voice and body to both loss and hope.

This is a song of those for whom the good news . . .
The good news, the good news, the good news!
Of the end of apartheid . . .
If it really is the end . . .
Amen.
Comes too late.
Amen. Hallelujah!

(Yourgrau, *The Song of Jacob Zulu,* pages 5–6)

One reviewer described this song in this way: "There is no irony in these simple, subtle words—just a fierce desire to embrace in song the paradox of a community on the verge of its precarious new beginning" (Lahr, "The Forest and the Trees"). In other words, the song embraces and celebrates life, its joys and its sorrows both.

The group's lead singer, Joseph Shabalala, knows from experience that singing brings healing to anger. His brother Headman was murdered in 1991 by a white security guard, who was convicted but never jailed for the crime. And for Shabalala, singing is proclamation, telling the world about the struggles and hopes of his people:

2. Write a reflection on this statement: *We cannot really celebrate joyfully without knowing sorrow as well.*

Nelson Mandela, who had been a political prisoner for more than twenty-five years, was elected president of South Africa in 1994.

"In our culture, we believe that music is something to make people know each other. Once you have a chance to stand and dance, the people are going to know who you are, where you're from, who's your father, who's your mother. You're not just dancing for yourself. When I sing, I know that I'm standing for my people, for my family. Now I must try to do a good thing, so my people will be known." (Lahr)

South African citizens celebrate Nelson Mandela's victory in 1994.

Since he was a young boy, music has filled Shabalala's life: the sounds of goats, sheep, cows, and frogs, the sound of a waterfall. All of this is music to Shabalala and an ever present reminder to celebrate life:

"Zulu people love to sing. Music is the life of the people. We use for *everything*. . . . Nobody composed it. It just came spiritually, because Zulus are spiritual. That's their way, their life. When you sing, you must *feel* the music and dedicate yourself to your dancing and singing. The music just takes over. The music makes you like you can fly. . . . Song is like a prayer. It's for praising and prayer. When you catch the right note, you feel it. The blood accepts it. Says, 'Yes, this is the right place.'" (Lahr)

Celebration for Thanksgiving and Renewal

In our quest to bring justice to the whole of creation, we face many challenges. The task can seem overwhelming at times, full of disappointment and frustration. Cynicism and apathy can easily take over. Celebrating life serves as a powerful antidote to cynicism and apathy by allowing us to give thanks for our gifts and to renew our spirits for the continuation of the struggle:

- Celebrations of life give us the opportunity to thank and praise God for the wondrous gift of life. They allow us to stop and take a deeper look at the world around us, to go beyond seeing only what is wrong or ugly in the world. Celebration opens our eyes to God's living presence in the world. Through celebration, we let God know that we see and value the goodness of creation.
- Celebrations of life renew us by constantly reminding us *why* we commit ourselves to justice efforts in the first place. By celebrating life, we keep alive our faith in the vision of justice. Celebrating life whenever and wherever we can brings new energy to our spirits, spurring us on to continue our efforts.

3. Think about some effort for justice you have made or could make. Imagine how your grandchildren might feel or benefit from your effort, years after you are gone. Write your thoughts on paper.

Celebration opens our eyes to God's living presence in the world.

Say Yes! to a Life of Justice

This course began by offering you an invitation to explore the Christian vision of a world of justice, to see if it was the kind of world you would like to be a part of. We continued by exploring what that world could look like.

Now, at the end of the course, the invitation is extended once again. Jesus proclaimed good news to the poor, release to captives, freedom for the oppressed. His proclamation needs to be renewed every day by women and men, children and teenagers, rich and poor, all ethnic groups and nationalities. You are invited to celebrate the gift of life in abundance by saying Yes! to justice and joining in the work of building a just community.

As you enter into the spirit of celebration, listen to these words of Vincent Harding, a civil rights historian, teacher, and advocate of justice. Let his words guide your journey and inspire your efforts:

> Living in faith is knowing that even though our little work, our little seed, our little brick, our little block may not make the whole thing, the whole thing exists in the mind of God, and that whether or not we are there to see the whole thing is not the most important matter. The most important thing is whether we have entered into the process. Like Martin [Luther] King talking to the old woman in Montgomery, Alabama, during the . . . boycott [of segregated buses in 1956], asking, "Mama, why are you walking like this, walking miles and miles to work? I mean, you're not even going to benefit much from this new situation yourself." And she said, "Dr. King, I'm not doing this for myself. I'm doing this for my grandchildren." That's why she could also say to him then, "Yes, Dr. King, my feets is tired, but my soul is rested."
>
> That's how your soul gets rested . . . when you stop thinking, working only for yourself, and start dreaming, as the Native Americans do, for seven generations beyond us. Your soul gets rested when you realize that your life is not meant to be captured just in your own skin, but that your life reaches out to the life of the universe itself. And the life of the universe reaches into us and demands of us that we be more than we think we can be, demands that we live out these dreams. ("In the Company of the Faithful")

Amen. Hallelujah!

Index

Italic numbers are references to photos, graphs, or illustrations.

A

Abel, 13, 14
abortion, 42
Abraham, 17
abundant life, 270–279
abused women, 45, 101, 195, 196–197
Academy Award, 69
Academy of Hope, 185
active nonviolence. *See* nonviolent resistance
Acts of the Apostles, 20, 75, 138
Adam, 12, 13
addiction. *See* substance abuse
advertising, 46–47, 142, 143, 173
aerial warfare, 115
affluent nations. *See* developed nations
affluent people, 160
Afghanistan, *60*
Africa
   chronic hunger in, 156
   drought in, 158
   infant mortality in, 169
   worldviews in, 238
African Americans. *See* black Americans
agriculture
   destructive, 102, *246, 247,* 254
   nurturing, *212,* 243
aid programs, 160, 167, 203–204
air pollution, 247
A-Khaw tribe, *47*
Alcoholics Anonymous, 185
Ambrose of Milan, 113
American Child Foundation, 29–31
Americans with Disabilities Act (1990), 44, 95
Amish farmers, *212*
angels, 200

anger, 92, 109–110. *See also* hatred
animal husbandry, *246*
animal sacrifices, 110
antibiotics, 246
anti-Semitism, 84–85, *86*
apartheid, 86, 276
apathy, 92, 278
Aquinas, Thomas, Saint, 113
Aquino, Corazon, 255
architecture, 262–263. *See also* building construction
Aristide, Jean-Bertrand, 63
arms. *See* weapons
Arnold, Nathan, 39
art activities, 29–31
Ashland (Ore.), 262
Asian Americans, 80, 81
Asian workers, 142–143
Asia-Pacific region, 156
assertiveness, 69–71
association rights, 216–218
athletes, 78, 80, 81. *See also* team sports
atmospheric conditions, 141, 247, 248
attitudes, 79–80, 91–92. *See also* prejudice; sexism
attorneys, 38, 43, 45
Audubon Society, 260
Augustine of Hippo, 113
average life expectancy, 171

B

Bangkok (Thailand), 203
Baranquilla (Colombia), 166
battered women. *See* abused women
Begin, Menachem, *122*
Berlin (Germany), *86, 95*
Bernardin, Cardinal Joseph, 42–43
Berrigan, Daniel, *42*
Berry, Wendell, 135, 261, 268

Bible
   on assaulted dignity, 34
   battered women and, 196
   Catholic social teaching and, 36
   on economic life, 135, 136
   on strangers, 201, 204
   See also Christian Testament; Gospels; Hebrew Scriptures
"Bill Hastings" (Jailer), 207
biological diversity, 247–248
biological literacy, 261
biological weapons, 114, 115
Birmingham civil rights protest (1963), *94*
bishops. *See* Catholic bishops; Lutheran bishops
black Americans
   athletic ability of, 80, 81
   in Brevard, N.C., 49–50
   in East Saint Louis, Ill., 228
   enfranchisement of, 86
   prejudice against, 82–83
   See also civil rights movement
black South Africans, *76,* 86, *274, 275–277*
bleeding woman story, 56–58
Bloods (gang), 117
bombing, 115
Bosnia, *102, 110*
Boston, *111*
boycotts
   in Berlin, *86*
   of buses, 120, 279
   of General Electric, 68–69
Brazil, *57,* 247
Bread for the World (organization), *167*
Brevard High School (Brevard, N.C.), 49–50, 51, 52, 53–54
Britain, 118
Brothers and Sisters to Us, 83–84
Buddhism, 121–122
Buechner, Frederick, 219
building construction, 152, 215, 258, 260, 262–263. *See also* housing
Burchby, Marcia, 231

Community Board Program (San Francisco), 121

community mental health programs, 184

community of life, 237, 245

companies. *See* corporations

compassion, 221–222

computers, 261

concentration camps, 67, 86

Concord Neighborhood Association, 260

conflicts, 100–101, 263. *See also* violence

Congress (U.S.), 44, 167

conscientious objection, 112

consensus, 121–122

conservation, 250

consistent ethic of life, 42–43

Constitution (U.S.), 37, 86, 140

construction work, 152, 215, 258, 260, 262–263

consumerism, 131

consumers, 68–69, 251, 266–267

conversion, 19, 91, 232, 256

cooperative businesses, 222, 223

cooperative creativity, 262–263

cooperative work groups, 223

Corinthian church, 162

Corinthians, First Letter to the, 77–78

corporations
    in capitalistic economies, 144, 145
    consumers and, *69*
    employee participation in, 222–223
    waste disposal by, 139–140
    See also businesses; multi-national corporations

courage, 119, 258

Covenant House (New York), *197*–198

covenants, 17

crack cocaine, 185–186

crazy living, 128–132, 145, 146

creation
    diversity of, 91
    divine intention for, 106
    economic aspects of, 135
    Genesis account of, *12*, 32–33
    goodness of, 29, 31, 32, 138–139, 236
    human work and, 208
    integrity of, 236–243, 245, 246, 248, 257–267
    stewardship of. *See* stewardship
    See also nature

creative cooperation, 262–263

crime, 46–47, 188. *See also* prisoners

Crips (gang), 117

Crite, Marion ("Mal"), 49–50, 53

cross bearing, 224–225

Crossroads program, 96

Cuernavaca (Mexico), 274

cure-over-care medicine, 175–176

cynicism, 102, 278

D

Daoust, Jerry, 155

Dardick, Geeta and Sam, 44

Day, Dorothy, *163*

death, 19, 273
    denial of, 173–174
    dignified, 177
    of infants, 169, 171
    medical technology and, 175–176

death penalty, 43–44

debt, 95, 138, 160

decision making, hierarchical, 145

Declaration on Christian Education, 226

dehydrated children, 169, 170

deinstitutionalization, 184

Del Monte Foods, 254

DeMatha Catholic High School, 96

denial of limits, 173–174

Deuteronomy, Book of, 137–138

developed nations
    children neglected by, *179*
    consumption by, 251, 266
    eucharistic vision and, 165
    exploitation by, 159–161
    government policies of, 166
    indebtedness to, 95, 160
    refugee crisis and, 203–204
    violence in, 105
    wealth of, 131–132

developing nations
    consumption by, 251
    indebtedness of, 95
    poverty of, 131–132, 159–161
    in Southern Hemisphere, 52–53
    violence in, 104

devil, 55

DeVille, Patrick, 39

dialysis, 176

diarrhea, 169, 170

diet. *See* food

difference, 91

digestive system failure, 175

dignity. *See* human dignity

dinner parable, 23–25, 155

diplomacy, 123

direct discrimination, 85–86, 87

disabled people, 44, *45*
    earning power of, 86–87
    exclusion of, *73*
    legislation on, 95

disasters, 158

discrimination (bias). *See* prejudice

discrimination (military science), 114

diseases, 169, 174, 175–176, 177, 224

diversity, 91

divorce, 9, 10

doctors. *See* physicians

Dolan, Jay, 93

Dole Food Company, 254

domestic violence, 102, 195–198

Donavan, Annie, 222

Donders, Joseph, 53

Dresden (Germany), *95*

droughts, 158

drug abuse. *See* substance abuse

Duccio di Buoninsegna, *88*

Duffy, John, 229–230

E

earth awareness. *See* environmental awareness
Earth Day, *240*
Earth in the Balance (Gore), 250
Earth Summit (1992), 263
East Saint Louis (Ill.), 227–229
Ecological Crisis, The (Pope John Paul II), 240–241
economic growth, 132–133, 145
Economic Justice for All, 20–21, 75–76, 133, 134–135, 141, 153, 213–214
economic life
    government policies on, 103, 213–214
    health care reform and, 179
    hospitality and, 204
    material resources and, 132
    moral aspects of, 149, 216–217
    unique callings and, 220
    U.S. bishops on, 20–21, 84, 133, 134–135
    See also businesses; international economy; workers
economic sanctions
    boycotts, 68–69, *86,* 120, 279
    embargoes, 123
ecosystems, 249
Eden, 12
education. *See* schools; students
Egypt, 17, 18
elderly people, 78
elementary school students, 262
El Salvador, *53,* 101, *204*
embargoes, 123
emergency famine relief, 165
emergency shelters, *190*–191, 196–198
emotional poverty, 61, 149
Empire State Building, 210
employees. *See* workers
empowerment, 56–58, 145. *See also* power
enemies, 108–109, 110, 119
energy use, *247, 252–253,* 263, *266*

environmental awareness, 27, 140, 212, 234–269. *See also* nature
Environmental Sabbath Program, 244, 251
environmental violence, 102, 244–256
    common good and, 242
    hunger and, 161
    self-destructive behavior and, 11
    unlimited resource assumption and, 141
    See also pollution
ethics. *See* morality
"ethnic cleansing," 86
ethnic conflict, 101
ethnic minorities, 156, 199
Eucharist, 161–165, 273
Europe, 52, 65, 93
euthanasia, 176
Eve, 12, 13
exam preparation, 100
exclusivity. *See* inclusivity
Exodus, Book of, 17–18
export crops, 159
Ezekiel, Book of, 91

F

factories. *See* businesses
factory farming, *246*
fair transactions, 140
faith
    assurance from, 256
    economics and, 133–146
    Harding on, 279
    healing through, 57
    integrity of creation and, 240–241
    justice and, 27
    of Solentiname *campesinos,* 58, 59
    work mission and, 219–225
families
    crazy living by, 128–130
    homeless, 183, 184
    of prisoners, 38
    provision for, 210–211
    wage injustices and, 45–46

family nursing, 170–171
family wage, 214
famine, 131, 156–167, 254
farming. *See* agriculture
farmland, 102
fascism, 65–68, *86*
fatal illness, 175–*176*
feast parable, 23–25, 155
federal government. *See* U.S. government
Fiesta, La (Moig), *273*
Fifteenth Amendment, 86
Filipino Catholic bishops, 255–256
Filipino forests, 254–255
firearms, *108*
Fletes, Ignacio, *59*
flood control, 248–*249, 251*
Flood of Noah, *13*
Flores, Ralph, 31
food
    church distribution of, 164
    factory farm production of, 246
    federal distribution of, 161
    myths about, 157–158
    plantation production of, 254
    plant production of, *239–240*
    wellness and, 168–169, 170
footwear factories, 142
foreign aid programs, 160, 167, 203–204
forests, 133, *141*
    in Africa, 158
    in Brazil, *247*
    in Mindanao, 254–255
forgiveness, 44, 256
fossil fuels, *247,* 263
foster children, 198
Francis of Assisi, Saint, 238
freedom of choice, 12, 50
free-market economies, 144–145
friendships, 97
fruit plantations, 254
fruit trees, *31–32*

G

Galatians, Letter to the, 90–91
Gandhi, Mahatma, *117,* 119, 120
gangs, 106–107, 117, 120
Garcia, Jose Salome, *113*

Garden of Eden, 12
garment workers, *218*
General Electric Corporation, 68–69
Genesis, Book of
    on creation, 12, 26, 33, 208, 241
    faith witness of, 17
    on sin origins, 11–13
German Nazism, 65–68, *86,* 95
Gestapo, 67
Giddens, Bill, 44, 45
Gift of Good Land, The (Berry), 268
global . . . *See* international . . .
God
    abundant life and, 271–272
    callings from, 219–220
    celebration and, 278
    covenant with, 17
    goodness of, 29
    grace of, 16, 19
    human power and, 50, 53–54, 71
    human wellness and, 155
    image of, 32, 33
    Kingdom of. *See* Kingdom of God
    known in Christ, 18
    natural law and, 17
    original intentions of, 12–13, 26
    providence of, 153
    rejection of, 256
    service of, 110
    testing of, 55
    trust in, 138–139
    vengeance of, 109
goodness of creation, 29, 31, 32, 138–139, 236
Good News. *See* Gospels
good Samaritan story, 89–90
Gordon, Frederick, 49
Gore, Al, 250

Gospels, 18, 19
    Catholic schools and, 232
    healing in, 57
    marginalized people in, 57, 58–59, 61, 75
    miraculous feedings in, 163
    on overcoming evil, 108–110
    See also individual Gospels by name
government, 31, 55
    economic policies of, 103
    famine relief by, 165
    foreign policies of, 166
    human rights and, 135
    inclusivity and, 95
    planning by, 156
    racism and, 84
    socialism and, 144
    violence by, 103
    warfare by, 112, 115
    wealthy elites in, 160
    See also U.S. government
grace, 16, 19
gratitude, 27, 278
Great Commandment, 88, 89, 241
Great Economy, 135–136, 153
great feast parable, 23–25, 155
Great Flood, *13*
greed
    hunger and, 161
    Jesus on, 139
    of Pharisees and scribes, 109–110
    as poverty, 61
    sinfulness of, 92
green architecture, 262–263. *See also* building construction
Guatemalan natives, 62, 63, 159, 169–170
guns, *108*
gym classes, 10

H

Habitat for Humanity, *191–192*
Haiti, 63
Hamilton, Steve, *209*
Hamlet (N.C.), 215
handguns, *108*
handicapped people. *See* disabled people
happiness, 127, 146, 147
Harding, Vincent, 279
Harvard School of Public Health, 108
harvests, *137*
Hastings, Bill, 207
hatred
    inner examination of, 92
    international, 119
    love vs., 111, 120
    See also anger
healing, 56–58, 89
health care, 168–179, 184
health insurance, 172–173, 215
heart renewal, 232. *See also* conversion; repentance
heart transplants, 174
Hebrews, Letter to the, 200
Hebrew Scriptures
    on creation, 238, 269
    on economic issues, 135, 138
    faith witness of, 17–18
    on poor people, 59
    on prisoners, 35
    See also Jewish Law
Heifer Project International, *166*
hemorrhaging woman story, 56–58
Heritage and Hope, 94
"hidden homeless," 189
hierarchical decision making, 145
high schools, 227–229, 232
high school students
    black, 49–50, 227–229
    diversity among, 97
    stereotypes about, 80, 81
high-tech medicine, *175–176*
Hitler, Adolf, 65, 112
Hmong, 201, 203

J

K

L

M

Mahony, Cardinal Roger, 201, 204–205

malaria, 169

malnourishment, 157, 168, 174

Man and Nature (Marsh), 250

Mandela, Nelson, 76, 275, *276, 277*

marginalized people, 75–76
  exploitation of, 77
  in Gospels, 57, 58–59, 61, 75, 272
  health care reform and, 178, 179
  housing for, 186–187, 194
  Jewish Law on, 137–138
  "seamless garment" philosophy on, 42
  wellness intended for, 155
  See also developing nations; poverty

Maria Guadalupe (ship), 58

marital violence, 102, 195–198

Mark, Gospel of, 138, 223

market economies, 144–145

Marsh, George Perkins, 250

Martin of Tours, 111

Marxism, 144, 145, 201, 202

Mass, 161–165, 273

massive war destruction, 114–115

Match-Two Prisoner Outreach Program, 41

material poverty. *See* poverty

material resources. *See* natural resources; possessions

Matthew, Gospel of
  chapter 6:138
  chapter 18:109
  chapter 23:110
  chapter 25:35, 191

Mayans, 159

Mayorga, Pablo, 162

Maywood (Ill.), 229–230

McCormack, "Mac," 7–8

McGeady, Mary Rose, 197–198

McGregor, Bill, 96

McMillan, John, 227

mediation, 119, 123

Medicaid, 172, 173, 174

medical care, 168–179, 184. *See also* healing

medical facilities, 69

medical personnel, 215, 224, 225. *See also* physicians

medical technology, *175*–176

Medicare, 172, 173

Mekong River, 202

Memphis civil rights protest (1968), *81*

men, 61, *78*, 195

Menchú, Rigoberta, *62*–63

mental illness, 183, 184–186

merciful works, 191

Mercy Nursing Home, 7

Mexican Americans, 96, 170–171

middle class, 189

migrant workers, 96, 216–*217*

military conflict. *See* war

military weapons. *See* weapons

Mindanao (Philippines), 254–255

minimum-wage laws, 214

Minnesota, 96, 188–189

minorities
  education for, 229
  ethnic, 156, 199
  housing for, 194
  in poor countries, 160

miracles, 58, 163

mission, 219–225, 233

Mississippi River, 248–*249*

Missouri River, 248–*249*

Mistral, Gabriela, 179

Moig, Manuel Garcia, *273*

Mondragon (Spain), 222

mononucleosis, 245

morality
  communal life and, 141
  economic lifestyles and, 149, 216–217
  individualism and, 140
  "seamless garment" approach to, 42–43

Moses, 17

motives, 100

multinational corporations
  labor for, 11, 133, 142
  local self-sufficiency and, 159
  in Mindanao, 254
  in Southern Hemisphere, 53

Muong Ja (Laos), 201

murderers, 36, 102

Murder Victims' Families for Reconciliation, 43

music, 236, 237, 239, 277

Muslim people, 85, 86

Mussolini, Benito, 66

N

Narcotics Anonymous, 185

National Coalition for the Homeless, 183

National Coalition to Abolish the Death Penalty, 43

National Conference of Catholic Bishops. *See* U.S. Catholic bishops

National Urban Peace and Justice Summit (1993), 106–107, 117, 120, *121*

Native Americans. *See* indigenous Americans

natural conflicts, 100, 101

natural disasters, 158

natural law, 16–17

natural resources
  common good and, 140, 141
  control of, 132
  factory production and, 144
  global consumption of, 131, 132, 251, 252–253
  on Mindanao, 254–255
  stewardship of, 212

nature
  power over, 55, 248–249
  separation from, 245–246, 248, 256
  simple living and, 150
  See also creation; environmental awareness

Nature Learning Center, 235

Nazism, 65–68, *86, 95*

negotiation, 123

neighbors, 88, 97, 241

Ness, Richard, 274

Newark (N.J.), 193

New Community Corporation (Newark, N.J.), 193

New Hampshire, *227*
New Testament, 17, 18, 135.
  See also Gospels
New Ulm (Minn.), 96
New York City
  homelessness in, 183–184,
    186–187, 191, 197–198
  street encounter in, 16
Nhat Hanh, Thich, 124–*125*
Nicaragua, 58–59
Nike shoes, 142–143
Nineteenth Amendment, 86
Noah, 13, 15
Nobel Peace Prize, 62, 125
nonviolent resistance, 117–120
  by Berrigan, *42*
  in developing nations, 104
  in international relations,
    123–124
  in Mindanao, 254
  in Norway, 65–68
  See also pacifism
North Carolina, 215
Northeastern University, 231
Northern Hemisphere, 52–53
North Sea, *215*
northwest states, 121
Norwegian teachers, 65–68
nourishment. *See* food
nuclear weapons, 68–69, 102,
  114, 115
nurturing homes, 195, 196
nutritional deficiencies, 157,
  168, 174

O

O'Donnell, Kathleen, 233
oil rig workers, *215*
older people, 78
Old Testament. *See* Hebrew
  Scriptures
On Human Work (Pope John
  Paul II), 208–209, 211, 213,
  214, 218, 224
On Social Concern (Pope John
  Paul II), 53, 91, 145
On the Condition of Workers
  (Pope Leo XIII), 217–218

On the Development of Peoples
  (Pope Paul VI), 25, 137
*On the Hundredth Anniversary
  of Rerum Novarum* (Pope John
  Paul II), *115*–116, 145, 148–149
opportunities, 76–77
oppressed people. *See* marginalized people
original sin, 12
outreach programs. *See* social
  services
overconsumption, 131
overwork, 215
Oxfam, 165

P

Pacific Northwest, 121
pacifism, 111–112, 113, 117. *See
  also* nonviolent resistance
parasites, 169
participation. *See* inclusivity
paschal mystery, 19
passion, 120
Passover, 273
patience, 120
Paul, Saint
  on Christian unity, 90–91
  on community participation,
    77–78
  on Eucharist, 162
  on overcoming evil, 109
Paul VI, Pope
  on justice, *23*, 116
  On the Development of Peoples,
    25, 137
peace, 27, 98–125, 240
peasants, 58–59, 159, 254–255
perseverance, 120
Persian Gulf war, 116
personal peace, 124–125
personal power, 63–64, 69–71,
  97
personal work mission,
  219–225, 233
pesticides, 216, 217
Peter, Saint, 56–57, 88–89, 109
Pharisees, 109–110
Philippines, 124, 254–255

Phoenix House Drug Treatment
  Unit, 44–45
photography, 29–31
photosynthesis, *239*–240, 248
physicians, 169, 170
  calling of, 219
  female, 45
  General Electric boycott and, 69
Picasso, Pablo, 210
Poland, *118*, 124
police, 82–83
politicians, 31. *See also* government
pollution, 139–140, 171, 247
poor nations. *See* developing
  nations
poor people. *See* poverty
popes, 218
popular culture, 173
population growth, 157–158
possessions
  domination by, 130–131, 133
  economic systems and, 145
  simple living and, 148, 149
  trust in God and, 138–139
  See also consumers
Poussin, Nicolas, *56*
poverty
  in ancient Israel, 137–138
  in Baranquilla, 166
  Catholic Worker houses and,
    155
  chronic hunger and, 156,
    158–161
  in Cuernavaca, 274
  economic growth and, 133
  educational opportunity and,
    229
  environmental stewardship
    and, 242
  green architecture and, 263
  health care and, 171–173, 175,
    178, 179
  in Hidalgo County (Tex.),
    170–171
  among migrant workers, 216
  minimum wage and, 214
  overconsumption and, 267
  power and, 58–61
  public education and, 87

simple living and, 147,
149–150, 151
U.S. bishops on, 135
wellness and, 168–169
women and, 45
worker ownership and, 222,
223
See also homeless people
power, 48–71. *See also* empowerment
powerless people. *See* marginalized people
power-over model, 50–51,
52–53, 55, 248
power-with model, 51–52, 53, 56
prayers
for the environment, 244, 251,
257
for homeless people, 205
of thanksgiving, 269
pregnant women, 161, 174
prejudice, 81–87, 196, 228, 276
Honeywell and, 92
in housing, 194
legislation banning, 95
overcoming of, 96–97
in poor countries, 160
premature infants, 174
prenatal care, 174
preventive health measures,
174, 175, 177
prisoners, 10, 34–41
Project RETURN, 41
Promised Land. *See* Israel
proportionality, 114
Psalms, 136, 238
public housing, 188, 190, *192*
public schools, 87, 226–229
public sector. *See* government

Q

**Queen of Angels Catholic
Church** (Newark, N.J.), 193
Quiché language, 159
Quinn, John, 114–115
Quisling, Vidkun, 65–67, 68

R

race relations, 96. *See also* civil
rights movement
race riots, 193
racism
American, 82–85, 228
South African, 86, 276
railroad routes, 64
rain forests, *247,* 254–255
Ramirez, Ricardo, 216–217
reconciliation, 120–122
recycling, *152*
Red Cross, *156*
Redig, Jane, 169
refugees, 95, 199–205
regional conflicts, 101, 102
rehabilitation, 36, 39
relief efforts, 165
Relieving Third World Debt, 95
religions, 238
remuneration. *See* wages
renewable power resources, *266*
renewal of the heart, 19, 91,
232, 256
Renewing the Earth, 241–242,
245–246, 251
repentance, 19, 256
Rerum Novarum (Pope Leo XIII),
217–218
*Resolution on Health Care
Reform,* 168, 178–179
resources. *See* natural resources;
possessions
respect
for the earth, 236–243, 246,
257, 268
in economic life, 21
for human dignity, 28–47, 124
for lower-ability students,
230–231
universal need for, 10
for work, 223
See also self-respect
responsibility, 27
Resurrection
death transformed by, 174
mission and, 224
power released by, 19
work enriched by, 225

retired people, 78
rich nations. *See* developed
nations
rich people, 160
rights. *See* human rights
ritual impurity, 89
rivers, 139–140, 248–249, 254
Robinson, Selena, 50, 52
Roman Empire, 109, 112–113,
271
Romans, Letter to the, 109
Romelus, Willy, *63*
Romero, Archbishop Oscar, 164
Roscoe, Molly, 89–90
rubber-shoe factories, 142
Rupprecht family, 242–243, 262
rural populations, 156, 188–189.
See also peasants
Rwandan refugees, *199*

S

Sabbath observance, 27, 215
sacramental world approach,
268–269
sacrificial animals, 110
Sadat, Anwar, *122*
Sadisah (Indonesian worker),
142–143
safety, 195, 215
Saint Mary's Catholic Church
(Sarajevo), *110*
salaries. *See* wages
Samaritan Inns, 185
Sand County Almanac, A
(Leopold), 250
San Francisco, 121, *182*
sanitation, 169, 170
Santa Fe (N.M.), 262
Sao Paulo (Brazil), *14, 147*
Sarajevo, *102, 110*
Savage Inequalities (Kozol),
226–228
schools, 225–233
Norwegian, 66, 67
public, 87, 226–229
racial imbalance in, *111*
violence in, 102
See also students

wetlands, 249, 258–260, 262
Wharton, Laura, 212
Wheaton College, 41
Whitley, John, 39
widows, 137
Williams, James, 49
Wishful Thinking (Buechner), 219
Wojda, Grace, 40–41
Wojtowicz, Anne Darlene, 170–171
woman with hemorrhage story, 56–58
women
  pregnant, 161, 174
  prejudice against, 160
  social contributions of, 78
  violence against, 45, 101, 195, 196–197
  voting rights of, 86
  wages of, 45–46, 142–143
  widowed, 137

worker-owned cooperatives, 222, 223
workers, 206–233
  Asian, 142–143
  economic systems and, 145, 222
  education of, 225–226
  female, 45–46, 142–143
  health insurance for, 172
  myths about, 158
  opportunities for, 83
  See also unemployment; wages
works of mercy, 191
work stoppages, 218
world . . . *See* international . . .
World Bank, 160
World War II, 65–68, 84–85

X

xeriscaping, 262

Y

Yang, Vang, 201–203
Yang, Youa, 202
young people
  cynicism among, 102
  homeless, 197–198
  prejudice overcome by, 96–97
  in public housing, 188
  social contributions of, 78
  See also students; urban gangs

Z

Zulus, 277

Acknowledgments

The scriptural quotations in this book are from the New Revised Standard Version of the Bible. Copyright © 1989 by the Division of Christian Education of the National Council of the Churches of Christ in the United States of America. All rights reserved.

The words of Oscar Romero on the cover and pages 2 and 164 are from *The Violence of Love: The Pastoral Wisdom of Archbishop Oscar Romero*, compiled and translated by James R. Brockman (San Francisco: Harper and Row, 1988), pages 212 and 64. Copyright © 1988 by the Chicago Province of the Society of Jesus. Reprinted by permission of HarperCollins.

The story by Kathy Petersen Cecala on page 16 is from *Of Human Hands: A Reader in the Spirituality of Work*, edited by Gregory F. Augustine Pierce (Minneapolis: Augsburg, 1991), pages 61–62. Originally published as "Meeting God in Others" in *Commonweal*, 14 July 1989. Copyright © 1989 by the Commonweal Foundation. Reprinted with permission of the Commonweal Foundation.

The excerpts on pages 21, 75–76, 133, 141, 153, and 213–214 are from *Economic Justice for All: Pastoral Letter on Catholic Social Teaching and the U.S. Economy*, by the National Conference of Catholic Bishops (NCCB) (Washington, DC: United States Catholic Conference [USCC]), numbers 28 and 77, introduction, and numbers 63, 364, and 136, respectively. Copyright © 1986 by the USCC, Washington, DC 20017. All rights reserved. Used with permission.

The excerpts on pages 25 and 137 are from *On the Development of Peoples*, by Pope Paul VI (1967), numbers 21 and 23.

The excerpts on pages 29 and 231–232 are from *American Dreams: Lost and Found*, by Studs Terkel (New York: Ballantine Books, 1980), pages 448–449 and 458. Copyright © 1980 by Studs Terkel. Used with permission.

The story on pages 29–31 is based on "Poor No More: New Beauty in Child's Pictures," by Daniel B. Wood, *Christian Science Monitor*, 5 Jan. 1988. Copyright © 1988 by the Christian Science Publishing Society. All rights reserved. Used with permission of the *Christian Science Monitor*.

The quotations from *The Church in the Modern World*, numbers 27 and 26, on pages 34 and 140 are from *Vatican Council II: The Conciliar and Post Conciliar Documents*, edited by Austin Flannery (Northport, NY: Costello Publishing, 1988), pages 928 and 927. Copyright © 1975, 1984, and 1987 by Harry J. Costello and Austin Flannery.

The quotations on pages 34–35 and 37 are from "Sounding Board," by Manning Moore, *U.S. Catholic*, August 1991, pages 16 and 18, and 14. Reprinted with permission from *U.S. Catholic*, published by Claretian Publications, 205 W. Monroe Street, Chicago, IL 60606.

The quotations on pages 35 and 40 are from *Behind Bars*, by Raymond G. Wojda, et al., pages 79 and 80. Copyright © 1991 by the American Correctional Association. Used with permission of the American Correctional Association, Laurel, MD.

The quotation on page 36 is from "Violence and Capital Punishment: A Reappraisal," by the Tennessee bishops, *Origins*, 14 June 1984, page 69.

The summary on pages 37–38 is from "Prison Reform Viewed from Inside," by Joseph Giarratano, the *National Prison Project Journal*, fall 1987, page 18.

The cartoon on page 38 is by Chris OBrion. Courtesy of *Free Lance-Star*, Fredericksburg, VA. Used with permission.

The information on page 39 is based on "Bringing Decency into Hell," by Jill Smolowe, *Time*, 14 Dec. 1992, pages 60–62.

The information on prisoner projects on page 41 is from "Getting Out, Staying Out," *Christianity Today*, 22 July 1991, pages 34–35.

The excerpt on page 42 is from "Cardinal Bernardin's Call for a Consistent Ethic of Life," by Cardinal Joseph Bernardin, *Origins*, 29 Dec. 1983, page 493.

The information on death row and the quotations on page 43 are from "Victims' Families: 'End the Death Penalty,'" by Tim Unsworth, *National Catholic Reporter*, 2 July 1993, pages 7 and 8.

The bishops' quotations on pages 43–44 are from the *U.S. Bishops' Statement on Capital Punishment*, by the USCC (Washington, DC: USCC, 1980), pages 7–8.

The story of Bill Giddens on pages 44–45 is from "The Detoxing of Prisoner 88A0802," by Peter Kerr, *New York Times Magazine*, 27 June 1993, pages 23–24 and 59.

The information on the Dardick family and the Americans with Disabilities Act on page 44 is from "Moving Toward Independence," by Geeta Dardick, *Utne Reader*, March–April 1993, pages 98–100.

The wage-gap information on page 45 is from "1993 Salary Survey," *Working Woman*, January 1993, page 43.

The story on pages 49–50 is adapted from "Civil Rights, 1990s Style," by Joyce Hollyday, *Sojourners*, July 1993, page 17. Reprinted with permission from Sojourners, 2401 Fifteenth Street, NW, Washington, DC 20009.

The paraphrased words of John Paul II on page 53 are from *On Social Concern*, number 16, and are taken from a translation by Joseph Donders as printed in the *National Catholic Reporter*, 26 May 1989, page 12.

The excerpt on pages 58–59 is adapted from *The Gospel in Solentiname*, vol. 2, by Ernesto Cardenal, translated by Donald D. Walsh (Maryknoll, NY: Orbis Books, 1978), pages 184–189. Copyright © 1978 by Orbis Books, Maryknoll, NY 10545. Used with permission.

The information on Rigoberta Menchú on pages 62–63 and the account of the Guatemalan family on page 159 are adapted from *Rigoberta Menchú: The Prize that Broke the Silence*, by the Resource Center of the Americas (Minneapolis: Resource Center of the Americas, n.d.), pages 14 and 9.

The information on and quotation by Willy Romelus on pages 63 and 71 are from "A Bishop Who Hears the Cry of Haiti's Poor," by Mev Puleo, *Saint Anthony Messenger*, May 1993, pages 34–41.

The diagram on page 65 is adapted from *The Seven Habits of Highly Effective People: Restoring the Character Ethic*, by Stephen R. Covey (New York: Simon and Schuster, 1989), pages 82–85. Copyright © 1989 by Stephen R. Covey. Used by permission of the publisher.

The account on pages 65–67 is adapted from *Nuclear Holocaust and Christian Hope*, by Ronald J. Sider and Richard K. Taylor (Downers Grove, IL: InterVarsity Press, 1982), pages 238–241. Copyright © 1982 by Ronald J. Sider and Richard K. Taylor. Used with permission of the authors.

The story about the General Electric boycott on pages 68–69 is based on information from "GE Finally Brings Good Things to Life: INFACT Declares Victory in GE Boycott," by Mary Morse, *Utne Reader*, July–August 1993, page 24.

The story on page 73 is by Kim Olson.

The excerpt on page 82 is from *Race: How Blacks and Whites Think and Feel About the American Obsession*, by Studs Terkel (New York: New Press, 1992), pages 402–403. Copyright © 1992 by Studs Terkel. Reprinted by permission of the New Press.

The quotations on pages 83–84 and 84 are from *Brothers and Sisters to Us: U.S. Bishops' Pastoral Letter on Racism in Our Day*, by the NCCB (Washington, DC: USCC, 1979), pages 10 and 10–14. Publication number 653-0. Copyright © 1979 by the USCC, Washington, DC 20017. All rights reserved. Used with permission. To order this publication, please call 800-225-8722 and ask for publication number 653-0.

The retelling of the parable of the good Samaritan on pages 89–90 was written by Molly Roscoe, a student at Billings Central Catholic High School in Billings, MT.

The quotation on page 92 is from "Rainbow Coalitions," by Winifred Honeywell, *Other Side*, January–February 1991, page 24.

The first excerpt on page 93 is from *The American Catholic Experience: A History from Colonial Times to the Present*, by Jay P. Dolan (Garden City, NY: Doubleday and Co., 1985), page 16. Copyright © 1985 by Jay P. Dolan. Used with permission of the publisher.

The second excerpt on page 93 is from "1492: The Discovery of an Invasion," by Enrique Dussel, *Cross Currents*, winter 1991, page 499.

The third excerpt on page 93 is from *The Rediscovery of North America*, by Barry Lopez (New York: Vintage Books, 1992), page 11. Copyright © 1990 by Barry Holstun Lopez.

The excerpt on page 94 is from *Heritage and Hope: Evangelization in the United States*, by the NCCB (Washington, DC: USCC, 1991), page 2. Copyright © 1991 by the USCC. All rights reserved.

The quotation on page 95 is from *Relieving Third World Debt: A Call for Co-responsibility, Justice, and Solidarity*, by the USCC (Washington, DC: USCC, 1989), number 48.

The information on migrant workers on page 96 is based on "Migrant Workers, Minnesota Teens Form a North-South Bond," by Maureen M. Smith, *Minneapolis Star Tribune*, 26 July 1993.

The football story on page 96 is based on "Huddle Up!" by Gelareh Asayesh, *Teaching Tolerance*, spring 1993, pages 14–22.

The folktale on page 99 is from *Peace Tales: World Folktales to Talk About*, by Margaret Read MacDonald (Hamden, CT: Linnet Books, 1992), pages 70–71. Copyright © 1992 by Margaret Read MacDonald. All rights reserved. Reprinted by permission of Linnet Books, North Haven, CT.

The quotation on page 106 is from the radio documentary "Increase the Peace," City Quest (University of Minnesota, June 1993).

The material on the gang summit on pages 106, 107, and 117 is taken from "A Time to Heal, a Time to Build," by Jim Wallis, *Sojourners,* August 1993, pages 10–19. Used with permission of Sojourners, 2401 Fifteenth Street NW, Washington, DC 20009.

The cartoon on page 107, copyright © by Michael Keefe, is used with permission.

The survey information on page 108 is from *A Survey of Experiences, Perceptions, and Apprehensions About Guns Among Young People in America* (Harvard School of Public Health, July 1993), page vi.

The words of Clement Alexandria on page 111 are quoted in *Catholics and Conscientious Objection,* by James H. Forest (New York: Catholic Peace Fellowship, 1981). Catholic Peace Fellowship, 339 Lafayette St., New York, NY 10012.

The quotations on pages 111 and 112 and the summary on pages 113–114 are from *The Challenge of Peace: God's Promise and Our Response,* by the NCCB (Washington, DC: USCC, 1983), numbers 114, 231 and 232–233, and 85–99, respectively. Copyright © 1983 by the USCC, Washington, DC 20017. All rights reserved. Used with permission.

The words of Martin Luther King Jr. on page 111 and Paul VI on page 116 are from *Peacemaking,* volume 1, by Pax Christi USA (Erie, PA: Pax Christi USA, 1983), pages 126 and 23. Copyright © 1985 by Pax Christi USA.

The quotation of Bishop Kenneth Untener on page 112 is from *Catholic Trends,* 2 February 1991, page 3.

The words of Augustine on page 113 are from *Nonviolence in Christian Tradition,* by Gerard Vanderhaar (London: Saint Francis of Assisi Center, 1983), page 9. Copyright © 1983 by Gerard Vanderhaar.

The quotations by Archbishop John Quinn on page 115 are from *Catholic Trends,* 16 February 1991, page 2.

The quotations on pages 115–116, 145, and 148–149 are from *On the Hundredth Anniversary of Rerum Novarum,* by John Paul II, numbers 52, 42, and 36, respectively. Copyright © 1991 by the USCC, Washington, DC 20017.

The sidebar quotation on page 116 is from "Waging Peace in a Decade of Power," by Archbishop Raymond Hunthausen, *Origins,* 4 April 1991, page 712.

The quotation on page 119 is from *Talking Peace,* by Jimmy Carter (New York: Dutton Children's Books, 1993), pages xi, 29, 116, and 119. Copyright © 1993 by Jimmy Carter. Used by permission of Dutton Children's Books, a division of Penguin Books USA.

The quotation on page 125 is from *Being Peace,* by Thich Nhat Hanh (Berkeley, CA: Parallax Press, 1987), pages 3–5. Copyright © 1987 by Thich Nhat Hanh. Used by permission of the publisher.

The statistics on affluence and poverty on page 131 are from *How Much Is Enough? The Consumer Society and the Future of the Earth,* by Alan Thein Durning (New York: W. W. Norton, 1992), pages 27 and 28. Copyright © 1992 by Worldwatch Institute. Used with permission.

The story on page 132 is based on *Stories for the Journey: A Sourcebook for Christian Storytellers,* by William R. White (Minneapolis: Augsburg Publishing, 1988), page 33. Copyright © 1988 by Augsburg Publishing.

The information on page 132 about consumption since 1950 is taken from "How Much Is Enough?" by Alan Durning, *Co-op America Quarterly,* winter 1991, page 11.

The principles from *Economic Justice for All* on page 135 were summarized in *Catholic Update,* January 1987.

The quotation on pages 136–137 is from *Stewardship: A Disciple's Response,* by the NCCB (Washington, DC: USCC, 1989), page 1. Copyright © 1993 by the USCC.

The material on pages 142–143 is based on "The New Free-Trade Heel: Nike's Profits Jump on the Backs of Asian Workers," by Jeffrey Ballinger, *Harper's Magazine,* August 1992, pages 46–47. Copyright © 1992 by *Harper's Magazine.* All rights reserved. Reproduced by special permission.

The quotation of Pope John Paul II on page 145 is from *On Social Concern* (1988), number 21.

The story about Christina on pages 146–148 is by Christina Puntel.

The words from Jeremy on pages 147–148 are from an interview by Sarah Freuh.

The story on page 155 is by Jerry Daoust.

The statistics on chronic hunger on pages 156–157 are from "Hunger Facts," by A. Cecilia Snyder, *Bread for the World Background Paper No. 124,* February 1994, page 1.

The statistics on food supply on pages 157–158 are from "Hunger Myths and Facts," by Food First, Institute for Food and Development Policy.

The quotation on page 163 is from *The Long Loneliness: The Autobiography of Dorothy Day* (New York: Harper and Row, 1952), page 285. Copyright © 1952 by Harper and Row. Copyright © renewed 1980 by Tamar Teresa Hennessy. Reprinted by permission of HarperCollins.

The quotations on pages 168 and 178 are from "Resolution on Health Care Reform," *Origins,* 1 July 1993, page 99 and pages 100 and 101.

The statistics on page 171 on health care spending in the United States are from "Health Care: A Planetary View," by James E. Hug, *America,* 11 December 1993, page 8.

The three cases described on pages 172–173 are based on "Six Good Reasons Why the Health-Care System Needs Reform," by Kelly Norton Humphrey, *SALT,* February 1993, pages 8, 11, and 12.

The cartoon on page 172 is by Ben Sargent. Used with permission.

The quotation on page 177 is from "When to Say No to Health Care," by Denis Wadley, *Minneapolis Star Tribune,* 7 November 1993, page 31A. Used with permission.

The quotation of Gabriela Mistral on page 179 is from *Bread,* March 1994.

The story on page 181 is from *Come the Morning,* by Mark Jonathan Harris (New York: Bradbury Press, 1989), pages 141–142. Copyright © 1989 by Mark Jonathan Harris. All rights reserved. Reprinted with permission of Macmillan Books for Young Readers, an imprint of Simon and Schuster Children's Publishing Division, and permission applied for to Barbara Lowenstein Associates for British rights.

The quotation on pages 182–183 and the statement of goals on page 194 are from *Homelessness and Housing: A Human Tragedy, a Moral Challenge,* numbers 14 and 12. Copyright © 1988 by the USCC, Washington, DC 20017. Used with permission. All rights reserved.

The stories on pages 183–184 and 186–187 are from *Rachel and Her Children: Homeless Families in America,* by Jonathan Kozol (New York: Crown Publishers, 1988), pages 1–2 and 42. Copyright © 1988 by Jonathan Kozol. Reprinted by permission of Crown Publishers.

The statistics on homeless families on page 184 are from "Despite US Law, Schools Eject Homeless Students," by James L. Tyson, *Christian Science Monitor,* 27 May 1994, page 6.

The account of Jubilee Ministries on page 185 is from "Samaritan Inns and Sarah's Circle: Specially Renovated Housing for the Homeless and the Elderly," *Jubilee Ministries,* October 1993, page 1. Used with permission.

The story about Tammy on pages 185–186 is from "Alcoholism and Substance Abuse," by Lisa Thomas, Mike Kelly, and Michael Cousineau in *Under the Safety Net: The Health and Social Welfare of the Homeless in the United States,* edited by Philip W. Brickner, MD; Linda Keen Scharer, MUP; Barbara A. Conanan, RN, MS; Marianne Savarese, RN, BSN; and Brian C. Scanlan, MD (New York: W. W. Norton, 1990), page 212. Used by permission of Philip W. Brickner, MD, and W. W. Norton. Copyright © 1990 by Philip Brickner, et al.

The quotation on page 192 is adapted from "Homes That Love Builds," by Joan Mitchell, *Spirit,* 21 November 1993.

The information on the New Community Corporation on page 193 is from the pamphlet "Against the Tide," by Robert Guskind and Neal Peirce (Newark, NJ: New Community Corp., 1993). Used with permission.

The statistics on page 195 on domestic violence are from the *Journal of the American Medical Association,* as printed in *When I Call for Help: A Pastoral Response to Domestic Violence Against Women,* by the NCCB (Washington, DC: USCC, 1992).

The story about Ricky on pages 197–198 is from *"God Isn't Done with Me Yet . . .": Letters from the Street,* by Mary Rose McGeady (New York: Covenant House, 1993), pages 92–93. Copyright © 1993 by Mary Rose McGeady. Used by permission of the publisher.

The quotations on pages 201 and 204–205 are from "You Have Entertained Angels Without Knowing It," by Roger Mahony, *America,* 27 Nov. 1993, pages 16 and 18. Reprinted with permission of Cardinal Roger Mahony and America Press, 106 West 56th Street, New York, NY 10019.

The story about Vang Yang on pages 201–203 is from *Dark Sky, Dark Land: Stories of the Hmong Boy Scouts of Troop 100,* by David L. Moore (Eden Prairie, MN: Tessera Publishing, 1989), pages 58–60. Copyright © 1989 by David L. Moore. All rights reserved. Used with permission.

The quotation about El Salvador on page 204 is from *The Big Picture: An Introduction to International Development,* by Catholic Relief Services (Baltimore, MD: Catholic Relief Services, n.d.), page 31.

The poem on page 207, by Todd Jailer, is used with the author's permission.

The quotations on pages 209, 210, and 220 are from *Working,* by Studs Terkel (New York: Avon Books, 1974), pages 488, 1–3, and xxix, respectively. Copyright © 1972, 1974 by Studs Terkel. Reprinted by permission of Pantheon Books, a division of Random House.

The first quotations on pages 211 and 224 and the last quotations on pages 214 and 218 are from *On Human Work,* by John Paul II, numbers 10, 27, 19, and 20, respectively. Copyright © 1981 by the USCC, Washington, DC 20017. All rights reserved.

The quotation on page 211 is from *Meditation in Motion,* by Susan A. Muto (Garden City, NY: Image Books, 1986), pages 130–131. Copyright © 1986 by Susan A. Muto. All rights reserved. Used with permission of the author.

The quotation on page 212 is from "Work of Human Hands: Fifteen People Talk About Faith on the Job," by Mary O'Connell, *U.S. Catholic,* September 1992, page 8.

The cartoon on page 213 is by Chester Commodore as published in the *Chicago Defender.*

The second quotation on page 214 is from *The Spirituality of Work: Unemployed Workers,* by Joseph Gossé (Chicago: National Center for the Laity, 1993), page 11. Copyright © 1993 by the National Center for the Laity.

The information on the Imperial Food Products fire on page 215 is from "Chickens Come Home to Roost," *Progressive,* January 1992, page 29, and the *New York Times,* 7 September 1991, 10 March 1992, and 15 September 1992.

The quotation on pages 216–217 is from "What Cesar Chavez Believed," by Bishop Ricardo Ramirez, *Origins,* 27 May 1993, pages 1, 19, and 20.

The quotation on page 219 is from *Wishful Thinking: A Theological ABC,* by Frederick Buechner (New York: Harper and Row, 1973), page 95. Copyright © 1973 by Frederick Buechner. Reprinted by permission of HarperCollins.

The excerpts on pages 220–221 and 221–222 are from *Of Human Hands: A Reader in the Spirituality of Work,* edited by Gregory F. Augustine Pierce (Minneapolis: Augsburg, 1991), pages 49 and 51. Copyright © Maxine F. Dennis. Used with permission.

The information on worker-ownership on page 222 is from "Minding Their Own Business," by David Scott, *Saint Anthony Messenger,* September 1993, pages 17–19.

The excerpts on the bottom of page 224 and on page 225 are from *Of Human Hands,* edited by Gregory F. Augustine Pierce, pages 97–98 and 97. Copyright © 1991 by Augsburg Fortress.

The quotation from the *Declaration on Christian Education* on page 226 is from *Vatican Council II: The Conciliar and Post Conciliar Documents,* edited by Austin Flannery (Northport, NY: Costello Publishing, 1988), number 1. Copyright © 1975, 1984, and 1987 by Harry J. Costello and Austin Flannery.

The quotations on pages 226–227 and the top of page 229 are from "Let's 'Throw' Money at the Pentagon and Allocate It to Education," by Jonathan Kozol, *Education Digest,* January 1993, pages 10–11 and 13–14. Used by permission of the author.

The quotations on pages 227 and 228 are from *Savage Inequalities: Children in America's Schools,* by Jonathan Kozol (New York: HarperCollins, 1991), pages 25, 27, 28, 29, 30, and 31. Copyright © 1991 by Jonathan Kozol. Reprinted by permission of Crown Publishers.

The quotations on pages 229–230 and 231 are from *Schools That Work: America's Most Innovative Public Education Programs,* by George H. Wood (New York: Penguin, 1992), pages 67 and 87. Copyright © 1992 by George H. Wood. Used by permission of Dutton Signet, a division of Penguin Books USA, and the author.

The quotation on page 233 is from *The Spirituality of Work: Teachers,* by William Droel (Chicago: National Center for the Laity, 1989), pages 22–23. Copyright © 1989 by the National Center for the Laity.

The poem by Stephanie Kaza on page 235 and the poems on pages 244, 257, and 269 are from *Earth Prayers from Around the World: 365 Prayers, Poems and Invocations for Honoring the Earth,* edited by Elizabeth Roberts and Elias Amidon (San Francisco: HarperSanFrancisco, 1991), pages 16–17, 70–71, 94, and 57, respectively. Copyright © 1991 by Elizabeth Roberts and Elias Amidon. All rights reserved.

Psalm 148 on page 238 is from *Psalms Anew: In Inclusive Language,* compiled by Nancy Schreck and Maureen Leach (Winona, MN: Saint Mary's Press, 1986). Copyright © 1986 by Saint Mary's Press. All rights reserved.

The quotation on pages 240–241 is from *The Ecological Crisis: A Common Responsibility,* by John Paul II, 1989, number 8.

The quotations on pages 241–242, 246, and 251 are from *Renewing the Earth,* by the NCCB (Washington, DC: USCC, 1991), pages 11, 6, and 9, respectively. Copyright © 1992 by the USCC, Washington, DC 20017. Used with permission. All rights reserved.

The first quotation on page 250 is from *Man and Nature,* by George Perkins Marsh, edited by David Lowenthal (Cambridge, MA: Harvard University Press, 1864). Copyright © 1965 by the Presidents and Fellows of Harvard College. All rights reserved.

The second quotation on page 250 is from *A Sand County Almanac: With Essays on Conservation from Round River,* by Aldo Leopold (New York: Ballantine Books, 1966), pages 243 and 261. Copyright © 1966 by Oxford University Press. All rights reserved.

The third quotation on page 250 is from *Silent Spring,* 25th anniversary edition, by Rachel L. Carson (Houston: Houghton Mifflin, 1987), page 13. Copyright © 1962 by Rachel L. Carson.

The last quotation on page 250 is from *Earth in the Balance: Ecology and the Human Spirit,* by Al Gore (Boston: Houghton Mifflin, 1992), page 295. Copyright © 1992 by Al Gore. All rights reserved.

The cartoon on page 251 is by Tom Engelhardt. Copyright © 1993 by Engelhardt and the *Saint Louis Post-Dispatch.* Reprinted with permission.

The account of Mindanao on page 254 is from "Halting the Plunder," an excerpt from *Plundering Paradise: The Struggle for the Environment in the Philippines,* by Robin Broad with John Cavanagh (Berkeley, CA: University of California Press, April 1993), in *Sojourners,* May 1993, pages 20–21. Reprinted with permission from Sojourners, 2401 Fifteenth Street, NW, Washington, DC 20009.

The quotation on page 256 is from "Environmental Degradation and Social Injustice," by James Malone, *Origins,* 18 March 1993, page 687.

The story about Andrew on pages 259–260 is based on *Kids with Courage: True Stories About Young People Making a Difference,* by Barbara A. Lewis (Minneapolis: Free Spirit Publishing, 1992), pages 143–150. Copyright © 1992 by Barbara A. Lewis.

The two quotations on page 261 are from *What Are People For?* by Wendell Berry (San Francisco: North Point Press, 1990), pages 5 and 6. Copyright © 1990 by Wendell Berry.

The quotation on page 268 is from *The Gift of Good Land: Further Essays Cultural and Agricultural,* by Wendell Berry (San Francisco: North Point Press, 1981), page 281. Copyright © 1981 by Wendell Berry.

The song lyrics on page 276 are from *The Song of Jacob Zulu,* by Tug Yourgrau (New York: Arcade Publishing, 1993), pages 5–6. Copyright © 1993 by Tug Yourgrau and Ladysmith Black Mambazo. Used with permission.

The second quotation on page 276 and the two quotations on page 277 are from "The Forest and the Trees," by John Lahr, *The New Yorker,* 12 April 1993. Copyright © 1993 by John Lahr. Reprinted with permission from Georges Borchardt, for the author.

The quotation on page 279 is from "In the Company of the Faithful: Journeying Toward the Promised Land," by Vincent Harding, *Sojourners,* May 1985, pages 15 and 17. Reprinted with permission from Sojourners, 2401 Fifteenth Street, NW, Washington, DC 20009.

To order a copy of any USCC publications, please call 800-225-8722.

Photo Credits

George Ancona, International Stock Photo: pages 75, 231 top

Dick Bancroft: page 62

Dick Bancroft, Resource Center of the Americas: page 53

Gunter Beer, Impact Visuals: page 147

The Bettmann Archive: pages 66, 86

Bread for the World: pages 167, 168

Bridgeman, Art Resource, NY: page 12

Paula Bronstein, Impact Visuals: page 276

Ernesto Cardenal: pages 59, 138, 162, 272

Simon Chaput, copyright © 1990: page 125

Vincent Cianni, Impact Visuals: page 183

CLEO Freelance Photography: pages 11, 21, 91, 225

Donna Decesare, Impact Visuals: page 204

Gail Denham: 146, 179, 235, 268

Paul Dix, Impact Visuals: page 205

Linda Dow Hayes, Courtesy of Fortkamp Publishing, Baltimore, MD: page 42

Dugout Sports Card Shop, Winona, MN: page 209

Earl Kogler Corp. Media, International Stock Photo: page 34

Chad Ehlers, International Stock Photo: page 29

Warren Faidley, International Stock Photo: page 244

Mary Farrell: pages 155, 192, 196

Harvey Finkle, Impact Visuals: page 187

Paulo Fridman, International Stock Photo: page 57

Frost Publishing Group: pages 136 bottom, 215, 233

Dan Habib, Impact Visuals: page 227

Haïti Progrès: page 63

Mike Howell, International Stock Photo: page 27

Marilyn Humphries, Impact Visuals: page 105

Karen Hurley, Sisters of Charity: page 170

Miwako Ikeda, International Stock Photo: page 31

International Stock Photo: pages 14, 245

Jewish Museum, Art Resource, NY: page 13

Marilyn Kielbasa: page 237

Phil Lauro, copyright ©: pages 64 top, 153, 210, 255, 273

Jean-Claude LeJeune: pages 47, 54

Robert Lentz, courtesy of Bridge Building Images, Inc., P. O. Box 1048, Burlington, VT 05402. Copyright © 1994. All rights reserved: page 164 top

Erich Lessing, Art Resource, NY: page 56

Ken Levinson, International Stock Photo: page 247 bottom

Andrew Lichtenstein, Impact Visuals: page 89

Julia A. Lopez, Habitat for Humanity: page 191

Mark Ludak, Impact Visuals: pages 182, 184

Marquette University Archives: page 163

Mary Messenger: pages 10, 96, 231 bottom

Steve Myers, International Stock Photo: page 246

John Neal, VAF, International Stock Photo: page 141

Nicaraguan Cultural Alliance, P.O. Box 5051, Hyattsville, MD 20782: pages 113, 274

Tom O'Brien, International Stock Photo: page 129

Dario Perla, International Stock Photo: pages 69, 127

Frederick Phillips, Impact Visuals: page 95 bottom

Gene Plaisted, OSC, The Crosiers: pages 70, 228, 263, 280

Bill Powers, Frost Publishing Group: pages 35, 37, 43

Resource Center of the Americas: page 169

Reuters, Bettmann: pages 52, 60, 76, 101, 102, 110, 115, 118, 156, 157, 199 top and bottom, 202, 249

Right Side Management: page 275

George Robinson: pages 30, 266

Steven Rubin, Impact Visuals: page 103

Scala, Art Resource, NY: page 88 bottom

Jeffry Scott, Impact Visuals: pages 106, 108, 121

James L. Shaffer: pages 9, 64 bottom, 73, 78, 88 top, 131, 152, 166, 178, 207, 208, 212, 217, 221, 238, 239, 242

Kay Shaw: pages 240, 259

Vernon Sigl: pages 50, 136 top, 137, 257, 269

Skjold Photographs: pages 16, 18, 24, 26 top and bottom, 83, 164 bottom, 262

Elliott Varner Smith, International Stock Photo: page 45

Ray Solowinski, International Stock Photo: page 32

Sean Sprague, Impact Visuals: page 247 top

Bill Stanton, International Stock Photo: page 33

Scott Thode, International Stock Photo: pages 134, 175, 176, 186, 190

2Maj/Teit Hornbak, Impact Visuals: page 95 top

UPI, Bettmann: pages 20, 81, 94, 111, 117, 122, 216

UPI, Bettmann Newsphotos: pages 23, 218

Wiley/Wales, ProFiles West: page 177

George Wirt, Covenant House: page 197

Grace L. Wojda: page 40

Gisele Wulfsohn, Impact Visuals: page 277